THE COMPLETE
GUIDE TO
KAYAKING

BOOKS BY RAYMOND BRIDGE

America's Backpacking Book

The Complete Snow Camper's Guide

Climbing: A Guide to Mountaineering

*The Camper's Guide to Alaska, the Yukon,
and Northern British Columbia*

The Complete Guide to Kayaking

THE COMPLETE GUIDE TO KAYAKING

Raymond Bridge

CHARLES SCRIBNER'S SONS / NEW YORK

Copyright © 1978 Raymond Bridge

Library of Congress Cataloging in Publication Data

Bridge, Raymond.
  The complete guide to kayaking.

  Includes index.
  1. Canoes and canoeing.   I. Title.
  GV783.B66   797.1'22   77-3230
  ISBN 0-684-15040-9
  ISBN 0-684-15041-7 pbk.

1 3 5 7 9 11 13 15 17 19 V/C 20 18 16 14 12 10 8 6 4 2
1 3 5 7 9 11 13 15 17 19 V/P 20 18 16 14 12 10 8 6 4 2

PRINTED IN THE UNITED STATES OF AMERICA

to Maddie

CONTENTS

THE COMPLETE
GUIDE TO
KAYAKING

White-water kayaking, a thrilling sport, and lots of fun if you don't mind getting wet.

Introduction

Like many other forms of self-propelled travel, kayaking in the United States has enjoyed a tremendous surge of interest in the last few years in all its forms, from white-water competition to paddling in quiet lakes. The reasons for the appeal of kayaking are easy enough to understand, since kayaking has all the attractions of an outdoor activity in a natural setting, a water sport, and a means of wilderness travel. In addition, it can be enjoyed at many levels of difficulty, ranging from a leisurely paddle around a local pond to the negotiation of powerful, boiling rivers. The level of physical strength, stamina, and agility required, together with the degree of skill and courage demanded of the paddler, ranges very widely. Kayaking can be equally appealing to those who enjoy difficulty and challenge and those who want nothing more thrilling than a peaceful glide around a neighborhood lake.

Modern kayaks evolved from the skin boat developed by the Eskimos for hunting seals in the ocean among floating blocks of ice. Because the hunting was done alone, the Eskimo needed a personal craft which could be paddled easily over long distances by one man, but which was also very seaworthy—in arctic waters, he could not swim back to shore, as the pioneer boat builders in warmer climates could. The Eskimo also had limited materials with which to work. Dugouts were impossible without large trees; the kayak was made with skin stretched over a frame.

The design which the Eskimos developed was ingenious—a long, narrow, closed boat. Since it was closed, it could be built low to the water because waves could not slop in—they merely splashed over the deck. The boat's long, narrow shape allowed it to be paddled

3

over great distances with a minimum of effort and made it ride easily over the swells. But the narrowness also made the boat very unstable from side to side, a tippy craft, in fact. The solution to this problem was the most original of all the kayak's features. The paddler sat in a cockpit which could be sealed off against the entrance of water, and he learned to use his paddle and body to roll the boat back upright if it should turn over. This development of what we now call the "Eskimo roll" allowed what seems at first glance a very unstable boat to be safely paddled out on the open northern seas by lone paddlers.

Despite the evolution of the kayak as a pleasure craft in recent years—the manufacture of designs made for negotiating very different kinds of water from those encountered by the Eskimo, kayaks accommodating more than one person, and other changes—the boat remains in many ways what it was from the start, a personal craft which is light and responsive, a delight to paddle, and suited for widely varying water conditions, sometimes very difficult ones.

It is somewhat ironic that modern Americans did not immediately recognize the virtues of the Eskimo kayak as a pleasure craft and a means of travel on wilderness waterways. Canoes modeled after the Indian birch-bark design, but made with many different materials, have had a continuous history of use in North America. The kayak, however, was first taken up in recent years in Europe, where models made with wood frames and treated canvas skins have been popular for years.

White-water boaters were the first modern Americans to begin to appreciate the virtues of the kayak. With its maneuverability, full deck, and easily handled double paddle, in difficult rapids the kayak has many advantages over the conventional canoe. In fact, modern white-water canoes are very similar to kayaks in many respects, having been modified to incorporate some of the kayak's desirable features.

U.S. boat builders finally reclaimed the Eskimo's invention when they began to use resin-impregnated fiber glass cloth to build white-water kayaks; and though Europeans remain in the forefront in many aspects of kayaking, the sport has begun to come into its own in Canada and the U.S.

THE MANY FACETS OF KAYAKING

One of the characteristics which makes kayaks particularly interesting is their versatility. Kayaks have been used by modern paddlers to cross the Atlantic, to tour down wilderness rivers over a thousand miles long, to explore chains of woodland lakes, and to ride some of the biggest and most turbulent rapids one could find. There is a special attraction to a lightweight, personal craft that gives a person the freedom to travel to many waters where he or she could not otherwise go, and to do it without large or elaborate vessels and other encumbrances.

Attitudes and approaches to kayaking are as varied as the waters suitable for the sport, and kayaks themselves take many forms. Kayaks are used by leisurely lake paddlers and heavy-water toughs

Kayaking on quiet water is one side of the sport, the one most enjoyed by many, though these paddlers expect more exciting water downriver.

who lust after the deafening roar of really big rapids. There are kayakers who bring the boat back to its original purpose as a craft for negotiating ocean waters along the coasts and surfers who specialize in riding the breaking waves along the beaches. Lake paddling can range from afternoon trips on a local pond to tours that may involve weeks of wilderness travel, including the crossing of long stretches of open water on lakes. There are fair weather paddlers in bathing suits and fanatics willing to break the ice on the pond to practice their strokes.

The boats of these diverse individuals vary widely, too. The perfect kayak for a three-week tour in the Quentico Lake country is quite different from the ideal slalom-racing boat. As the versatility of the kayak has been recognized and technique has become more sophisticated, specialized designs have developed for various purposes.

The main point for the beginner is that there is a wide range of boats and a wide range of water available, and that there is no need to be frightened of the sport or the craft after hearing wild tales of hair-raising white-water runs. The joy of kayaking common to all the facets of the sport is having a small craft, perfectly responsive to the paddler, light and readily portable to all sorts of waters, small enough to give the boater a feeling of joining the flow of the water, and so seaworthy that the skilled paddler can, if he or she chooses, learn the thrills of paddling really wild water.

WHAT THIS BOOK IS ABOUT

The purpose of this book is to provide a thorough introduction to the sport and the craft. A number of books have considered kayaking briefly as an adjunct to canoeing. There are obvious similarities, but the boats are really quite different. Both the traditions of the sport and the normal learning progression are quite different, too, though knowledge of river lore can be acquired in either a canoe or a kayak, and really skilled paddlers of one generally learn to handle

White water is what kayaking means to many paddlers, whether they prefer touring or racing. This boater is competing in a slalom race.

the other craft quite quickly. For the beginner, however, learning to paddle a kayak will be completely unlike getting to know a canoe, for reasons that will be explained in the first chapter.

Most of the best American literature on kayaking has concentrated on slalom competition. It is true that competition has been the cutting edge of kayaking, improving techniques and design of boats and paddles enormously. It is also clear that every paddler can benefit from racing, because it encourages perfecting his or her own technique. Nevertheless, the majority of those interested in kayaking are not thinking about racing, particularly when they first take up the sport. The emphasis in this book is on touring, ranging from short local trips to long wilderness treks, whether on flat or white water.

One aspect of touring that has been neglected is equipment, particularly for kayakers traveling unaccompanied by rafts. This book pays considerable attention to methods of building equipment stowage bags that will hold up under the rough treatment they normally receive on long tours. The float bags currently available that can be opened to allow packing equipment inside are far too flimsy to hold up well, and they are generally cursed almost constantly by their owners. Some plans for making your own flotation bags are included.

Kayaking is not a particularly expensive sport, once you are equipped, with transportation expenses accounting for nearly all the recurring costs involved, but boats and accessories are quite high-priced, and they are getting even more costly. For this reason considerable information on building your own equipment is included in this book, to help those who wish to save money. There are reasons for building your own equipment other than financial, however. It is possible to build stronger and lighter boats than those commercially available for a relatively low cost, if you are willing to provide the labor involved. Those who enjoy building their own equipment for the satisfaction of it need no further justification. There are also many boaters who are interested in working out designs of their own, but this demands some work and skill that can only be acquired by building some boats first from others' molds. Information is also provided on making various accessories, like spray skirts and wet suits.

Most of all, however, this book is intended to help others to share the pleasure and joy I have found in paddling some of the waters of North America, rough and smooth, particularly those surrounded by wilderness. The peace of quiet lakes, the stirring of the blood as you come around a bend to hear the crash of white water against the boulders ahead, the joys of camping by a river running through trackless wilderness, are special and irreplaceable. If you learn to love them too, then you must also join in the fight to preserve the wild rivers we have left and to revivify as many of our polluted waterways as possible.

1

The Kayak

A kayak is a small boat, generally designed for one occupant, which is paddled from a sitting position with a double-bladed paddle. This particular definition serves to distinguish kayaks from modern white-water canoes, which are paddled with single-bladed paddles, generally from a kneeling position. For the purposes of racing classification, canoes and kayaks are designated with the letters *C* and *K*, followed by a number indicating the number of people carried. Thus, a K-1 is a one-person kayak, and a C-2 is a two-person canoe. There are also many rules governing the dimensions and designs of canoes and kayaks for various racing events, but these do not concern us here.

Historically, canoes and kayaks were developed from quite different roots, though modern builders have created a range of boat designs which overlap a good deal. The modern slalom C-1 has more in common with the Eskimo kayak than with the birch-bark canoe, though both are its ancestors.

The hybridization of modern watercraft and the rules of competition produce a good deal of confusion for the beginner trying to sort out canoes and kayaks. There are open flat-water racing kayaks with four places, and there are closed one-person canoes. To make matters that much worse, the English use the word *canoe* to designate what Americans call a kayak, referring to our canoes as "Canadian canoes."

Despite this confusion, kayaks are for our purposes those boats deriving from the brilliantly conceived Eskimo hunting craft—boats paddled from a sitting position by one or two people, decked, normally fairly narrow and not too stable, usually capable of being com-

A kayak (on the left) and a C-1, or one-man white-water canoe. The two are easily confused by the inexperienced. This is a very large-volume kayak, but note how much bigger the canoe is, though the two are exactly the same length. The kayak is paddled from a sitting position with a double-bladed paddle, and the C-1 from a kneeling position with a single-bladed paddle.

pletely sealed off so that they can be rolled over and righted without shipping water. Some of the fairly stable "foldboats" are discussed in this book, but flat-water racing kayaks are not.

A PERSONAL WILDERNESS CRAFT

As a wilderness craft, the kayak has both advantages and disadvantages, compared with the traditional type of canoe. It is lighter and can be paddled with impunity on rougher water. It is the ideal white-water boat; many more rapids can be run. It is low and is therefore not too much affected by wind. Paddling is more efficient

A kayak in the foreground and an open canoe in the background. The kayak is a personal wilderness craft, giving the paddler an intimate contact with the water and superb control in difficult rapids, but far less carrying capacity, less comfort on flat water, and no ability to carry passengers.

and easier to learn, because it is done symmetrically with a double-bladed paddle. However, kayaks are generally not suited to poling, making for difficult work in traveling upstream and in very shallow water. The canoe has larger carrying capacity, both in weight and volume, and it is easier to load and unload. In general, open canoes are more suitable for carrying large quantities of equipment, particularly on relatively quiet water, for family groups, for fishing, and for utilitarian purposes. The open canoe is the workhorse of wilderness waters. The kayak is the ideal lightweight craft for traveling distances with minimal effort, particularly when each person wants to paddle alone. Besides its being a much better craft for white water and for touring on the sea, its responsiveness is a delight—the paddler and the kayak become one unit. Even in rapids that can be run in an open canoe, the kayaker will often have more fun, playing in the rapids, working his boat up, down, and across the swift water, and "surfing" along the standing waves.

Designing boats is an extremely complicated subject, too technical to discuss in detail in an introductory chapter, but some basic vocabulary and notion of the different kinds of kayaks is necessary from the start. An extensive examination is included in Chapter 9.

MATERIAL FOR CONSTRUCTING KAYAKS

Kayaks can be built with many different materials, and a lot of combinations have been tried. Eskimo kayaks were made with wood and bone for the frame and sealskins to cover it. A similar construction was used in Europe when kayaks first came into vogue, substituting rubberized or painted canvas for the skin, and this remained the standard method of construction until quite recently, although veneer, plywood, metal, and other materials have been used with varying degrees of success.

The introduction of kayaks constructed with molded fiber glass cloth, bonded and given rigidity with hardening resins, was a revolutionary event in kayak building and design. With these and similar

A C-1 in the river. Note the single-bladed paddle, the higher position of the paddler (who is kneeling), and the fatter profile of the boat, compared with the preceding photograph. Like most white-water kayaks, this canoe was made by molding plastic-reinforced fiber glass cloth.

materials, it is possible to make boats far stronger than any other type. Since speed is most influenced by very smooth hull surfaces, which are easily achieved with fiber glass, these boats were also very fast. Most important, the boats could be molded into almost any shape, and the shape could be changed fairly easily, so a period of continuous experimentation in kayak design was ushered in.

Kayaks made from fiber glass and polyester resin laminates and similar materials have displaced other constructions for most purposes, but for certain specialized needs other designs have some advantages. One version of the European wood and rubberized canvas kayak is the *foldboat,* which has a collapsible frame that allows the whole kayak to be taken apart and packed in a couple of carrying bags. Such kayaks are considerably heavier than their fiber glass counterparts, but they save storage space and are easily transported under circumstances where a rigid kayak would be too large and bulky. *Inflatable kayaks* have begun to make an appearance in the last few years, as something of a cross between a kayak and a raft. Their main advantage is also portability, since they are quite light and fit into a small space. They are generally known as *rubber duckies.* Inflatables are fun to play with, and have some uses now, but the models that have appeared so far are too flimsy for more serious use. (Klepper has recently introduced a closed, high-pressure inflatable that may be suitable for moderately difficult white water—if it proves not to trap the boater should the kayak become wedged against a rock.)

SOME TERMS FOR DESCRIBING KAYAKS

Some terms are needed for even a rudimentary discussion of kayak design. The *hull* is the lower part of the boat, the part that is in contact with the water but may extend well above it. The *deck* is a surface held above the bottom of the boat and covering at least part of the inside volume of the boat. In canoes and kayaks decks are not weight-bearing surfaces—they are intended to keep the water out of the boat and may also be an important part of the structure, in the sense that the hull and the deck may strengthen each other. The *gunwales* are the upper edges of a boat's sides, which may or may not extend above the deck. In kayaks the hull and the deck generally form a continuous curved surface, and the gunwale is simply the place where the top of the kayak starts to curve back over the inside. There may or may not be a sharper curvature at the gunwale. A *keel* is a protruding fin running along the center of the bottom of the hull to make a boat run straighter in the water and to resist sideways motion. In kayaks keels are either very shallow or completely absent. The *keel line* refers to the shape of the bottom of a boat. The keel always runs straight in the direction of travel of the boat, but to say that a boat has a straight keel line for all or part of its length means that the keel does not curve up or down along that length. *Rocker* is the amount of curvature of the bottom of the boat along its length. The *bow* is the front of a boat and the *stern* is its rear.

Many factors are important in the design and handling characteristics of a kayak, and not all of these will even be mentioned here. Some will come up later in this chapter and in the others that follow, and a more rigorous discussion of kayak design will come later in the book.

BASIC DESIGN FEATURES

In general, a longer boat will be faster and more directionally stable, that is, it will tend to keep on a straight course, rather than veering from side to side as it is paddled. A keel will lend directional stability also, and the deeper and sharper the keel, the more true this stability will be. Besides keeping a boat from veering, a keel helps prevent its sliding sideways. A V-shaped hull tends to make a kayak fast and has the same effects as a keel as well. It also makes the boat very tippy in its normal position, though stability improves as the boat is leaned. All these features giving a kayak directional stability make it hard to turn, so the desirability of such features depends somewhat on how the kayak is to be used. If you are winding your way down a boulder-strewn rapid, ducking in and out of little patches of quiet water, then maneuverability is a great asset, directional stability or "tracking ability" is definitely unwanted, and speed is of no importance. If, on the other hand, you are paddling across a wide lake or working down a long stretch of slow flat water, a boat that turns on a dime is a burden, whereas good tracking is a

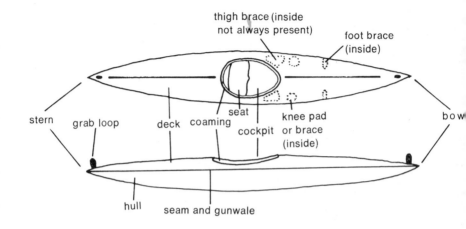

Some of the parts of a normal single-seater white-water touring or slalom kayak. Most such boats are made of resin-impregnated fiber glass in several parts. The two largest ones, the hull and deck, are joined along a visible seam, which may be covered with tape. The coaming around the cockpit is a flange onto which a spray skirt can be fitted to seal water out. The seat and the various braces are important; taken together they form a bracing system which enables the kayaker to hold the boat rigidly for proper control, and yet slip out easily in an emergency. The grab loops permit the boat to be held easily, even when its surface is wet and slippery.

great help, as is a hull design that slides easily through the water. Some of the characteristics that make a boat easy to turn are a more rounded bottom, a pronounced rocker, and a shorter length. Stability in the normal sitting position is aided by a broader bottom.

These basic statements need many qualifications which will be made later. There are also a lot of other important kayak characteristics to be discussed. The effects of wind on various parts of a boat can be important, for example, and turns are not always executed with the boat sitting straight up in the water. To begin with, however, we will consider some of the basic types of kayak.

SOME TYPES OF KAYAK

Single-seater kayaks are the normal type for various reasons. They are versatile; a *two-seater* is difficult to paddle alone. Couples generally paddle separate kayaks, retaining the natural maneuverability of the one-seater, and gaining more carrying capacity. (This is partly a question of definition, since the two-person white-water canoe has many features derived from the kayak, such as a closed deck, but is classified as a canoe because it is paddled with single-bladed paddles from a kneeling position.)

Two-seater cruising kayaks, whether made with wood frames and coated skins or fiber glass laminates, can be very pleasant for taking trips on easy water. They are lighter, easier to paddle, and less affected by the wind than comparable canoes, but they will not carry so much. Because of their purpose, they are designed to be directionally stable, with fairly straight keel lines. Often they are equipped with rudders for easy steering.

The *Eskimo kayak*, besides referring to the craft actually made by the Eskimos, designates the type of boat most commonly used by northern hunters—a very long and narrow kayak with a keel and a straight keel line running much of the length of the boat. Eskimo kayaks are very good for the purposes for which they were designed, traveling long distances quickly without tiring the paddler and allowing safe travel on the open sea and in inlets. The ends have a long, narrow taper and rise somewhat.

The *slalom kayak* is a short, very maneuverable kayak with a lot of rocker, a rounded bottom, and no keel. The "slalom" refers to a race through gates set over white water in which complete control of the boat and the ability to move it in any direction in rough water conditions are the ideals. A slalom boat is thus the most pronounced example of a kayak in which virtually all other features are sacrificed for good handling characteristics in rough water. There is no one slalom boat, however, since techniques differ and change. Under the pressure of competition, designs change faster in slalom kayaks than in any other type. Yesterday's slalom boat is today's touring boat. Slalom boats are widely used for recreational paddling, particularly on white water.

The *downriver kayak* is another type of craft designed for a specific kind of racing. A downriver race is a speed race from one point of a rough river to another downstream. Maneuverability is of importance only to allow the competitors to avoid rocks. Speed is all-important, and the experts for whom downriver boats are designed can manage kayaks that are difficult to maneuver and very unstable. Modern downriver boats are not of any use for any other kind of paddling, although some of the older downriver designs are satisfactory for experienced paddlers on the sea and on long lake trips.

The *flat-water racing kayak* is a long, very lightweight boat with a rudder, designed solely for speed on lakes. It is unusable for any purpose other than competitive paddling on nonturbulent water and is very fragile.

The *touring kayak* is the catchall term that is used to describe a wide variety of boats. "Touring" always refers to some kind of recreational, noncompetitive kayaking, but it is unfortunately not much more precise than that. For some, touring means paddling around lakes, ponds, and rivers without any really fast water. For others, it means going down white-water rivers that require more than a day to negotiate. For still others, it refers to any sort of paddling that is not either competitive racing or training for the same. Since "touring" means so many things to different people, the kayaks that might be used for it show just as much variety. As an additional complication, the boats that are likely to be chosen for the same sort of river trip will be quite different, depending on the paddler's skill, experience, and style. For clarity, I will use the term *cruising kayak* to talk about a boat that is suitable for lakes, some sea use, and easy white water, with lots of room for camping equipment, and perhaps designed for more than one paddler. Such a boat is likely to be fairly long, have a wide, stable hull with some keel, and to be designed to

A white-water touring kayak in turbulent rapids. This boater is on a multi-day trip and has all his camping gear, clothing, and food in his kayak. The boat must be maneuverable enough so that it can be handled in the river and buoyant enough to carry the kayaker and his gear through rough water.

track quite well. It will be a poor boat to take into difficult white water. By a *white-water touring kayak* I mean a boat that is fairly agile, and therefore more tiring to paddle through long stretches of flat water, but that has the capacity to carry well-chosen camping equipment for one person and food for at least a week.

CONSTRUCTION

Strength and durability are the most important considerations for the majority of kayak purchasers, with cost and weight important secondary considerations. Buying a secondhand kayak or shopping carefully are good ways to save money, but buying a poorly made boat is very bad economy. It will not stand up, and so it will cost more in the long run—and it may give the purchaser a chance to walk a long way after his boat breaks up as well.

Extremely light weight is very important for the serious slalom racer, so he or she will pay premium prices for rather flimsy boats. The beginner is not well advised to buy such a kayak; he cannot take advantage of the weight saving in a really light boat, and he is not skillful enough to give it the gentle treatment it requires. The beginner wants the lightest weight he can get and afford, but only without a sacrifice in toughness and durability.

The best fiber glass boats use cloth in their construction, rather than matt, which is a feltlike material that results in weak, heavy kayaks. Matt is often used in seats, coamings, and other pieces that have sharp bends, but it should not be used in the basic layup of the kayak. Seams are the weak point in most kayaks, and they should be inspected carefully. It is difficult to tell much about the construction of commercially made boats, but the beginner can find out a good deal by asking around among experienced boaters and by learning to recognize good and bad workmanship before buying a kayak. Bad workmanship is likely to be a sign of poor materials as well.

For foldboats, the skin should be of a very sturdy material, and it should fit perfectly on the frame. The frame should be made of prime quality wood with sturdy, noncorrosive fittings. Aluminum will corrode rapidly in salt water. All the pieces should go together easily—again, bad workmanship is probably an indication of inferior materials too. It is best if the fittings are all of a type that stays permanently attached to the frame or ladder. Small pieces of hardware that detach are all too likely to become lost.

CHOOSING A KAYAK

It should be clear from the preceding discussion that the use you plan to make of a kayak is the most important consideration in buying a boat. The beginner always has the problem of having to decide what he is going to like before being able to really try it. There are some definite pitfalls to avoid, however.

Try to make a realistic appraisal of what you really want to do. If you have your heart set on running white water, don't get a two-person foldboat or a long, stable cruising kayak. A real expert can paddle a bathtub through serious rapids, but even he doesn't enjoy it, and most paddlers cannot manage to maneuver in white water in a kayak that has good directional stability.

Probably the beginner who wants to paddle in white water should buy a fairly large-volume boat that was originally designed for either slalom or recreational white-water paddling. Such boats can also be used on long tours and on lake trips, though penalties will have to be paid in speed and effort.

Those who want to do lake touring, coastal paddling, and easy river running will be happier with a "cruising" or "touring" boat, generally a little longer than the 13-foot slalom kayak, and with a straighter keel line. Such boats are fast, still relatively maneuverable, and can be rolled well. An experienced boater can take them through difficult white water, though he will not have as much fun. It is important to be honest with yourself, however. If you really aren't interested in trying anything harder than easy rapids but will be paddling around a lot on lakes, this type of boat will be much more fun than a slalom kayak.

If your main interest is in lake touring, and you want to be able to carry more equipment in the kayak, or you want a boat in which you can paddle safely without learning the Eskimo roll, get one of the touring foldboats or the fiber glass equivalent. They are hard to tip over, have a good load capacity (though not as great as a canoe), and they are really very rugged, seaworthy craft. Remember, though, that these wider, more stable boats sacrifice much of the maneuverability that is one of the main attractions of the kayak. The two-man versions are less maneuverable than the canoe.

A great deal can be learned about which boats are best by talking to kayakers in your area, particularly those who do the kind of boating you would like to do. They may be able to point you in the direction of a used boat that will suit your purposes. You may be able to borrow a kayak, at least for initial practice sessions.

When pricing kayaks, be sure to take shipping costs into account. Particular companies often dominate the market in their own areas, simply because boats are so expensive to ship. If you are interested in the boats of a particular manufacturer, be sure to find out if there is a dealer anywhere near. Driving a few hundred miles to get a factory price from a dealer is a good deal cheaper than paying over a hundred dollars in packing and shipping costs.

Be sure to ask around about local boat makers. There are some poor kayaks made by garage manufacturers, but most of the best boats available are made by them too, often at considerably lower prices than those of the big factories. Again, the best source of information is the local paddling community.

2

Paddles and Other Essentials

The kayaker relies on his or her paddle as much as on the boat—it is the means of control and propulsion through the water. Without a paddle, the boater and kayak will drift aimlessly or crash disastrously. The paddle is also one of the major sources of stability on rough water, and the kayaker is likely to use it almost constantly for balance in large waves.

Just as there are differences in kayaks, so there are many differences in paddles, but they tend to be more subtle. It is easier to choose a paddle that will be satisfactory than it is to pick a boat, because paddles for most purposes are less specialized. The kayak paddle has two blades mounted on opposite ends of a fairly long shaft. The blades are normally *feathered,* that is, they are mounted at right angles to each other, so that when a kayaker is paddling with one blade, the other goes forward with minimal air resistance. There used to be some controversy over the desirability of feathering, but it is now generally agreed that the advantages of feathered paddles far outweigh their disadvantages.

The materials from which paddles are made spark a good deal of controversy, and new types are tried every year. Wood paddles remain among the best, providing they are well made—laminated with properly chosen woods to combine strength with light weight. Unfortunately, good wood paddles are very expensive, and, when they are broken, they are harder to repair than some other kinds of paddles. Nevertheless, the wood paddle remains as the standard against which others are measured. A good wood paddle has just the

23

A feathered paddle in use; the blades are angled at 90° to each other to reduce wind resistance while paddling. In the photograph, the kayaker has just completed an Eskimo roll, coming up on the left side of the picture, and is about to make a forward stroke using the blade on the right side of the photo. The blades of this paddle are slightly spooned. Note that the paddler's right hand is tilted back to put the left blade in position for a stroke, showing the paddle is a right-control one. The life vest in the picture is made with closed-cell foam sewn into channels and is a popular type among kayakers.

right balance of springiness and stiffness; it is lightweight and not exceptionally cold in chilly conditions, and it is a beautiful tool that is a pleasure to use. Probably the most commonly used paddle is one made with a tubular aluminum shaft, covered with plastic shrink-tubing, flattened at the ends and extending into fiber glass blades. Basically, this is a good paddle. It is relatively inexpensive and light, and it will float unless the shaft is completely broken. The blades are easily repaired. The shaft is colder than wood, though the plastic helps. Aside from aesthetic considerations, the main disadvantage to most such paddles is that the blades are thin and sensitive to the angle at which they are held in certain maneuvers. Another problem is that the aluminum alloy is prone to crack where it is flattened at the end. There are some good paddles made with shafts of fiber glass or similar materials. Ultimately, fiber glass–like materials wrapped around a foam core may provide the best replacement for wood, but the design of the paddle itself is even more important than the materials.

Some paddles are made so that they can be taken apart in the center, permitting easy storage. The joint is a potential weak spot in the shaft, however, and unless the take-apart feature is absolutely essential, it is probably best to avoid it, except for spare paddles. Another feature that has dropped out of fashion is the installation of drip rings along the paddle shaft to prevent water from running down over the hands.

The shaft should not be perfectly round, but should be oval in cross section in the areas where the hands grip, with the long dimensions of the ovals perpendicular to the nearest blade, so that when that blade is being pulled through the water, the fingers wrap around the narrower end of the oval. This means that the oval sections are offset from one another, just as the blades are. The purpose of this shaping is to give the hands a positive feel for the exact orientation of the paddle and the angle of the blade.

Paddle length depends partly on the kind of kayaking one does and on kayak width, partly on one's height, and partly on individual

preferences. For most paddling, particularly in white water, a paddle about 82 inches long is about right for a person of average
height, 5 feet 6 inches or 5 feet 7 inches. Shorter people may want
paddles one or two inches shorter, and taller people one or two
inches longer. If one is planning on paddling primarily on lakes,
paddles should be about three inches longer than the lengths given
above. Those using older-style cruising kayaks with wide beams may
need as much as a foot of additional length to reach the water easily.
The shorter lengths are desirable for white-water use because a
shorter paddle is easier to move quickly to make rapid sequential
maneuvers.

Blade area can also vary somewhat. Stronger paddlers generally
prefer larger blades, which encounter greater water resistance and
therefore make strength an advantage. Paddlers with less sheer
physical strength normally use paddles with smaller blade area and
increase their paddling rate to offset the decreased power of each
stroke. Smaller blades are generally used for long-distance paddling,
whereas competitors in short-distance events use paddles with large
blades. Area is difficult to measure without considerable effort, since
the shape of paddles varies a good deal, but an average size might
be 8 inches wide at the widest point and 18 inches long from tip to
throat (junction between the blade and the shaft).

The shape of the blade is not so easy to recommend. The amount
of rounding at the corners is probably not terribly important.
Square corners at the end allow the blade to bite quickly
when you are paddling hard, but they also are easier to nick on
rocks. Blades may be curved somewhat along either the length or
the width, or both. A completely flat blade is probably easier for the
beginner to manage, but most experienced paddlers prefer blades
that are curved along their length, because they allow power to be
transmitted through the paddle more evenly during the entire
stroke. (This is because the lower part of the curve is more nearly
straight up and down in the water at the beginning of the stroke,
when the shaft is at an angle to the water, so there is less energy

wasted—there is less of a vertical component at the beginning of the stroke. As the paddle moves back, the vertical components resulting from the curve balance against each other and cancel out, and the stroke ends before the top of the paddle comes out of the water.) *Spooned blades*, those that are curved in both directions, are advocated by some. My personal opinion is that they give no advantage, while making rolling and certain strokes more difficult. I recommend that most people buy paddles with curved but not spooned blades.

Curving or spooning the blades results in a difference between *right-control* and *left-control* paddles, and the neophyte must also choose which of these to buy or make. Since kayak paddles are normally feathered, the paddle must be turned through 90° each time the blade on one side of the boat is raised from the water and the blade on the other side dipped in—twice in each normal cycle. To maintain exact control of the angle of the blade, one hand always grips the shaft firmly, and that wrist is bent back and forth to control the blade. This hand is called the *fixed hand* or the *control hand.*

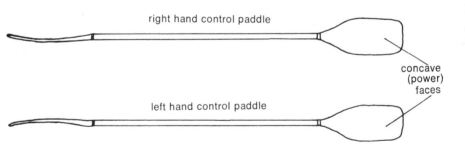

right hand control paddle

concave (power) faces

left hand control paddle

Two paddles with curved blades, one made for a paddler who controls the blade orientation with the right hand, and the other for a kayaker who uses the left hand. The blades must be oriented differently. With flat-bladed paddles there is no difference.
The blades of the paddle are set at 90° to one another to reduce wind resistance against the blade that is raised from the water.

The other hand holds the shaft loosely except when it is exerting force. If a flat-bladed paddle is chosen, it can be used by anyone, but if the blades are curved or spooned, the blades must be differently oriented for right-hand-control paddlers and left-hand-control paddlers. It does not matter much which a beginner chooses, but the choice will be permanent, since all strokes will be learned using the control with which he or she starts. Most people choose their normal writing hand as the control hand.

An experienced paddler can tell simply by picking up a paddle which type it is. For a beginner looking at a paddle or making one, the following rule can be used: hold the paddle in front of you with the concave side (power face) of one blade pointing toward your feet; the power face of the blade in front of your face will then be oriented to the right on a right-control paddle or to the left on a left-control one.

Paddles that are jointed in the middle of the shaft or have removable blades can usually be assembled as either right- or left-hand control, but because of the potential weakness at the joints, these are usually reserved for spares.

SPRAY SKIRTS

The *spray skirt* or *spray deck* is the cover used to seal the cockpit against the entry of water. The cockpit itself has to be large enough to allow easy entry and exit from the boat and to permit enough freedom for the torso to move in various paddling maneuvers. The space left between the cockpit rim and the body is covered by the spray skirt. Spray skirts are made from flexible materials and must be designed to form good seals both with the rim around the cockpit of the kayak (the *coaming*) and with the waist of the paddler. The coaming is normally formed in a curve that faces away from the cockpit so that some kind of elastic seal can be snapped over it to form the seam with the boat. An elasticized seal is also used at the kayaker's waist. Spray skirts are normally designed to be worn by the paddler and fastened around the coaming after the paddler is seated in the boat. Thus, the skirt may fit quite snugly at the waist, but it should be removable in case of emergency.

Like the Eskimo originals, most kayaks are designed to be paddled with spray skirts. They are built low to the water, so that waves

Spray skirt in use. The cockpit of the kayak must be closed off to permit the paddler to lean without filling the boat with water. This skirt is made of neoprene rubber. Note that it fits tightly around the paddler's waist, and an elastic band holds it onto the coaming of the boat (cockpit rim). If the kayaker has to exit, a loop attached to the front of the skirt can be grabbed to pop the elastic off the coaming.

may often pass over the boat and leaning turns may immerse part of the cockpit. The seaworthiness of the craft depends on a seal to prevent water from entering over the coaming. Only a few types of kayaks, such as flat-water racing boats and some of the wider folding kayaks, are designed to be paddled much without spray skirts. With most kayaks, spray skirts are as much a part of standard equipment as the boat itself.

Spray skirts can be made of many materials. They must be water-repellent and are usually waterproof. A skirt should fit the paddler snugly enough to form a good seal with any of the clothing combinations that may be worn without hampering normal movement of the torso in the boat. The lower part of the skirt has to be shaped correctly and have a strong enough elastic to form a tight joint with the coaming, yet it must come off the boat easily and without fail when tugged by the boater in an upset. When in use, the lower part of the skirt should form a flat, tight deck for the cockpit, so that water will not collect in a great sag or exert a lot of force on the skirt in turbulent rapids. Bagginess is also undesirable for anything that may be worn by a swimmer in white water.

The material used for the best spray skirts at the time of this writing is spongy neoprene rubber backed on one or both sides with nylon fabric bonded to the rubber. The rubber's own stretch is used to form the waist seal, with a stronger elastic sewn in at the lower edge, to go around the coaming. Coated nylon fabric is commonly used for less expensive skirts. Instructions for making a spray skirt are included in Chapter 10.

FLOTATION

In many circumstances, flotation is nearly as important as some of the basics already mentioned, although this importance only becomes apparent in the case of an upset. Flotation is simply a means of holding large air spaces inside the boat even if it is submerged, so that it cannot completely fill with water. The most obvious case of a boat requiring flotation is the standard fiber glass kayak, which will sink if it fills completely, since the resin–fiber glass lamination is heavier than water. Even a boat only half-filled and in a quiet lake is a nuisance to handle, since it may contain close to a quarter-ton of water. Improper emptying can damage the boat. In white water, flotation is far more important, since a boat going through a rapids with a thousand pounds of water in it has a lot of inertia. It will be virtually impossible to rescue in fast water, and it is likely to come out somewhat the worse for wear after any encounters with rocks.

Flotation for a boat can be managed in a number of ways, most of which will be discussed later in the book. The cruiser who is on a week-long camping trip, carrying all his own gear, for example, will carry clothing and much camping equipment in waterproof bags. Some modern boats are constructed with foam bulkheads that provide a good deal of flotation, in addition to their structural purpose. Everything has been used from inner tubes to beach balls or custom-made air bags. The beginner should simply be aware of the need to keep the water out of his boat, especially when he begins to paddle in white water.

LIFE VESTS

For many kinds of kayaking, life jackets or vests are essential for safety. A flotation device is now legally required on many bodies of water. Unfortunately, there is sometimes a conflict between regulations and the requirements for safe boating.

Though anyone who wants to learn to kayak should be a good swimmer, one cannot rely solely on one's swimming ability to provide a margin of safety in case of an accident. The strongest swimmer will find himself nearly helpless in heavy white water without something to keep him afloat—if he should fall out of his boat, the flotation must be provided by the life vest or jacket. Similarly, kayakers on the open sea or on lakes that are big, cold, or subject to severe winds need life vests to provide a reasonable safety factor.

Life vests may be superfluous for good swimmers out for a jaunt on a small, warm local lake, but for many kinds of paddling they represent an absolutely essential piece of equipment.

What has just been said would elicit agreement from nearly all experienced kayakers, but the choice and design of life jackets is a problem that is considerably more controversial. This is true because the degree of protection provided by a flotation device must often be balanced against the restrictions it makes on freedom of movement and on comfort. Also, materials have changed a good deal in the last few years. Finally, to complicate the matter still further, the U.S. Coast Guard now regulates the type of flotation devices used on small craft, including kayaks, in many waters, yet the regulations have probably had a negative rather than a positive effect on the safety of kayak paddlers. The regulations require that a Coast Guard–approved personal flotation device be carried in the boat for each person, and that it be readily accessible. Obtaining approval is so costly and time-consuming that it is not always feasible for those wanting to make devices for specialized groups like kayakers, so that improvement of life jackets for kayaking has been hampered by the regulations. Worse yet, some approved devices are not only restrictive, but are unsafe as well. The rest of this section will consider life vests strictly from a safety point of view, ignoring regulations. In many places anyone wearing a nonapproved vest would have to carry an approved device in the boat as well in order to comply with the law.

The purpose of a life jacket is to give the body enough buoyancy so that the wearer can breathe in difficult circumstances. Some people have little natural buoyancy, and no one has more than a few pounds in normal fresh water. When the water is rough, it may take considerable effort for a good swimmer simply to keep breathing, and the situation is considerably more difficult if he is being swept down a rough stretch of white water or through difficult surf where a lot of attention must be devoted to staying clear of rocks and other obstructions. Many other complications may exist. In white water, air is mixed in with the turbulent river, lowering its density. The tendency of the body to float is proportional to the density of the water, so in aerated water, you tend to sink, while there is less for your hands and feet to push against in the effort to swim to the surface. In cold water, the numbing effect will interfere with your efforts (see section on wet suits, below).

The most important attribute of any life jacket or vest, then, is the amount of flotation it provides, the flotation being the upward force that the device exerts on your body in the water. The flotation is equal to the weight of water displaced by the device, minus the weight of the materials. Thus, the only way to increase the flotation of a vest is to increase the volume of water displaced, since most of the materials used are very light to begin with.

The amount of flotation needed is dependent on the weight of the individual and on the conditions expected. The more turbulent the water, the more it will tend to buffet a swimmer about, often beneath the surface. In addition, flotation will be reduced in more turbulent water, because of aeration. Experience seems to indicate that a flotation of about one-tenth of a person's body weight is a minimum in normal circumstances, including white water of moderate difficulty. In heavy water, considerably more flotation is desirable, but thirty to forty pounds of flotation is likely to be the practical maximum, if the paddler is to have any freedom of movement at all. Anyone selling life jackets or other flotation devices should clearly state the flotation of each one, since this is the most critical feature of such items. Hardly anyone does.

Almost as important as the amount of flotation is its location around the body. Since breathing is not done by osmosis, the boater who has been unceremoniously dumped from his or her kayak tends to be concerned about getting his head above water—that's what the flotation is for. This may seem obvious, but the fact tends to be ignored by the makers of some kinds of flotation devices. Belts, for example, tend to make things worse rather than better in turbulent water, since they are about as likely to bring the feet to the surface as the head. Large quantities of flotation on the back, unbalanced by greater amounts in front, tend to force the face into the water. On the other hand, an ejected kayaker swims in rapids on his back with feet pointed downstream, and only the flotation on the back of the vest is useful in this situation. The front flotation is up in the air. It is also vital that the vest not tend to slip up over the arms and head. One sometimes wonders whether some devices are designed to improve the chances of body recovery rather than survival.

The ideal for a life vest is one that would provide large flotation forces, float even an unconscious individual face-up in the water, and not hamper body movement. Durability and comfort need to be considered as well, and it is essential that the jacket be easy to get off in case of the rare emergency where it becomes a hazard—for example, if it becomes snagged on an underwater branch. In practice some compromises of these ideals have to be made. A jacket with a lot of flotation has to be bulky; to float an unconscious person face-up, most of this volume needs to be concentrated in the chest area and in a fairly tight-fitting collar, but adequate amounts must also be provided on the back. Ease of movement and comfort would tend to be impaired. Individual fit is of considerable importance both for comfort and for the function of the device. Neither Coast Guard stamps nor manufacturers' claims can be taken at face value. Some vests that supposedly turn an unconscious person face-up do not in fact do so, or do so only with those who are of a certain build.

There are several construction methods used for flotation devices. The most common, used in most of the less expensive life vests sold in discount stores and elsewhere, uses kapok-filled plastic bags sewed into cotton vests, which are then tied or snapped on with cotton webbing. The kapok keeps the bags from deflating even if punctured, but prolonged soaking eventually wets the kapok, and once this occurs, the vest must be retired. The plastic bags are uniformly made of very thin material, so they are fairly easy to puncture or pop. (Never sit on a vest of this type.) The cotton also tends to rot fairly quickly with exposure to sun and water, so this type of device tends to be rather short-lived. Those made with nylon instead of cotton are somewhat better. Also, since the bags of kapok are made fairly large, these vests are quite unwieldy compared with some other types with comparable flotation. They are cheap, however, and they are often a good initial choice for beginners on a tight budget.

Also available are inflated vests, which have one or more pockets for air and are inflated either by mouth or by a carbon dioxide cartridge. If inflated by mouth, they must be blown up before they are needed; the carbon dioxide inflation can theoretically be accomplished by pulling a cord in case of need. This type of vest has several disadvantages. It tends to be bulky and unwieldy unless divided into many chambers, in which case it is complicated to make and weighs a lot. Materials that are durable enough to stand up to hard wear are rather heavy and uncomfortable. Carbon dioxide inflators need to be regularly checked and maintained if they provide the only source of flotation. In general, this type of vest is not used much anymore, and probably the only really good purpose for it would be auxiliary flotation—to be worn in heavy water in addition to a regular vest.

The type of construction in the devices now used by most kayakers is one with blocks of closed-cell foam sewed into a vest made of a lightweight nylon fabric. With enough separate blocks and compartments to hold them, the vest is fairly flexible and comfortable to wear, while providing enough flotation for moderate protection. Such vests normally zip up the front and have an additional tie to keep them snug about the waist, although snaps can easily be substituted for these closures. Closed-cell foam will not absorb water, since each bubble is separated from the rest and is watertight. Hence, when flotation is composed of closed-cell foam there is no need to seal the compartments into which the foam is sewed, and it is relatively simple to make a comfortable vest from lightweight materials. The longer vests of this type are not suitable for kayaking,

Typical river gear. Many types of helmets are used, from rock-climbing models to the one made for kayaking (in the foreground). A helmet protects the head of a kayaker going through a rapids upside-down from passing rocks. A short-length wet suit is being worn by the boater to the left for protection against cold water, which can be particularly important on extended river tours. The life jacket worn by the kayaker on the right is a "Grand Canyon" type, preferred by many paddlers on very large turbulent rivers because of the extra flotation it provides. The same type is being worn by the kayaker in the picture on page 19 but most paddlers in other kinds of water prefer a lighter vest like the one shown in the first photo in this chapter.

because the sitting position of the paddler and the spray skirt at waist level limit the length of the trunk that can be covered by the life jacket. The better vests of this type will normally satisfy the requirements for minimal flotation on moderate water, somewhat over a tenth of body weight.

LIFE PRESERVERS AND U.S. COAST GUARD REGULATIONS

At the time this book was written, all boats used on Coast Guard–regulated waters, including boats driven by paddles, were required to have at least one Coast Guard–approved personal flotation device aboard in an accessible place for each passenger (federal regulation 33CFD 175). Such devices must have official Coast Guard approval stamps, listing the approval number.

All U.S. coastal waters and "federal" rivers are under Coast Guard jurisdiction, and these flotation device regulations apply. Federal rivers include any passing through national parks or monuments and those crossing state boundaries. Thus, most of the waters in which kayakers are interested fall under these regulations. In addition, many state codes simply copy the federal regulations and require Coast Guard–approved devices on pleasure craft traveling on any waters under state jurisdiction. In particular, boaters taking trips on rivers governed by the Park Service and requiring permits can expect to have their equipment checked.

When, in 1972, it was proposed to include paddle-driven craft under the regulation, white-water boaters called attention to some of the problems involved and the Coast Guard exempted them from the regulations. Now that the rule is on the books, the exemption has been removed.

The actual devices permitted include life vests, life jackets, and seat cushions. The cushions, in fact, present both an example of the absurdity of the regulations as applied to white-water craft and an excellent method to achieve legality if the vest you use is not an approved one. A boater can legally paddle with an approved cushion or vest tucked behind his seat, which will be totally worthless in case of an upset on white water or in surf. (Some administering agencies do require that the device be an approved *vest*.)

Legal vests include many that are too bulky for reasonable use in kayaks, because they extend too far down the torso to fit or inhibit safe movement. There are many other inadequacies. In checking one recently approved vest, I easily slid out of it in the water, after having fitted it on correctly as it was intended to be used. In turbulent white water, this vest could have come off completely or just enough to pin the arms of the wearer above his head.

In my opinion, the kayaker should take care to choose or design his flotation device with his own safety as the primary consideration. If a suitable vest is found which is also approved, then no problem exists, but if not, one's life seems more worth preserving than the egos of Washington bureaucrats. A cheap approved device can always be carried in the boat, and when passing muster with various inspectors, this device can be exhibited.

One difficulty with the regulations is that there is no practical way to have homemade devices inspected and passed—the machinery is far too expensive and cumbersome. Most really good white-water and ocean gear for kayaks has been developed by boaters making their own equipment. This has been true of everything from kayaks to clothing. Even when really good vests are available commercially, they will be far overpriced because of the expense of obtaining approval. If all these annoyances and costs really contributed to the safety of the white-water paddler, they would be worthwhile, but since they clearly do not at the moment, kayakers would be well advised to do the work necessary to get rid of them.

WET SUITS

A *wet suit* is a garment made of spongy neoprene rubber, designed to keep the wearer warm even in cold water. Wet suits are essential for paddling in really cold conditions, and they are desirable in chilly water.

The kayaker is bound to get wet even if he never tips over. The kayak and its paddler ride low in the water, and the boat is designed to keep afloat in rough water not by having sides high enough to prevent water from getting over but by having a sealed deck over which waves wash easily. They are likely to wash over the occupant as well. Add to these factors possible rain, spray, dripping from the paddle, and contact with the water in some leaning strokes, and you cannot depend on staying dry when paddling a kayak.

Given the fact that the kayaker can be fairly sure of getting wet, together with the rapid cooling effect of cold water running over the skin, some protection is obviously essential if you contemplate paddling in cold water. Even if you can stay fairly dry when paddling, the best kayakers can go in the drink sometimes, and prospects for survival of a swimmer in very cold water are almost nil after only a few minutes of exposure without adequate protection.

For conditions that are not too cold, wool clothing together with wind shells or paddling shirt and pants may be adequate—when water temperatures are in the fifties, for example, and the air is at a moderate temperature. Wool clothing retains some insulating value even when wet. If you are swimming or soaked from immersion, however, cold water is actually running over the skin, draining away your body's reserve of heat. For this reason, wool or polyester-insulated clothing alone is not enough to provide safety in cold water—a wet suit is essential. The wet suit does not seal the water out completely, but it prevents any significant water circulation from occurring, so that the suit keeps you warm, though damp.

Wet suits are made in a number of configurations, and different paddlers have different preferences. A number of factors need to be considered. Wet suits are not particularly pleasant to wear, even at their best. Chafing at the armpits and inside the bend of the elbow is particularly common. Short-sleeved or sleeveless tops are thus preferred when they give adequate protection. Thick suits interfere with movement more and are uncomfortably hot when the weather is not too cold, but they are necessary in really harsh conditions. Compromises thus have to be found. A few recommendations are summarized here, and there is further discussion of wet suits in Chapter 10.

The amount of insulation provided by the suit depends on the thickness, the parts of the body covered, design, and fit. The thicknesses generally used in suits for kayaking are ⅛ inch and ³/₁₆ inch. Both are advocated for various purposes, but most commonly, short jackets, which are used in moderate conditions, are made from ⅛-inch foam, while full-length suits are generally made of ³/₁₆-inch material. Jackets with short sleeves and short suits are more comfortable for paddling. Some prefer the short suit, which is of one piece with short legs and sleeves, while others favor a jacket with a crotch piece that can be snapped in to hold the jacket down and provide additional warmth, or can be left hanging like a tail when less protection (or more comfort) is needed. Such jackets, particularly when combined with other clothing, can provide perfectly adequate protection and comfort until the water temperature drops into the forties.

Full-length jackets of ³/₁₆-inch neoprene become necessary for water temperatures in the low forties and upper thirties, and such jackets are preferred by some at higher temperatures, particularly if the wet suit is worn without other clothing and in very wet conditions. Full-length pants to go with the top become essential if water temperatures are in the thirties.

Pants are less essential than jackets, mainly because the lower part of the body is given a good deal of protection by the boat as long as the paddler stays in it, even if his legs are wet. Cold winds will not reach the legs, and even if water is sloshing around in the bottom of the kayak, it will not be doing nearly as much cooling. Pants do become necessary for very cold conditions, however, and they are also sometimes used in preference to jackets by racers, who want maximum freedom of movement and are kept warm during a race by heavy exercise.

Neoprene gloves or mittens and neoprene socks are widely used to add comfort even at higher temperatures, and they become necessary at water temperatures near freezing. Mittens are warmer than gloves, but they are also more of a nuisance.

Wet suits are expensive, even when they are homemade. (Plans are included in Chapter 10.) Unfortunately, they are likely to take quite a beating from the kayaker, since the neoprene material is easily torn, whether on rocks during an unexpected swim or on branches and brush. Seams are better fastened and the material is more durable if it is bonded to nylon fabric. If this fabric is facing out, the suit will be more resistant to snagging; if it is on the inside, the garment will be more comfortable and easier to get on and off. Ideally, nylon should be bonded to both sides of the neoprene material, but this type of construction is rare and expensive.

Probably the wisest purchase for most beginners would be a short suit of some kind made of ⅛-inch material. When combined with long underwear of wool, a sweater, a paddling jacket, and a pair of light wind or rain pants, this type of suit will keep most people safe and comfortable in fairly cold water and weather. Beginners do not usually paddle in really cold conditions. If, however, you tend to chill easily, or if you expect to paddle in cold conditions, you may prefer a full suit of $3/16$-inch material, preferably with separate top and pants. It will keep you warm and safe in any reasonable paddling circumstances.

PADDLING JACKETS

Some sort of light shell is very helpful in keeping water from running over the body, in reducing chilling from the wind, and in gen-

A paddling jacket in use. The jacket is made of coated nylon and provides protection against wind chill together with some insulation. In moderate weather the jacket is worn alone, and in cold weather it can extend the range of a wet suit. Cuffs and neck are normally closed with neoprene, but the jacket will not keep water out completely. The poles in the foreground form a slalom "gate," through which the competitors are required to maneuver. Note the curve of the paddle blade. The boat is a low-volume slalom design made for rapid maneuvering and high performance in the hands of a good boater.

eral keeping the paddler considerably warmer than he would otherwise be, while interfering only minimally with movement. Such a shell should be lightweight and loose enough not to hamper paddling or swimming.

The best paddling jackets are made of waterproof nylon material with neoprene cuffs and neck closure, but any lightweight nylon shell will do. The bottom is generally held closed by the spray skirt.

HELMETS

Lake paddlers and oceangoing kayakers who avoid surf do not need to bother with helmets, but most surfers and white-water paddlers choose to wear them. A kayaker who is properly trained does not fall out of his boat or immediately exit if he turns over—he orients himself underwater and rolls back up. During the intervening period, no matter how short, he is traveling along the river channel with his head below his body and his boat, where it will strike any rocks that happen to be in the way. A helmet will prevent serious injury.

Various kinds of helmets are sold and worn for kayaking, including many designed for other sports, such as rock-climbing or football. The choice does not seem to be really critical, since the forces likely to be involved if a boater strikes his head are not nearly so great as those that may be encountered by a motorcyclist or a climber. The ideal helmet would be very light, would not interfere with vision, would be adjustable so that a hat could be worn in cold weather, would be well ventilated to be cool in warm weather and ensure rapid drainage of water in a roll, and would permit installation of a face guard. Such a helmet does not exist.

One thing to be sure of when using a helmet, even one sold specifically for kayaking, is that the suspension will keep the hard hat on your head. A surprising number of helmets are very easily dislodged.

OTHER ITEMS

A large *sponge* should be fastened to the seat of the boat, to be used for bailing out water that manages to get into the kayak. A number of arrangements can be used to attach it so that it cannot be lost if you leave the kayak; perhaps the simplest is to make a hole through the center and tie the sponge with very light cotton string. *Do not use long lengths of nylon cord, which might become tangled around your leg in an emergency.*

Old sneakers are the standard shoes for kayaking; those that have acquired too many holes for any other use are perfect, since water drains out easily as you step into a boat. Shoes should be worn as protection against fiber glass abrasion, sharp rocks, broken bottles, and many other objects you will find your fellow citizens have tossed into the water.

Wearers of eyeglasses should always remember to use *glasses retainers;* an Eskimo roll will knock off unrestrained glasses every time. Contact lens wearers should take the same precautions as for diving and swimming with their eyes open. Goggles may be needed.

Some paddlers dislike the loss of sensitive feel for the paddle when wearing gloves or mittens in cold weather. They prefer *poagies,* which fit over the hand and paddle shaft at the same time, leaving the palm of the hand directly on the shaft. These usually close with Velcro fasteners. It is important that they release easily in an emergency.

3

Learning to Paddle

This chapter discusses the basic kayak strokes and gives some recommendations on the best way to learn them, but a few points need to be made first. The discussion of strokes is arranged systematically, but learning will not really proceed in as orderly a fashion as this, or in the same sequence. For example, the Eskimo roll, which is discussed separately in the next chapter, should be learned very early, if at all possible, for several reasons that will be mentioned here. Mastery of one stroke will not be achieved by practicing it alone; rather, since the various maneuvers with the paddle are interdependent, continuous work on all the strokes is needed. Progressive improvement will take place in all of them.

Though anyone can manage to move one of the more stable kayaks through the water on the first attempt, learning to paddle modern kayaks well requires a certain amount of effort and application. It is not overly difficult, but some things, the roll in particular, may be discouraging, because some people have to make many fruitless attempts before acquiring the knack. Great physical strength is not essential, nor is any unusual athletic ability, but a fair measure of determination may be. The beginning kayaker will feel as awkward when he first gets into a kayak as the novice skier does the first time he puts on skis.

All of the strokes discussed in this chapter, as well as the paddling principles, apply to any kind of kayak, but different types of boats can be maneuvered or propelled more or less effectively by various techniques. A downriver racing boat, for example, is normally turned by leaning the craft to the side away from the turn, and allowing the shape of the hull to steer the kayak. Big, stable touring kayaks are more difficult to turn using braces. Most of the discussion here, for simplicity, will assume the use of a boat that is neither extremely unstable and hard to turn, like a downriver racing boat, nor very broad of beam and stable like most of the currently imported folding kayaks. The former should only be paddled by experts anyway, and the foldboats are simply less responsive to many modern paddling techniques than most other current designs.

KAYAK STABILITY

The reputation kayaks have for being tippy results from an element of truth plus a good deal of misunderstanding. Most kayaks are not particularly unstable once the passenger has gotten into the sitting position from which the boat is paddled. This sitting position makes the center of gravity of the boat and passenger combination quite low, so that the beam of the kayak can be fairly narrow without making the craft likely to roll over. The greatest element of kayak stability, however, is similar to the stability of a bicycle while it is being ridden—it is a dynamic stability. When one is merely sitting in a kayak, it remains upright with no trouble, all by itself, but during active paddling, particularly in rough water, the paddler creates his or her own stability by leaning on the water with the paddle. Instead of carefully trying to maintain a delicate balance position while paddling hard, the kayaker leans against the paddle, sometimes very heavily. A paddle blade is large enough so that the water will resist its movement with a great deal of force, and this force at the end of a long lever arm (the paddle shaft) is sufficient to allow the paddler to lean as far over as he likes, because he can simply push himself back up. An amazing degree of stability is achieved once the kayaker has learned to use the paddle as a brace, because one can reach far out with a paddle at will, giving the effect of a seven-foot beam in stability.

The use of leans, often quite severe ones, is at the heart of modern paddling technique, but a paddle blade is two-edged. It gives

The key to stability in most modern kayaks is the ability of the boater to lean on the paddle. Stability is provided by the kayaker rather than the hull. The farther out the paddler reaches with his blade, the more stable he is.

the paddler complete control over the boat's stability, but such control only becomes an asset after one has learned to use it. The paddle can be used to tip its holder into the water as well as to push him out of it; it is an instrument of destabilization as well as the opposite. The beginner is bound to find, again and again, that a correct motion and blade angle will support him easily as he reaches over to move the boat behind a rock or into a current, while an error will flip him into the water before he even knows what happened.

GETTING STARTED

It is quite possible to learn the rudiments of kayaking by yourself. It is much better and more enjoyable to learn with a group of other inexperienced people. By far the most efficient and enjoyable way to learn to paddle, however, is from experienced kayakers. They can provide guidance and assistance that will ease the way to proficiency and speed your progress immeasurably. If you have a friend who is a good paddler, you can seek his or her help. The other alternative— one that will probably be recommended by your friend, anyway—is to join a club. Nearly all kayaking clubs (which are generally made up of canoe paddlers and perhaps rafters, too) have more or less formal instruction programs for beginners. Such programs provide a very good way for the neophyte to learn to paddle while allowing old hands to teach new boaters in a way that wastes as little of their time as possible. If you do have an experienced friend who teaches in a club program, he will probably want you to come to that, rather than having him duplicate his effort by taking you out alone.

Another advantage to club programs is that in most parts of the country, where it is too chilly for much boating in the winter, swimming pool time is arranged by clubs for training, in order to waste as little of the paddling season as possible on getting into shape. Such pool time is a valuable commodity that is impossible for most individuals to obtain by themselves, so if there is a club within reasonable driving distance, be sure to get in touch with it. The pool sessions generally begin several months before the boating season.

Kayaking is not really a solo sport anyway, particularly for beginners. Although a competent swimmer can paddle around small lakes by himself with no problem, most of the more interesting kinds of trips are not safe to undertake alone. Even experts rarely run serious white water by themselves, and when they do, they know that they are undertaking a much greater risk than they would paddling with a group. Kayaking alone on big lakes and on the sea is risky, too, and it is foolish for the neophyte. Besides the safety factor, there are a number of practical reasons to get to know as many other boaters as possible. Most river tours require a shuttle, since paddlers and boats start at one point on the river and end up at another, and such shuttles are hard to arrange without several boaters. The best way to get to know other boaters is to join a club.

Clubs usually have organized schedules of training, cruises, and races, all with competent leaders and a good progression of difficulty to allow the beginner to develop his paddling skills as rapidly as possible.

Finally, a new boater may be able to save a good deal of expense and end up better equipped by joining a kayaking club. He may be able to use borrowed or club boats in initial practice, allowing him to put off the expense of buying equipment until he has learned enough to avoid expensive errors. The advice of people with long kayaking experience is bound to prove valuable, and for those who are interested in making their own boats, a club is bound to provide the best introduction both to owners of kayak molds (the club itself may own them) and to experienced boat makers.

The actual order in which you learn various kayaking skills may be determined by your teachers. But for those who start on their own or in a less formal situation, some recommendations may be helpful. The first thing that has to be done is simply to become acquainted with the kayak: you must learn to get in and out of it and get the basic feel of paddling around, becoming familiar with the way to hold the paddle and the way that the boat turns, its balance and handling characteristics. This is likely to take a few hours in a swimming pool or a local stretch of quiet water. Once you are comfortable with the boat and have some idea of the basic strokes, it is time to begin learning how to roll. Rolling was once thought to be an arcane and advanced skill, but it is really the foundation of modern technique for several reasons, just as it was an essential technique for the Eskimos who originated the design of the kayak. It is fundamental partly because the ability to roll provides much of the kayaker's security. The closed, narrow-beam boat is safe, even in deep water far from shore, because if you become careless and tip over, you can always roll back up again, never leaving the boat. Kayaks are hard to empty out and hard to enter if they become swamped in deep water. The Eskimo roll is a basic safety factor both in white water and in large bodies of flat water, and it is a prerequi-

A strong Eskimo roll is a fundamental skill for the kayaker, and it can be acquired only with lots of practice. In winter a swimming pool is a good place to learn. Here the paddler is practicing falling into the water from an awkward angle after paddling hard, after which he will orient himself and roll up. Rolling is normally learned in conjunction with paddling.

site for any of the more advanced kinds of kayaking, from surfing to river touring to slalom racing.

The second reason that the Eskimo roll is fundamental is that it both enables the paddler to recover easily from his mistakes and develops his ability to brace against the paddle. Many strokes, to be used effectively, require that the paddler lean well beyond the balance point. Beginners who have not learned to roll are timid about leaning out, acquiring bad habits. Those with a good roll are far less hesitant about falling into the water, since they know they can recover easily. Besides, it is very inefficient to have to bring the boat in to shore, empty it, and get in again each time you overbalance.

This chapter and the next one are complementary. The beginner should first experiment with the basic strokes, while becoming familiar with the boat, but should proceed to develop the ability to roll along with the strokes. Generally, these will proceed together, since most people spend several sessions learning to roll, and the strokes can be worked on during each practice, after you have become so waterlogged that it is time to give up rolling for a little while.

ENTERING THE KAYAK

A kayak tends to be rather awkward until you are actually seated in it, so it is worth taking some pains to enter the boat carefully. Many beginners end up unceremoniously dumped into the water before they are fairly in their boats. The spray skirt and any other paraphernalia should be donned by the paddler before the boat is put in the water. There are various tricks for entering kayaks in awkward situations, but normally the boat is placed in the water with the keel line parallel to the shore or the edge of the pool or pier on which the paddler is standing. The paddle should be held in the opposite hand from the kayak. Don't let go of the boat once it is floating, particularly in moving water. It is easiest to get into the kayak without scraping the bottom if the water gets deep quickly, but on gradual shores, it may be necessary to wade out a little way into the water before getting into the boat.

Once the boat is in the water, face in the same direction as the bow, and squat down next to the boat, as close to it as circumstances permit. Pass the paddle around behind you and place it across the boat, so that the shaft lies just behind the cockpit, the blade angled up in the air just beyond the cockpit, and the other blade lies flat on the ground, as far onto shore as its length permits. With the hand next to the boat, grasp the paddle shaft and coaming together at the rear of the cockpit. With the other hand, hold the shaft a couple of feet farther in toward shore. Place the foot next to the kayak into the

a

Getting into the kayak.

a. The paddle has been rested on the shore and across the boat, in order to provide a handrail and to hold the kayak steady. The paddle is held behind the body and the hand nearer the boat holds both the shaft and the coaming. The paddler is already wearing a spray skirt.

b. With the paddle supported on both ends, the kayaker puts his weight on the shaft and puts first one foot and then the other into the boat, and then lowers himself into the seat.

c. The paddle is moved around in front of the cockpit, so that it can be grabbed quickly if the boat drifts away from shore, and the spray skirt is attached around the cockpit, first at the rear and finally in front. The paddler is now ready.

b

c

boat in front of the seat on the other side of the centerline, and carefully shift your weight over the boat, using both hands on the shaft of the paddle for support. Put the other foot in the boat next to the first, and lower yourself into the seat.

After you are in the boat, you can shift the paddle around in front of you. A grip on the shore is no longer important, normally, but try not to lose the paddle. The spray skirt should now be sealed around the coaming. In most cases, this is most easily done by pushing the elastic down around the back part of the coaming first, pulling the grab loop on the front forward, and pushing the rest of the elastic in. The grab loop or ball must be out where it can be easily yanked to release the skirt.

Variations of the method for entering the boat in water up to a depth of mid-thigh are a simple extension requiring a little more practice and balance, because one end of the paddle cannot be braced on shore, but the procedure is not too different. Sit on the rear of the cockpit to get the second foot in, before lowering yourself into the seat. Getting out gracefully simply involves reversing the steps used to get in. When the water next to the shore is running swiftly, it is common to place the kayak so that it is slightly aground, pushing off after you are seated. But gravel and rocks make this technique hard on the bottom of the boat, so it should not be used except when required. Similarly, it is sometimes necessary to drive the boat up onto the shore with hard paddling when making a landing.

GETTING OUT OF THE KAYAK

The way to make a dignified landing has already been mentioned. The more interesting problem for the beginner is getting out of the boat when hanging upside down in the water. In properly constructed kayaks, the "wet exit" is really very simple, but practice is essential at an early stage, both to make sure that the method of debarking from the boat is instinctive in case it is needed and to convince the student that turning over in the kayak is nothing to fear, since it is easy to slip out.

The beginning boater should deliberately turn over several times and practice getting out of the kayak under water. Since one is held in the boat only by the pressure of the legs against braces inside the boat, all that is necessary is to release the spray skirt by tugging on the grab loop or ball, relax your legs, and push yourself easily forward out of the boat. After the first couple of times, you should stay in the boat for thirty seconds or a minute, orienting yourself underwater. You should also start to develop the habit of hanging on to the paddle with one hand and the coaming of the boat with the other. Later on, if an accident should occur which forces you to leave the boat, it is important instinctively to keep hold of both paddle and kayak, so that you can swim to shore with all your equipment, perform self-rescue, or at least leave your companions with only one floating assemblage to assist, rather than three.

SWIMMING WITH THE KAYAK AND EMPTYING IT

After a few exits in shallow water, the novice should take his boat into deeper levels, tip over, and swim with the kayak and paddle to shore or to the edge of the pool. Getting used to keeping with the boat even after a dunking is very important. Losing a boat on a wilderness trip can be a serious matter, and rescuers will always have to assist a person before a boat. If the kayak has been abandoned, it may be smashed in a rapid or carried away by the river or the wind.

Float bags and life jackets may or may not be used in practice sessions, though the beginner should be sure to get some experience with them before going out on moving water. Whether or not float bags are used, it is always best to leave a boat floating cockpit-down in the water after a wet exit. Turning the boat over while swimming with it will allow water to rush into the cockpit, partly filling the boat. This is always undesirable, whether you are in still water near shore, so that you merely have to swim to the water's edge to empty the boat; out at sea, where it must be emptied by other means; or in rapids, where extra water in the boat will make it harder to tow to shore and more likely to be damaged in a collision with a rock.

Grab loops, painters (lines attached to the end of the boat), and other devices to enable you to hold the otherwise smooth and slippery kayak are discussed in another chapter, but the swimmer should switch from the coaming to whatever gripping device the boat has, and, holding the boat and paddle in one hand, swim to the edge of the pool or the shore. Backstrokes and sidestrokes are usually the most effective.

If there is not too much water in the boat (there should not be unless it was turned back over, particularly if float bags are in), one end is placed on the shore and the other is tipped up, keeping the cockpit pointing straight down so that all the water runs out. Lowering the end that is being held up will let any remaining water run back and out the cockpit. With some coaming designs, several tilts may be necessary to drain the boat. *Do not lift up the boat in this way if it is very heavy.* If there is too much water in the boat, levering it in this manner may damage it. Instead, empty most of it before trying to get the boat out of the water. This can be done by going to the center of the kayak, getting a shoulder under one side of the coaming, and slowly lifting it out of the water, keeping the bow and stern level with one another, so that water does not simply run down into one end. The kayak can then be carried onto shore or one end put on the side of the pool, to be emptied as described above.

THE FIT OF THE BOAT

One can begin to learn the rudiments of paddling while just sitting in a kayak, but any serious training requires that the boat fit the paddler. Although a kayaker relaxing in his boat may just be sitting in it, when he is really paddling he is virtually wearing it. He is locked into the boat by muscular pressure exerted against a number

of braces, so that every motion of the body and the forces transmitted through the paddle from the water can be communicated to
the boat. In order for this to be possible, the boat must fit.

The seat has to be comfortable, once the kayaker is used to the
position that paddling requires, and it has to be designed so that
when the hips are twisted, the kayak follows them, rather than simply allowing the buttocks to slide off to one side. This may be accomplished with a deep molded seat, with foam side braces for the
hips, or in various other ways. Foot braces of some sort are necessary, placed at the right distance from the seat, so that the paddler
can push against them and lock his knees up against the knee pads
or braces in front of the coaming. Most commercially made boats
and those used by a number of people have adjustable foot braces of
one kind or another; if you borrow a boat from a friend whose height
is different from yours, you may have to improvise. In a properly fitting boat, the paddler should be able to lock himself easily into the
kayak, yet when the muscles are relaxed, exiting should be simple.
Kayaks that are too tight for an easy bail-out are very dangerous in
white water.

THE FORWARD STROKE

The forward stroke is relatively simple to learn, though the
serious paddler will continue to refine it for years. Hold the paddle
so that the fixed hand grips the shaft naturally; the knuckles of that
hand will be pointing up when the paddle is held across the body,
and the middle joints of the fingers will be pointed forward. (It was
mentioned in Chapter 2 that paddles with curved or spooned blades
must be chosen for right- or left-hand control. But even if a paddle
with flat blades is picked, the beginner must decide which hand he
will use from the beginning, because the most important thing to be
learned with every stroke is the control of the blade angle on each
side—this angle is determined by the control hand.) Most paddles
have an oval cross section, so that the angle is naturally determined

a

b

c

The forward stroke.

a. The paddler is beginning a stroke on his left side. You can tell the paddle is right-control, because the paddler's right hand is bent back at the wrist to angle the left blade correctly; compare with **e,** where the left hand is holding the shaft loosely in normal position, since it is not the control hand. The paddle is dipped well forward and near the hull, and the upper hand is in front of the face.

b., c. As the stroke proceeds, the shoulders rotate, and the muscles of the back and torso are used for as much of the power as possible.

d. The paddle is flipped out of the water to the side as it comes back to the position of the hips.

e. The paddle is now swung forward and rotated with the right hand to make a stroke on the paddler's right.

d   **e**

by a comfortable grip with the control hand. Those who use round-shafted paddles have come up with various devices to give the hand a feel for the angle, such as tape wrapped in a particular way, or bicycle handlebar grips on the shaft. The beginner will be best off with oval cross sections.

The control or fixed hand always maintains this same grip on the shaft. The other hand keeps a loose hold between strokes, so that the shaft can rotate back and forth. Start with a forward stroke using the blade on the control side. The two hands hold the paddle at a little over shoulder-width apart. Lean forward somewhat, and drop the blade into the water as far ahead as possible, the control arm at full extension. Dip the paddle all the way into the water, not just scraping at the surface with half the blade. The angle of the shaft to the water should be at least 45°, often more, depending on the width of the boat, the length of the paddle, and other factors. Pull and push the blade back against the water, levering the boat forward. The blade is giving you purchase in the water so that the kayak can be pushed forward, and the more turbulence created in the water, the less efficient the stroke is. The control hand should pull back on the shaft, while the other hand pushes straight forward away from the paddler's face.

At the end of the stroke on the control side, the off-side hand is extended all the way forward, with the arm straight and the body twisted somewhat forward to that side. The paddle on the control side is pulled from the water. The control-side hand, still gripping the shaft firmly, turns back, the wrist bending upward 90°, so that the off-side paddle blade is twisted to be at right angles to the direction of travel as it enters the water. The off-side hand then drops the blade into the water as far forward as possible, and the stroke on that side duplicates the one on the control side, except that the fixed hand is bent back at a somewhat greater angle than would be natural, maintaining control of the angle of the blade. Thus, in each full paddling cycle, the control hand rotates the paddle shaft through 90° and turns it back again, going back and forth as strokes are made on each side of the boat. This action soon becomes instinctive, and in the forward stroke it causes little trouble even for beginners.

As much as possible of the force that goes into forward strokes should come from the strong muscles of the trunk, shoulders, back, and legs, not just from those of the arms. For this reason, the body should be put into the stroke, and the paddle should be held well ahead, so that the arms do not bend excessively; halfway through the stroke the arms are both completely extended, and the power of the stroke is all coming from the back, abdominal, and leg muscles.

The blade is pulled neatly up out of the water as it gets back to the hips. Extending the stroke beyond this point simply wastes energy lifting water and pulling the stern of the kayak down. The action of slipping the blade from the water should be smart. Slowness and sloppiness at this point may unintentionally steer the boat the wrong way. Most of the releasing motion is sideways, though the blade is also pulled up somewhat.

The new kayaker will find very quickly that his boat does not want to go in a straight line, though some designs tend to veer off course much more than others. Slalom boats, which are made to turn easily, will do just that; the beginner is bound to be frustrated by the boat's tendency to turn at its own initiative, not his, and to continue to turn once it has begun. The experienced paddler finally learns to control the direction of the boat automatically with subtle adjustments of the forward stroke, and the effort and method will not be apparent to the watching novice. The technique comes with time and practice.

A lot of training work on the forward stroke is worthwhile right from the beginning, and lakes, slow rivers, and similar spots are useful for this. It is one of the defects of pool practice that extended forward paddling is impossible, so you have to do the best you can. Ideally, in the process of learning the basic skills, the beginner should try to do some distance paddling both forward and back. Distance paddling with occasional sprints is the best way to develop proper rhythm and efficiency.

The forward stroke in moving water, again with a right-control paddle. The paddler, viewed from behind, has just reached forward for the catch in a right stroke. Note that the kayaker is wearing a helmet, a large-flotation life vest, and a full wet suit.

The body should lean slightly forward during the whole forward stroke. Try to avoid slouching or leaning back in the cockpit. Although these positions are often used to relax cramped muscles on long tours, the normal posture for the forward stroke should be a fairly straight back and a forward lean.

The forward stroke should move parallel to the keel line of the boat, not to the curve of the hull, so that the force is in line with the desired direction of travel. The blade angle should be perpendicular to the direction of the stroke. Variations from these lines are made only to change the direction of movement and to steer the kayak.

THE BACK STROKE

The back stroke is as important for the kayaker as the forward one, and it deserves as much practice. It is not used so much, but when it is needed, the need is often critical. The stroke itself is inherently weaker and more difficult to control. As with the forward stroke, practice over long distances is very worthwhile, and so are rapid alternations between forward and backward paddling.

As with the forward stroke (and all others), the control hand determines blade angle. For the back stroke, the motions of forward paddling are simply reversed. The blade is planted in the water at about the position of the hips, pushed well under the surface of the water, and driven forward toward the bow of the boat, using as much energy from the trunk and leg muscles as possible, and keeping the angle of the blade perpendicular to the keel line of the boat, which is along the desired direction of travel during these pure forward and back strokes.

Control of the blade angle is more critical in the back stroke than in the forward one, since it is easy to capsize with a powerful stroke if the lower edge of the blade is tilted forward. At first, particularly after a dunking or a near miss, the beginner is likely to be reluctant to put his heart into the stroke or may deliberately tilt the blade forward, at a climbing angle. Eventually, however, it is important to develop a strong, reliable, and automatic back stroke. Work at it.

Note that the paddle is not reversed for the back stroke; only the direction of paddling is changed. Thus, if the paddle is curved or spooned, the back stroke is made on the nonpower face of each blade. There is no time to reverse the paddle in the complex paddling situations that demand a back stroke. In fact, the position of the hands on the paddle remains virtually unchanged in all strokes, and severe problems are likely to result when the paddle is not correctly oriented. From the beginning stay out of the bad habit of reversing the paddle.

A slight backward lean is helpful in back paddling, just as the forward lean is the best position for paddling ahead. Try to learn to paddle straight back while looking forward or over either shoulder; this will require much practice. Obviously, the problem of not being able to easily see where you are going is one of the difficulties of the back stroke.

SWEEPS

The sweep is the most obvious way to turn the kayak and the simplest. For the regular forward sweep, the paddler reaches as far forward as possible and puts the blade in the water near the bow, so

The forward sweep stroke.

a. To turn to his left, the paddler places his right blade in the water next to the hull as far forward as possible, power face out.

b., c. The paddle is swept around near the surface of the water, describing a half-circle as far out as possible; the boat turns the opposite way.

d., e. As the blade reaches the hull at the stern end, it is pulled quickly out of the water, and is ready to be moved forward for another sweep or a different stroke.

that the blade is immersed just a couple of inches. The paddle is then swept out in an arc, as far from the boat as possible in the center, and sweeping back in toward the stern. A strong sweep should turn the kayak well over 90°. Practice the sweep on both sides (pushing the boat in opposite directions). See how many sweeps are required to turn the boat completely around; no more than four should be needed if you are doing the stroke properly, and you should rapidly reach the point where three sweeps turn the boat at least 360°.

As soon as you have the knack of the forward sweep, work on the back sweep, which is simply the reverse of the forward. Like the back stroke, the back sweep can result in a rapid dunking if the blade angle is poorly chosen. Practice back sweeps on both sides of the kayak, and then try various combinations of back and forward sweeps and regular forward and back strokes. A forward sweep on one side and a back sweep on the other should turn the boat at least 180°.

Forward and back sweeps are often used in modified form. To make slight course corrections while paddling either forward or

A backward sweep, similar to the forward one, but less powerful.

backward, you can introduce a little sweep on one side or the other.

The sweeps complete the basic inventory of strokes. The beginner should be able to manage a rudimentary attempt at the forward and back strokes and the various sweeps after an hour or two in the kayak and to get around the swimming pool or the shallow water of a lake enough to begin feeling at home in the boat. This is the time to start with the preparatory drills for the Eskimo roll. Most of the other strokes covered in this chapter require the paddler to lean on the paddle and the same drills are required to develop the confidence and skill necessary for rolling and for the leaning strokes. From this point, as has been mentioned already, practicing the various strokes will probably alternate with work on the roll.

THE DRAW

The draw and its variations may be the most important of all kayaking strokes. Many of the hanging strokes, eddy turns, and braces develop from it. It has to be practiced for long periods. The beginner will at first be timid in executing the draw, and real confidence will not develop until the Eskimo roll has also been mastered. Eventually, however, persistence in working on the draw will be rewarded, because when this stroke is executed well, the paddler is well on his way to true expertise in handling the kayak.

Reach out to one side of the centerline of the boat, drop the paddle into the water with the blade parallel to the keel line, and pull the boat toward the paddle with the paddle side arm, the other (now upper) arm acting mainly as a fulcrum. As the paddle and the boat come together, slip the paddle quickly to the rear and out of the water. At the end of the stroke, the paddler either regains balance or reaches out for another draw.

The effectiveness of the draw depends on the paddler's reaching well out from the side of the boat and putting full power into the stroke, which in turn requires actually putting a good deal of his weight on the paddle—he leans out beyond the balance point and

The draw, which is used to pull the kayak to the side or to give the paddler stability.

a. The kayaker has reached out to the side for a left draw, dropping the blade into the water and leaning out on it. The right hand, which is the control hand, is bent back at the wrist to bring the left blade parallel to the hull. The right arm is high and pushes on the shaft while the lower (left) arm pulls.

b. The kayak is pulled toward the paddle, with the blade's push on water under the surface stabilizing the boat and paddler, despite the lean.

c. As the paddle nears the hull, the blade underwater is swept back and the shaft forward, so that the blade knifes out of the water, and the paddle is quickly reached out for another draw.

d. The draw should be practiced at all angles until the paddler can lean far out on it comfortably, his lower side completely in the water. This would be an exaggerated position in which to do the draw, but not for using it as a support.

then pulls the kayak underneath to regain balance, using the paddle
for leverage on water a foot or two below the surface. There are a
number of pitfalls in the draw, but the paddler is all too well aware
of most of them from the beginning, and timidity is usually the
major problem that needs to be overcome. Recovery is a bit tricky
and requires some practice. It means slicing the paddle out of the
water just before the boat rides over it, but not too soon, since that
would sacrifice much of the effectiveness of the stroke. Waiting too
long before pulling the paddle out, however, results in an almost
certain upset, particularly if the boater is still overbalanced from the
lean.

Everything about the draw improves with a strong lean. Both
arms are brought out over the water for maximum power and a
proper vertical placement of the paddle. As long as the paddler
remains timid about leaning out over the water, the reach is limited,
the off-side arm is in an ineffective position, and much of the force
that is developed is wasted on a downward pushing against the
water. If you don't fall into the water quite a few times while working on your draw, you aren't really trying.

Practice a repeated draw for some distance on each side, back and
forth across a pool or for equivalent lengths in a lake. Once the basic
draw begins to come along, try intentionally drawing slightly forward and back of the centerline of the boat. (You'll have done it a lot
accidentally while trying to get the basic stroke.) The draw can be
used to move the boat to the side and turn it simultaneously, and,
like the sweep, it can be combined with regular forward and backward strokes. This sort of maneuver is common in white water,
where the draw may be employed to move the kayak to the side to
avoid an obstacle and to make course corrections of all kinds. As the
draw becomes more powerful, you will find that the position is
becoming very stable, more stable than sitting upright in the boat,
because you are supported by both the boat and the paddle, at some
distance from each other.

Another method of moving the kayak one way or another is to

vary the angle of the blade. A draw directly in on the centerline
with the bow edge of the paddle angled out will move the boat
backward, while the opposite angulation will move it forward. This
exercise also begins to develop the precise control of blade angle
that is important in many advanced strokes.

RUDDERS

The paddle can be used directly to steer at either the front or the
back of the boat, and it is worth practicing these rudders as part of
your basic inventory of strokes, though they are seldom used as distinct maneuvers. A rudder is normally used in conjunction with a
regular stroke to make minor course corrections. The paddle is simply held as a deflecting vane beside the boat, sometimes directly to
the side, more often toward the bow or stern.

A rear rudder, useful mainly for minor course corrections when the boat is
moving with respect to the water. This technique comes quite instinctively,
but active paddle strokes are usually preferable. This is the same position as
the low brace, except that in the latter, the paddle is turned 90° so that the
flat of the trailing blade pushes down on the water.

A rudder is not effective for making any major change in course, and obviously it will work only if the boat is moving at a fair speed with respect to the water. It is interesting when experimenting with rudders to note the effects of attempts to steer from the bow and stern ends of the boat. A bow rudder while the boat is going forward will easily start the boat off a straight-line course, but after the initial deflection it will have little effect on the direction of the turn. The stern rudder will have considerably better effect. A stern rudder is also fairly easy to use at the end of a forward stroke. For both these reasons, a stern rudder is normally used when the boat is going forward and the bow rudder when the direction of travel is reversed. A bow rudder is used while going forward only to initiate a turn and almost immediately blends into another stroke, such as a draw at the bow end of the kayak. A stern rudder during backward movement has a similar effect.

A forward rudder like this can be used to initiate a turn when the kayak is moving with respect to the water, but it is limited in use, except when it is used at the start of a high brace in eddy turns, as discussed in Chapter 5.

SCULLING

Sculling is something like a continuous draw stroke. The paddle is moved back and forth parallel to the keel line of the boat and near the centerline, with the paddle always angled somewhat, the leading edge away from the boat, so that the kayak is pulled toward the paddle. The angle is changed at each zig and zag, so that the pull is always away from the boat. The scull can be executed with both arms fairly low, but a really effective sculling action for the kayak is only achieved when the paddler leans out on the stroke, with the off-side hand out over the head.

To begin the scull stroke, lean out and place the paddle in the water well away from the hull of the boat, as if for a draw. Angle

Sculling, which is a continuous form of the draw. The lower blade is kept in the water and the kayaker leans on the paddle, moving the blade first forward, then back, then forward again, turning it at each stroke so that the leading edge is always angled away from the boat, thus pulling the kayak across the water.

a. The kayaker is forcing the blade in the water forward, using the upper hand as a pivot. Note the angle of the upper blade, which is leaning back, indicating the climbing angle of the lower one.

b. The lower blade has reached a forward position, and the paddler is starting to turn it for the reverse sweep, drawing on the shaft a bit to maintain support while the angle is changed.

c. Reversing the direction and pushing the lower blade backward through the water, while also rising to a somewhat more normal position. Note the angle of the upper blade, which is now canted forward instead of back, so that the printing on the power face can now be seen. As with the draw, the paddler should be comfortable sculling with various degrees of lean.

the blade with the sternward edge out from the boat, and push the blade back through the water parallel to the keel line, using the upper hand as a pivot for the paddle shaft. As the rear limit of the stroke is reached, turn the blade to angle back the other way, and push it forward. The back and forth action can be continued as long as is necessary to move the kayak the desired distance. The scull can be finished in a number of ways, but the simplest and most common is with a draw stroke that restores the paddler's balance and brings the paddle out of the water.

Once the scull has been practiced on both sides, variations can be worked out, just as with the draw stroke. One can scull somewhat toward the bow or the stern instead of on the centerline, so as to turn the kayak at the same time that it is being moved to the side. One can go into a scull from another stroke or finish another stroke by going into a scull.

The use of the scull is similar to that of the draw. The latter is more often used, but the scull does have the advantage of being continuous. A strong scull should be a very stable position for the paddler, like a draw. Since it is continuous, there is no break like that of the draw where balance may be lost. Both should be practiced extensively, for both will contribute to the control of the paddler over blade angle and to his or her confidence in leaning strokes. Be sure to practice equally on both sides.

BRACES, SUPPORTS, AND HANGING STROKES

The draw and the scull serve as a good introduction to a whole class of maneuvers: the hanging strokes and braces. Modern kayaking technique is founded on the use of these strokes; they permit the skilled paddler to achieve control and stability in the roughest water even with very narrow boats. They allow the canny river runner to use powerful crosscurrents to advantage, instead of being swamped by them, and the competent coastal paddler to move with impunity in powerful breaking surf.

The first element in all the braces and hanging strokes is the use of the paddle to allow the paddler to lean on the water, reducing his dependence on balance to prevent a capsize, while enabling him to gain power and reach at the same time. Sculling, drawing, and Eskimo rolling all use the paddle for support, although support has been incidental to other purposes in the discussion so far.

A brace or support is the use of the paddle to lean against the water. One can brace in a number of ways, at any point within reach around the boat; different braces at different points will have varying effects. A hanging stroke differs from the corresponding brace only in that the paddle moves. The distinction is a rather narrow one, and in the United States, at least, the various terms are used somewhat interchangeably.

The reason that there is no real dividing line between the various hanging strokes and braces is that the result of any of them depends on a complex series of factors. In the simplest situation, the paddle may be used to regain balance while the boater is sitting still on flat water and absentmindedly begins to tip over. The paddle blade on the side of the boat toward which he is tipping can be pushed down flat on the surface of the water and the shaft used as a lever to push the kayaker back into balance. This maneuver is commonly called the *slap support,* and it can also be used in moving water.

In another simple case, a stroke may be used simply to move the boat over flat water, but the stroke may be most effectively executed by leaning out and using the paddle for support while pulling on it. Thus, the type of draw already described can be called a *hanging draw* to distinguish it from the less effective draw in which the paddler does not lean much and the off-side arm goes across the chest instead of over the head.

In many cases, however, the relationships are more complicated. When a boat is moving with respect to the water, a support stroke can exert rotational force on the kayak through the paddle shaft and the body of the boater, and this rotational force may combine with other effects of the stroke. Thus, to give one possibility, if you are practicing your forward stroke on a lake or in a swimming pool, and while you are traveling at a good rate of speed you reach out and do a strong draw stroke with the leading edge of the paddle angled away from the boat, you will find that this is not only a very powerful brace against tipping over, but that it also causes the boat to turn around the paddle blade. You are using the resistance of the paddle in the water to provide a rotational center for a turn. The farther you lean, the more leverage goes into the turning action. Another factor is at work too: as you lean onto the paddle, the kayak turns onto its side. The side has much more curvature (rocker) than the bottom of the boat, so there is less resistance to the boat turning. Such *hanging turns* can be very effective.

The combination of bracing action to stabilize the balance of the paddler and turning action on the boat can be a very useful amalgam, allowing the paddler to avoid potential spills in fast turns by leaning into the inside of the turn against a firmly braced paddle. In difficult water the braces are ideal, because they enable the skillful boater to use violent current differentials—which would normally be working to upset him in turbulent white water or surf—to his advantage. The long reach of a hanging stroke can be exploited to place the paddle in water flowing at a different rate or in the opposite direction from the water in which the kayak is moving, and to use the resulting rotational force to maneuver the kayak very swiftly, while at the same time bracing the boater in a stable position.

The use of such braces is the key to kayaking on difficult water, and it will be discussed in detail later. Hanging strokes are introduced here because of their importance in moving water. The beginner can get a good deal of practice even on flat water, however.

THE LOW BRACE

The simplest of the braces, this one is most commonly and easily used in the stern quadrants. To begin, paddle forward to get up speed and then place the nonpower face of one paddle blade flat on

the water near the boat and behind you. Lean over on it hard, pushing down on the shaft with the hand at the end near that blade, and
pulling up with the other hand. You will find that the boat will tend
to turn around the paddle blade and that you will be able to put
quite a bit of weight on the paddle. Experiment with the brace on
both sides of the boat. Reach out farther from the boat with the
paddle, angling it up out of the water slightly at the leading edge,
and keep working on the brace until you can lean far out on it. The
more you lean, the more effective it will be as a turning stroke.

The low brace in one of the rear quadrants can also be used for
turning strokes when the kayak is not moving with respect to the
water. Start the stroke next to the boat toward the stern, with the
outside edge of the blade angled up. Lean hard on the paddle, and

A low brace in use on moving water. The paddler is leaning some of his
weight on the paddle extended back, pushing the *nonpower* face of the
blade against the water. This is one of the most common uses of this brace,
giving the boater stability in moving water. To maintain balance as he hits
the waves below, he will simply lean harder on the paddle.

sweep it out away from the boat. The stroke can be continued all the way forward or stopped at any point by simply pushing the body back up into balance against a flattened paddle.

It should be apparent that the low brace can be either a pure support or a stroke. Usually it is both, like most of the braces and hanging strokes. The low brace is very handy for minor course corrections when paddling forward, particularly when one does not want to slow the boat very much. Bracing turns, including that using the low brace, tend to slow movement less than other turns, too. Low braces are excellent aids to balance in many situations in rough water, easy to apply and to recover from. They are most often used in the rear quadrants, but they should be practiced toward the front of the boat also. Note that the slap support already described is simply a special case of a low brace of short duration used at the centerline of the boat.

THE HIGH BRACE

The high brace is the true keystone of modern kayak technique. At its highest stage of development, it is the method for making the most elegant of turns in heavy water and for flipping up out of a big breaker while surfing. It is also the most powerful of the braces, the perfect support of the kayaker in many difficult situations.

Essentially, the high brace is simply a refinement of the high draw stroke. A stationary high brace is performed by holding a paddle at shoulder level or over the head, the forearms pointing either straight up or slightly backward, and reaching out to brace on the water with the power side of the blade as far out from the hull as possible on the centerline of the boat. To regain an upright position, the paddler can push the paddle down on the water, pull it toward the boat in a draw stroke, or scull in either direction. The high brace in its simplest form is very similar to the draw, except that the intent is to support the paddler rather than to move the boat over, and the paddle blade is likely to be somewhat more horizontal. With the draw it is important to get the paddle fairly near the vertical, so that the force on the water is exerted in the direction one wants to go. You can get plenty of support even on a perfectly vertical shaft, because you are pulling on the lower part of the shaft and pushing with the upper hand high on the shaft, producing a rotational force counter to the lean of the body. However, for a pure bracing action it is preferable for the shaft to be at an angle of 45° or so to the vertical, since this allows the paddle to be placed farther out in the water, giving better leverage and a stronger support. The longer reach is also helpful when the high brace is modified for use in turns.

In addition to practicing the high brace with the paddle flat and at the centerline of the boat, the kayaker should try it toward the stern and the bow on both sides. The next step is to brace with the blade at a climbing angle (backward and forward), and to move it in the direction of climb while leaning on the shaft. The motion is like scull-

Practicing the high brace or Duffek stroke while the boat is moving. The kayaker has paddled the boat up to speed.

a. He leans over on the paddle with the blade placed in the water at a climbing angle, and the boat pivots around the blade.

b. The boat has slowed down as it turned, and the paddler is finishing with a slight draw to right himself and the kayak.

c. The high brace in moving water. The kayaker has reached the paddle out into a fast current and is bracing on it while it turns the boat.

ing, but the shaft is less vertical, and the stroke does not normally go back and forth. This brace with an angled blade should be practiced on both sides at the centerline and fore and aft of it. One can practice leaning far back and forth from one side to the other, bracing in each direction in rapid succession. With this sweeping motion, either from the rear sweeping forward, or from the front sweeping back, one can lean very far over for some time and still recover. Work at it at least until you can lie over with the side of your body in the water and recover without strain, with either a forward sweep or a backward one on either side of the boat. These sweeps also turn the boat in the opposite rotation from that of the sweep.

The *Duffek stroke,* named after its originator, is simply the high brace used as a turning stroke, when the kayak is moving at a good speed with respect to the water. Paddle forward until the kayak is going at a good clip, and lean over onto a high brace, with the blade inserted into the water at a climbing angle. A good lean is required to make the stroke really effective. After you have worked at it for a while on each side, try it toward the bow and the stern on each side. To continue the turn as the boat begins to slow, a sweep forward can be made. Recovery is made either with a sweep or a draw stroke. When you are quite confident using the high brace turn going forward, try it going backward. Since you will not be able to get up as much speed paddling backward, you will probably have to incorporate some sweep in the turn practicing this way. Also, you will find the blade angle harder to control at first, and you'll take even more dives than in learning the forward stroke. It's a good opportunity to practice your rolls, which should be fairly reliable by this time.

The Duffek is most useful in moving water, especially where there are strong shifts in current speed and direction, because in these cases, one reaches out into water moving with respect to that under the boat and uses the current differential to turn the kayak. These techniques will be discussed in Chapter 5. They are mentioned here only to indicate the importance of the high brace. All the variations of this stroke can and should be practiced extensively on flat water, but it is in surf and in rapids that they become really important.

PRACTICE

Many variations of strokes have been mentioned in this chapter, and there are many more that you will find as you work on your management of the kayak. There is nothing like getting out and paddling for long periods to develop the instinctive control of the paddle that is necessary for progress and the physical conditioning that will enable the kayaker to develop his or her technique. Paddle forward and backward for several miles at a stretch, taking sprints every little while. Experiment with leaning back and forth while paddling to develop better balance and the ability to paddle on either side while the boat is being tossed about. First try leaning toward the side on which you are paddling, tipping back and forth each time you dip the paddle for a few hundred strokes, forward and back. Then try tipping the boat away from the paddle with each stroke.

Practice drawing and sculling on each side for considerable distances. Much of the control needed in the more complicated turns can be developed from assiduous drill with the draw and sculling strokes. Train yourself to use them when the boat is moving and to apply them from various positions. It is often necessary to throw a quick draw to avoid a rock or to brace after losing your balance. Practice getting into draw strokes and all the various braces from as many different paddling positions as you can create. Try to catch yourself by surprise, so that you can develop the control of paddle position and blade angle that you will need on difficult water. Make sure that you really lean on the hanging strokes. A timid high brace will not do the job when the real thing is needed.

Work on all of the turns, learning to maneuver your boat as well as possible in the water, practicing around some sort of slalom gate or buoy. An empty Clorox bottle or two anchored with cord and rocks will do nicely at first. Work for mastery of all the turns on either side of the boat, backward and forward. The English gate, an exercise described at the end of the chapter, makes a very good drill once you have developed all your basic strokes.

Watch the way experienced paddlers handle their boats, and try to imitate them. Ask good paddlers to criticize your technique, and work to improve it. Once you have a really good command of all the standard strokes and their variations, you may want to try some more exotic strokes and combinations that other paddlers will show you. It is good exercise to work on the various canoe strokes with the kayak. They are not normally used, but some drilling with them will develop better control of the paddle and more body flexibility. One is the *pry*, which is the reverse of the draw stroke: the paddle is inserted in the water, blade parallel to the keel line, just next to the hull, and pushed out away from the boat. The canoeist, who has only a single-bladed paddle, often has to use the pry to keep paddling on the same side of the boat. The draw is a better stroke for the kayaker, but the pry is good practice. Try the *cross draw,* too. This is a draw executed on the opposite side of the boat from the hand doing the drawing. The paddle crosses the hull and dips into the water for a draw on the other side. Again, this is mostly useful as an exercise, and if you work at it, you'll certainly have some chances to practice your roll. Try it on both sides.

A more useful canoe stroke is the *reverse sweep.* Start with a draw from as far out as you can reach forward and to the side of the kayak, continue with a forward stroke along past the centerline of the boat, and finally push the paddle back and out away from the hull at the end of the stroke. This stroke can be used to turn the kayak toward the paddling side. To practice it, keep paddling on the same side of the boat for a while, using the reverse sweep to keep it moving in a straight line. Then work on the other side.

As you continue to practice paddling, you will gradually develop control of the kayak and will move effortlessly from one stroke into the next. In rough water pure strokes often yield to combinations. Forward strokes, draws, and braces blend into one another with smooth control of the paddle. However, working on each separate stroke for a time in each training session will benefit you as a beginner, keep you from getting sloppy, and develop your weaker strokes. The canoe strokes just discussed, and others that you can find, are helpful as exercises, but don't neglect practice of the basic tools of kayaking. Finally, take your skills out onto moving water, where you can really begin to test them, following the safety precautions discussed later in the book, When you begin to use your paddling technique on moving water, the fun and challenge of kayaking really begin.

THE ENGLISH GATE

A good training exercise is a sequence of maneuvers performed around a single gate hung over a pool or lake (see Chapter 8 on gates), or a pair of floats anchored there. Begin practicing without the rolls until you have learned to do them. The sequence is: Paddle straight through the gate, turn 180° to the right, paddle straight back through, turn 180° to the left, and paddle straight back through a third time. Next, paddle backward past the gate outside both poles, keeping them to your left; do a complete roll to the left, paddle forward through the gate, paddle backward past it with the gate on your right, roll to the right, paddle forward through the gate, reverse past it with the gate on the right, continue in reverse through the gate, double back clockwise and paddle through backward again; paddle forward on the outside with the gate on your left, roll left, paddle backward through the gate, paddle forward past the gate on your right, roll right, and paddle through in reverse for the finish. The object is maximum speed without hitting any poles or floats. You won't be able to manage the sequence at all for a while, but a champion can do the whole routine in a minute.

4

The Eskimo Roll

The technique of rolling the kayak back up after a capsize without having to leave the boat is a basic skill that must be mastered by anyone who wants to do any kayaking beyond the level of flat-water boating close to shore. With most kayaks, rolling is the primary safety measure for recovery from an upset, although some folding kayaks designed for moderate touring are hard to tip over and hard to roll back up. The ability to roll is also vital to beginning and intermediate kayakers trying to perfect their paddling skills. Working on the hanging strokes and braces discussed in the preceding chapter is bound to result in lots of spills if the paddler is making a real effort, and he will quickly become exhausted if every capsize requires a trip to shore to empty the kayak and get back in.

Most kayaks are fairly easy to roll and are therefore suitable for use by beginners in training. Some specialized boats should not be used, however, including downriver racing craft, which are very tippy; flat-water racing boats, which are not intended for rolling; and touring boats with very wide beams, such as most foldboats, because they are very difficult to roll.

There are several methods of rolling and many variations of each, but they all have certain common principles. Normally, the paddle is used to brace against the water and to lever the kayaker and his craft back into an upright position. A properly executed roll requires little force in normal circumstances, and the paddle gives a great deal of support, so that a well-performed roll is very reliable. A good kayaker can even roll with his hands only (or with only one hand), but this type of roll is less effective. It cannot be relied on in unfavorable circumstances, such as turbulent white water.

Regardless of the method of rolling, the first step in righting your-self from a capsize is to orient yourself underwater. The experienced roller often does not pause at all; he has trained himself to make all the correct motions from the beginning, but this self-orientation is one of the beginner's key problems, and it is usually best for him always to pause for a few moments while upside down in the water to figure things out, perhaps with a face mask to enable him to see what he is doing. Even the experienced kayaker may need to pause occasionally after a confusing capsize—it is better to pause a second and to roll up successfully than to make a quick and ill-fated at-tempt.

After orienting himself, the kayaker uses his paddle (in one of the ways to be discussed) to pull his body up to a horizontal position in the water in the direction he wants to emerge, and the boat turns around with him. However he does not yet try to lift his body out of the water at all. The next stage, the "hip-flick," is to begin to roll the boat upright with the hips, and this stage continues as the roll is completed; the body follows the boat up, and the head follows the body, so that the boat has been rolled completely upright while the body and head are still horizontal, barely out of the water. The novice's most common error as he begins to succeed at the roll is to reverse the sequence, trying to bring his head up first, his body sec-ond, and the boat last.

A correct hip-flick makes the roll almost effortless, requiring only a light thrust on the paddle, and keeping the blade close to the sur-face, so that the paddler can brace on it after emerging, if necessary.

Many rolls, particularly those without paddles, require the pad-dler to lean close to the deck of the boat, either backward or for-ward, to reduce the force needed to bring him up. Such leans are usually combined with the motions required for the paddle stroke.

LEARNING TO ROLL

The desirability of having a seasoned instructor to help the begin-ner learning to roll has already been mentioned. Various kayakers have their own preferences in teaching rolling, and anyone lucky enough to find a teacher should be happy to use the method he or she prefers. There are many sequences that will ultimately bring the neophyte to proficiency in rolling. The one suggested here is the one I personally find effective. Eskimo rolling is one of those tricky physical skills for which the student's learning difficulties may lie in his conception of the motions that need to be performed, in confusion about the body's orientation, in coordinating the muscles and the mind, in lack of flexibility and strength, or in various other areas. Often some tiny change in method, a trick used by an instructor, or a learning device suggested by a book will suddenly turn the tide for one student, while it will be of no use at all to another. Thus, the sequence suggested in this book may work perfectly for one person, while a completely different program will be found far superior for another. It is doubtful whether there is any one "best way" to learn to roll.

Fortunately, with a little persistence, any reasonably well-coordinated person can learn to roll well. Some will learn much faster than others, and the fastest learners will not always be either the best athletes or the best paddlers. Do not become discouraged if your roll does not succeed right away. Go back to the beginning, and keep working. When you get too waterlogged, practice your strokes for a while and come back another day. The Eskimo roll is a particularly odd skill; even when you understand exactly how it is done, your muscles are frequently intractable and will not perform. It is often especially difficult to analyze what you are doing wrong.

My own experience may serve to illustrate some of the typical frustrations of the novice roller. I taught myself the right-hand roll quite quickly, going through the sequence without much difficulty in one practice session with no instructor. After a few more work periods some time later, the right-hand roll was quite reliable. However, even though I obviously understood the actions required, it took me three sessions to be able to roll to the left with any reasonable probability of getting up in that direction. This was true even though I had a great advantage in learning the second side, because

I could always roll up the other way after a failure. Most kayakers have had some such problem when learning to roll, even if they have since forgotten the difficulties.

Patience and perseverance are therefore often the most important elements in learning to roll. Next in priority is careful attention to fundamentals before attempting complete rolls. A lot of drill in the hip-flick is important, so that it can later be managed without thought while the kayaker is worrying about what he is doing with the paddle. Careful observance of properly executed rolls, analysis of them, and dry-land drills may help a great deal.

Many people may be helped by a face mask through much of the initial practice of rolling, but this is not essential. It does allow the beginner to see what he is doing and keeps the water out of his nose. Goggles will serve the first purpose, and many experienced paddlers like to use nose clips and sometimes ear plugs during extensive rolling practice. Wearers of glasses will need retaining bands, and contact-lens users may require goggles. If there are many beginners in a small area, particularly in a swimming pool, the ends of the kayaks should be padded with ethafoam bumpers fastened with boat tape.

As described in the last chapter, the first step for beginners is to become familiar with their boats, gaining some skill in paddling forward and back, turning with sweep strokes, getting in and out, attaching spray skirts, and making enough wet exits to be comfortable about turning over. After these preliminaries, rolling practice can begin.

THE HIP-FLICK AND SUPPORTED ROLL

The action of turning the boat up with the hips is fundamental to all rolls. Until it has been mastered, there is little point in going on with other stages. In a swimming pool, the hip-flick can be learned along the side. In a lake or other quiet waterway, a pier or the edge of a large platform float may serve as well. If a helper is available, whether he is an instructor or not, he can serve the same purpose by standing in waist-deep water and holding out his hands or the paddle shaft for a support.

Whatever means of support is used, the student needs to practice leaning over into the water and rolling the kayak down under and up out of the water. This has to be practiced on both sides until it is really learned, and it may take a short time or a couple of hours. The successful beginner should be able to support himself on whatever he is using, with his body half in the water, and then roll the kayak in one quick motion from a position almost completely turned over to one turned nearly upright.

The next step is to maintain a hold on the support with both hands and to submerge the body as far as possible in the water, wait a second, and roll up, using the support and concentrating on the hip-flick. If the hips are rolling the kayak as they should, this should require little effort. Practice for a while on each side.

Now roll completely over, maintaining a grip on the support only with one hand (the one that starts farther from the support and is nearer after you are upside down in the water). Wait for a few seconds to get the feeling of the vertical position under the water, and then roll back up. The second hand can grab the support on the way up, if you wish. Practice this as before, pausing underwater and making sure that the hips roll the kayak up each time, before the body and head are lifted all the way out of the water. Again, the best gauge is the effort required. With a proper hip-flick, there should be no straining or hard pulling. If a helper is providing the support, he should be able to tell the student who is leaning too hard.

Finally, the student should capsize away from his support, reaching up on the support side when he reaches a vertical position underwater and rolling up on the support side. This is a full roll. Practice on both sides until the motion is fluid and unstrained.

THE EXTENDED SCREW ROLL

The student is now ready to work on an actual roll, and the type of roll taught at this stage is the major point of disagreement among instructors. Some prefer to teach the layout roll (see pages 107–108) first, and others teach the screw roll with various modifications. I prefer to start with a screw roll in which leverage is increased by holding one blade of the paddle. This gives the beginner easy command of the blade angle, but the motion is essentially the same as with the regular screw roll, which is the standard roll for most situations. The extended screw roll is also known as the *Pawlata roll*, after Edi Pawlata, who learned the technique in the 1920s.

In the screw roll, the kayaker leans forward and pushes the paddle up toward the surface on the side of the kayak he wants to roll up on, shaft parallel to the gunwales of the kayak, with the hand opposite reaching across the kayak and out of the water. The leading edge of the forward blade is angled up on the side away from the kayak, "up" being away from the kayaker, who is upside down in the water. Still leaning forward, the kayaker sweeps his blade out until the paddle is at right angles to the kayak, and the resulting sculling action begins to bring him toward the surface of the water. He then pulls himself up on the paddle, and levers himself out of the water. The kayak leads the body of the paddler out of the water, and the body leads the head. The sculling sweep may continue into the rear quadrant or may stop at the midline of the kayak.

In the *extended screw*, the opposite blade of the paddle from that being used for the roll is held in the hand. This gives the kayaker good control of the blade angle, and it means that the working blade is a foot and a half farther away from the boat, giving much better leverage. The reason that the extended position is not used normally is that the hands have to change position on the paddle, which is time-consuming and might cause loss of the paddle in rough water.

For the extended position, it is possible to practice the motions on dry ground, before the session in the pool or lake. Put the boat

The extended screw roll. These drawings should be compared with the photographs on pages 101–105 of the screw roll, which is performed identically
except for the position in which the paddle is held, and with the following
set of drawings showing the extended screw from a point of view under
water.

a. The kayaker preparing to practice the roll sets the paddle in position
before turning over. The forward blade, which will perform the sweep, is
held at an angle roughly parallel to the hull, the outer edge of the blade
down, so that it will angle up after the boater has turned over. For a full
roll, the kayaker turns over toward the paddle, which then comes out of the
water on the opposite side.

a

b. The boater is shown here after turning over, looking from the opposite
side. The beginner should wait a few moments before starting the sweep, to
be sure that he has reached this position, with the paddle parallel to the surface of the water.

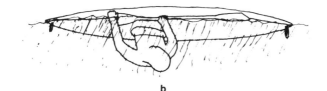

b

c. The kayaker begins the sweep, the active blade planing at an angle close to the surface of the water, while the hand and blade near the hull are clear of the water. The body and the sweeping arm swing outward toward a position perpendicular to the side of the kayak.

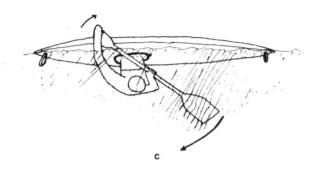

c

d. As the paddle reaches a position perpendicular to the hull, the kayaker stops sweeping it backward and pulls directly down on the shaft, pushing up with the hand holding the blade. The planing action of the paddle has already raised the boater and kayak some distance from the vertical. The boater has turned the hull ahead of his trunk by rotating his hips, and the paddle is now used as a lever directly down against the water to raise the boat and body the rest of the way. The hull is turned up first, and if the roll is executed properly, the paddle blade will remain near the surface.

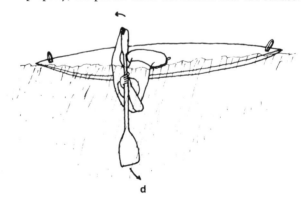

d

e. The kayaker emerges at the end of the roll with the paddle in a sculling position high in the water. A paddle deep in the water is an indication of a weak roll.

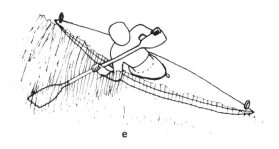

e

on grass or somewhere else where undue stress will not be placed on the hull. A right-handed paddler using a right-control paddle will probably want to start with a right-hand roll, which is the one described here. A left-handed paddler using a left-control paddle may wish to reverse sides to start. Ultimately, every kayaker should be ambidextrous in rolling; he should have no weak side.

For the right-hand roll, get in the kayak, lock your feet and knees into the braces, and hold the paddle along the left side of the boat. Here is where the confusion in rolling begins: the paddle sweeps out to the side that is on the left of the upside-down paddler, and it remains essentially fixed, while the kayaker rolls up on it, so that the paddle ends on the right side of the boat. It is really the kayaker and his boat who have rolled to the other side of the paddle, however. In land practice this orientation problem can only be imagined, but the novice should try to visualize the situation as it will be in the water.

With the paddle along the left gunwale, grasp the end of the sternward blade with the left hand, the heel of the hand on the power face and the fingers wrapping around the tip to the other side. Hold the shaft with the right hand about two feet away. Lean as far forward as possible. Now sweep the paddle out so that the active blade describes an arc from the bow of the kayak out to the midline. The blade should stay just above the ground, a level that corresponds to the position of the water surface in a true roll. The power face of the active blade will face upward, because you and the blade will be upside down in the water. The outside edge of the blade—the leading edge—should be angled somewhat downward, so that it will be up in the water. Practice controlling the blade angle with the hand holding the inactive blade, which remains next to the kayak, held as far down as possible. Practice until you have a good feeling for the motion of the trunk.

As the paddle sweeps to a perpendicular position at the centerline of the kayak, the right arm pulls the paddle straight up in the air—the motion will be down in the water. From this point the land simulation begins to fail, since this is where the kayak must be rolled over with a hip-flick and the body pulled up out of the water. Visualize the differences that would affect the motion in the water as you continue to practice the whole motion of the roll on land.

Once land drill is finished for the extended roll, get someone to help with the real thing, ideally an individual who knows how to roll, though any assistant will do if an experienced kayaker is not available. If the person helping you can roll well himself, the best thing for him to do the first few times is to guide your paddle through the proper motion, then provide some support for it while you complete the roll up. If not, have your assistant watch the paddle, so that if you have trouble, you may be able to find out what is going wrong by talking to him. Have him watch from the bow, ready to give you a hand when you need it. Tell him not to try to help you up until you ask by releasing the paddle and holding a hand up out of the water. When he grasps your hand, you can roll up on this support, just as you have already done in previous practice sessions.

When you are ready to try the roll, remind yourself of the whole sequence of motions you will make. Hold the paddle along the left

gunwale, just as in the dry-land drill. Lean forward and capsize to
the right; you will roll back up the same way. Give yourself enough
time to orient yourself underwater, and then go through the same
motions you did on shore, sweeping the paddle out, so that you
swing your bent trunk around from a forward to a leftward lean,
keeping the paddle blade angled so that the leading edge will ride
up in the water. When the paddle is straight out, roll up on it, flipping the hull up with the hips first, pulling the body up with the
right arm, and leaving the head lying in the water until last.

It will probably take more tries than you anticipate before you roll
successfully. After each failure, sit in the kayak and try to analyze
your mistakes. If you have a face mask, watch the paddle during the
stroke to see if the sweep is correct—the active blade of the paddle
should sweep out in a quarter-circle near the surface of the water.
Keeping your eye on the paddle is a good idea, anyway—your head
follows the paddle as it should. Talk with your assistant to try to find
your problems, and listen carefully, even if he does not know how to
roll. He can see the relation of the paddle to the water surface,
while you cannot. The paddle should make a quarter-circle sweep
with the active blade near the surface from the starting position near
the bow until the paddle is at right angles to the boat. Then you
should pull up with the right arm while holding the end of the other
blade with the left hand. Remind yourself that the hip-flick is essential at this point. You will have to fight to keep from trying to lift
your head and body out before rolling the kayak.

Keep working until you can roll this way at every attempt. The
hardest part is the initial one—rolling up unassisted the first time.
Then things will begin to get easier. It is important not to be satisfied until the roll is perfect, however. The paddle should end fairly
high in the water, with lots of bracing room to spare. If the paddle is
deep at the end of the roll, then it is a marginal safety factor, and
you must continue to work on it before going on to the next stage.
You should be able to manage at least a dozen rolls without a failure
before continuing.

The extended screw roll seen from underwater.

a. Corresponds to **b,** page 93. The kayaker is in position underwater, ready to begin the roll.

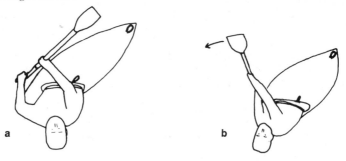

b. Corresponds to **c,** page 94. The boater has begun his sweep.

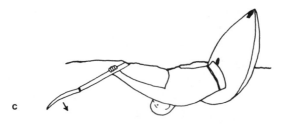

c. Corresponds to **d,** page 94. The sweep is complete, and the boater starts to roll the kayak up with his hips and to pull up on the paddle.

As soon as you can roll back up after turning over to the right, put your paddle in the same position along the left gunwale, capsize to the left, and roll back up on the right. This is no more difficult than rolling up on the same side. In fact, it will be easier, once your roll is stronger and faster, because you can use your own momentum to help bring you back up.

It is probably best to continue to develop a regular screw roll on your right side before moving to the left-hand roll. If you develop a completely reliable roll to one side first, you will be able to work on your second side without assistance, since you can always recover to your strong side after a failure on the weak side.

TROUBLES WITH THE EXTENDED ROLL

Here are a few of the possible difficulties in developing the initial roll, together with some suggestions about how they may be corrected:

1. *Paddle slices down into the water in the middle of the sweep, so that it is deep down when the pull-up begins.*

This problem results from an incorrect blade angle, not turned up enough to plane in the water. The slice will be aggravated if you have a spooned paddle. The sweep is important not only to get the paddle in position but because the sculling action begins to roll the body up.

2. *You get partway up out of the water and then fall back in.*

This is the usual result when an earnest attempt is made at the roll, but it is not executed correctly. Careful review is necessary since many mistakes can be involved. Consider the sweep first. Is the paddle traveling out in the long quarter-circle close to the surface as it should? Have someone watch and tell you. Are you reaching far out through the whole sweep, from near the bow to the midline of the boat? Are you rolling the boat up first and following with your body and head?

3. *Paddle is out in a good brace position, but you have to strain to get up and may not make it.*

This problem is probably caused by your trying to lever your body and the boat up at the same time, not using a hip-flick. Not leaning forward and then over may contribute, or the sweep may be incomplete.

4. *Boat turning partway around instead of rolling up all the way, and paddle going down into the rear quadrant too deep for you to get all the way up.*

You are probably disoriented and are digging the paddle down into the water too soon instead of sweeping it all the way out before pulling on it. If possible, an experienced teacher should run the paddle through the proper arc a few times while you hold it loosely, rolling up when the paddle reaches the proper angle, while the teacher holds the blade. It may also help to hold the paddle right against the deck, near the gunwale, before rolling over, the line of the deck determining the orientation of the shaft and the curve of the deck determining the angle of the forward blade. The pulling on the paddle must not be started too soon. The right arm should be fully extended and next to or behind the ear before the pull-up is started.

5. *Left hand or the blade it is holding is hitting the hull.*

The left hand should reach up to clear the boat, and during the pull-up on the right arm, the left completes the motion by pushing and providing a fulcrum.

THE SCREW ROLL

Once the roll has been thoroughly learned in the extended position, the novice is ready to go on to the standard *screw roll*, which is precisely the same, except that the paddle is held with the normal grip used when kayaking. The roll is intended for recovery from surprise upsets, often in turbulent water. Shifting the paddle into special position would require too much time; it risks loss of the paddle in strong currents; and it leaves the kayaker with his paddle out of position when he rolls back up, unprepared for the next problem and thus subject to another spill.

For these reasons, the preferred method of rolling is always with the paddle in a normal grip. This paddle position allows plenty of le-

verage for a correctly executed roll. The novice may prefer to use
one additional extended stage, not grasping the end of the paddle
with his left hand, but moving that hand down the shaft so that it is
against the blade. This position gives a still better feel for the angle
of the paddle and somewhat more leverage than when the hands are
in normal paddling position. If the extended roll has been practiced
thoroughly, the transition from the normal paddling position first to
this intermediate stage and then to a roll should be quite easy. The

The screw roll. (The photographs are a composite sequence from several
rolls turning over to the left and coming up on the right.)

a. To prepare for the roll (which can be done underwater later on) lay the
paddle along the deck on the side toward which you are going to roll,
forward blade on the deck, as the kayaker here is doing.

b. The boater falls into the water, paddle still in position.

c. The kayaker waits until the boat has turned completely over and raises the blade on the deck to the surface of the water. The angle is maintained, so that the outer edge, which was angled down, is now at a climbing angle.

d. This is the beginning position for rolling up as seen from the side; the blade to the right in the photograph is the active blade, angled up at a slight climbing angle. Note that the paddle is still in essentially the same position as it was on the deck, pushed out only slightly.

e. Beginning the roll. The active blade, still held at a climbing angle, is swept out in an arc away from the hull, which begins to roll the boat up.

f. The paddle is approaching a straight-out position, the paddler's body has been turned up to near the surface, and the kayak has rotated about half-way up. The blade is still near the surface and still at a climbing angle (note the angle of the upper blade).

g. The paddle is now straight out, and the blade is still near the surface. The kayaker is rotating the boat out of the water with a hip-flick. Note that the hull is already rotated over halfway up, since the front part of the coaming is already out of the water, and the lower part of the kayaker's torso is coming out, but the head is still fully submerged and most of the upper torso is still underwater. The boat should come up ahead of the kayaker.

h. The paddler emerging from the water, head coming up last. The hull is already rotated three-quarters of the way back up, and the paddle is still extended with the blade near the surface.

i. The roll is finished, and the paddle ends in a draw or high brace position, still near the surface, so the paddler can still lean on it. If the roll finishes with the blade buried deep, it is marginal and may not work in turbulent water.

motions are exactly the same, and they should come without much trouble. If problems are encountered, go back to the extended roll and analyze the differences. If the inactive blade is hitting the side of the boat during the sweep, concentrate on pushing up with the left hand. The angle of the blade is felt with the oval grip of the shaft just as in normal paddling.

Hard practice is very important in making the roll completely reflexive and reliable. For several sessions after the roll is first learned, at least thirty or forty rolls should be done. Work on your left-hand roll after the right-hand one is reliable. If a roll on the weak side fails, roll back up on the strong side and try again. With serious practice, the paddler should soon not be able to remember without thinking which is the strong side and which the weak. Ambidexterity in rolling is critical, because in strong currents there is usually one side toward which it is easier to roll, and often it is impossible to roll up the other way.

Once rolls are reliable on both sides with preparation, try sprinting along and courting a capsize at an unexpected moment, so that you are caught with the paddle in odd positions and are out of breath when you fall into the water. Get up to full forward speed and turn over with the paddle held in one hand. Reorient yourself underwater and roll back up. Devise as many exercises like this as you can. The roll must become instinctive under the most difficult conditions, as normal a reaction as recovering your balance after stumbling when you are walking. When sitting in the boat in the water, float your paddle in the water on one side of the boat, let go, capsize to the other side, reach up and get the paddle, and roll up.

OTHER ROLLS

There are several other types of rolls and countless variations. You should be absolutely comfortable with the screw roll before working on any others, but once you are, practice the others. Only a few are discussed here, because these basic methods are all the kayaker

The layout roll requires that the paddle be shifted, but provides a great deal of leverage, so that it is preferred by some paddlers as a last resort. The principle of the hip-flick is the same.

needs to learn. Finding still other techniques is a good game to while away the time in pool sessions, and they will be left for the paddler to discover for himself.

The *layout roll* gives good leverage and requires no sculling action, but it does require shifting the grip on the paddle. It is often taught as the first roll, but it is agreed that in actual capsizing situations it is far less versatile than a screw roll. Some have found it useful for a second attempt after a screw roll fails. Directions are given here for the right-hand roll; simply reverse them for the left.

To get the feel for the action of the roll, sit in the kayak, push the paddle all the way over to the left, holding one blade in your left hand, raised just to the left of your face. The palm of the hand should be toward you on the other side of the blade, holding the top edge. Reach over your head with your right arm, grasp the shaft and pull on it, using your left hand for a pivot. The long lever-arm of the paddle allows you to roll up on it, but a forward or backward lean and a good hip-flick are important for a strong roll.

To practice the layout, you can get the arms into position, begin to fall over to the right, and recover with a slap of the paddle. Then try getting into the position, turning over to the right, and rolling back up the same way. To get into the position underwater, slide the paddle out to your left, grasp the blade in the left hand, reach with your right over the top of your head, lean forward, and roll up.

The *backward screw* is a really useful roll, since it can be used immediately to right the boat if the paddler is pinned back on the rear deck in turbulent water. In principle it is exactly the same as the screw roll, except that the sculling sweep is started from the stern end of the boat instead of the bow, and the paddler's lean is backward instead of forward. This roll can be difficult to visualize at first, even after you have mastered the normal screw.

The starting position for the backward screw is to lie back on the rear deck. For a right-hand roll, the paddle is laid back along the left gunwale, the left elbow bent as much as possible, and the left hand holding the paddle shaft near the shoulder, while the right arm

Starting position for the backward screw roll. The paddler is lying backward on the deck for a roll starting by falling into the water to his left and coming up on the right, as with the screw roll shown earlier. As with the screw, the paddle is laid on the deck to orient it, but the right blade, still the active one, is laid on the back of the deck this time. The power face still faces up and will be at a climbing angle when the kayak turns over. The execution of the roll is exactly the same, except that the sweep is 90° from the stern end instead of from the bow. A useful roll if currents pin one to the rear deck.

reaches over the head to hold the shaft on the opposite (left) side of the boat. The angle of the active blade (which is back toward the stern) can be determined by the angle of the curve of the deck, as with the regular screw. To roll, the active blade is swept around in a quarter-circle near the surface, just as with the regular screw roll, until it is perpendicular to the hull, at which point the paddler rolls up with a hip-flick and a pull. If the body is kept bent back somewhat, the roll can be done with very little effort.

Rolls without paddles are excellent training, since they require perfect technique. In case of loss of a paddle, you might be able to get back up if this roll has been practiced enough, but a no-paddle roll is too unreliable for unfavorable water conditions. Rolling without a paddle is often practiced first with a Ping-pong paddle and then with the hands only. The motion of either type of screw roll can be adapted for recovery without a paddle.

For a roll with no paddle, dog paddle up to the side you want to roll up on, and, leaning along the deck either forward or back, use a strong hip-flick to bring the boat up. Often, it is easier to throw the opposite arm over the boat if you are leaning backward, not forward. Some kayakers performing this roll with a backward lean like to slide down into the kayak to reduce the effort required to turn the boat and body up.

THE ROLL ON MOVING WATER

Once you feel completely at ease rolling in still water, it is time to go out and practice on a river or in the surf. Powerful currents will sometimes hinder and sometimes help your roll, but they will nearly always tend to disorient you, to pull at the paddle, to whip you around. In white water, your early practice will begin to pay off, but don't become confident about your ability to roll in turbulent water until you have actually taken a number of white-water spills. The same comments apply to surf—start with small swells. After a spill in moving water, it is important to roll up as soon as possible, because you may be buffeted about underwater, encountering rocks and crosscurrents. Don't try to roll up precipitately, however. Make sure you are oriented and that your blade position is right first, so that your first roll will work. An aborted roll consumes far more time and energy than a short pause before a successful one.

5

River Cruising and White-Water Touring

For most enthusiasts, running rivers is the greatest pleasure to be had in a kayak. The sparkle and movement of white water, the roar of the rapids, the challenge of finding a way through pouring channels and a maze of rocks, together with the ever-unfolding mystery of what is around the next bend—these are what kayaking is all about.

The level of difficulty of the rapids that can be run varies a good deal, ranging from riffles that will thrill the novice and scarcely be noticed by the old river rat to great roaring torrents that leave even the expert in awe. So, too, the run may be a stretch of a few miles along a well-traveled road or a journey of hundreds of miles through remote wilderness. The common denominator is the magic movement of the river.

This chapter discusses the phenomenon of moving water and the skills needed by the kayaker venturing into it. The subject is a broad one, and even more than for the subjects of the previous chapters, a book can only begin to prepare the reader for what he or she must learn on the water. It takes years of experience to learn to read rivers well and even to begin to understand their ways. River running is a safe sport, but its safety rests on the judgment of the paddler and his precautions. The first and most important element in safe kayaking is the recognition of your limitations in skill and experience. Paying attention to learning what you *cannot* run is even more important than learning what you can. Rivers have a lot of tricks; learn them with care.

Those aspects of river running specifically concerned with multi-day trips and with racing are discussed in later chapters.

RIVERS

The variety of rivers in North America is truly astounding. The continent is seamed with waterways great and small, and much of the early exploration and trading by Europeans followed the example of the Indians' use of canoes to travel via the great river systems.

Rivers may be wide or narrow, flow quickly or slowly, and carry large or small amounts of water. The same river may change rapidly in a short distance or a short time. The differences between rivers and the metamorphoses that one river may undergo make river cruising interesting. They may also present dangers to the foolish or the unprepared. Some understanding of the characteristics and dynamics of the river is as important to the kayaker as his paddle.

Rivers flow downhill. This fact is obvious, of course, but not all of its consequences are so apparent. The whole surface of a river is inclined downward, aside from wave motions and turbulence that may develop in isolated spots. The amount of slope is one of the most important characteristics of the river as a whole and of particular sections of it, because this slope is the main determinant both of the velocity of the water in the river and the speed that a kayak will travel down it. The slope at a given point may range from 90° at a vertical waterfall to near zero on the surface of a lake. Even a lake on a river that is running has to have some slope, however; the foot of the lake is lower than the head. In a dammed lake where the outflow does not go over the top of the dam, letting water out at one side of the reservoir lowers the water level there, while the addition of water at the source raises the level there, and water will flow down the incline.

Both the water traveling down the river and a kayak floating on it slide down this incline. One important point is that as long as it is floating freely, the kayak tends to travel faster than the water on the surface, which is generally the fastest-flowing water. Both are being acted on by gravity. The motion of the kayak is slowed by drag against the water, just as the water is slowed by drag against the bottom or against a lower layer of water. The kayak hull will not experience any drag, however, until it slides down the incline faster than the water on which it is floating.

A related major feature of a river is the drag, friction, and interference with its flow by the surface of its bed and obstacles in the channel. Even when the river is flowing down a straight slot with a gravel or sand bottom and sides, there is friction between the water and the surface of the bed, and the water coming in contact with the bed is slowed down. This in turn drags against the faster-flowing water in the next layer up. In such a channel, the fastest-flowing water will be in the center and at or near the surface.

River channels are not generally so smooth, however. The river twists and turns, goes over boulders, or flows against rocks that are too high to go over, and so on. And the drag is twofold: the bottom and banks pull at the river, but the flowing water pulls at them too. When a piece of gravel causes enough drag on the moving water, it is carried downstream. Rocks or banks standing in the path of the water are eventually worn away, and debris plucked from them is deposited farther downstream.

The erosional effects that the river has on its channel eventually determine much of its shape and form, and since these follow very definite patterns, the river runner learns to anticipate many common river features. Maximum erosion will occur where the river flow is faster, so steep drops will be free of silt, sand, and fine gravel that is easily washed away. These will be deposited where the river slows down and has less carrying capacity.

When a river turns a corner, the water continues to flow straight until it is forced to turn by the bank on the outside of the bend or the buildup of water against the bank. The turbulence of the water running against this bank and the fact that the water moving around the outside of the turn must go faster (just as a rider travels faster on the outer edge of a merry-go-round than near the center) causes more erosion there. The erosion on the bank of the main channel of the river is normally on the outside of a turn. The kayaker learns to expect this and to use it to his advantage in running the river. If the river is rather shallow, so that he is looking for the main channel to avoid running aground, he will stay to the outside. If the river is high and fast, he will expect more turbulent water and a faster ride

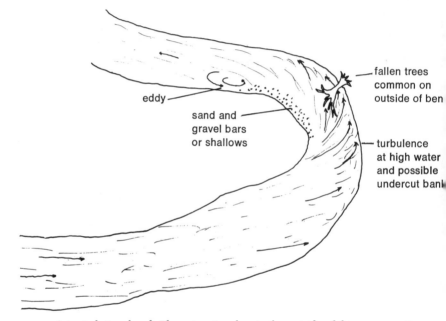

eddy

sand and gravel bars or shallows

fallen trees common on outside of ben

turbulence at high water and possible undercut bank

A typical river bend. The current rushes to the outside of the curve, particularly in high water, causing turbulence and undercutting the bank, so that fallen trees are likely if the bank is forested. Gravel bars and shallows can be expected along the inside of the bend and eddies around the inside on the downstream side, because slower water flows back into this area, the water level of which is lowered by the rush of the current to the outside. In high water, boaters should hug the inside of the bend, while in low water they will move to the middle or outside, keeping watch for sweepers.

on the outside. Fallen trees hanging over the water waiting to sweep the kayak clean of its occupant, "sweepers," will be far more likely on the outside of a bend. Bars formed by the dropping of silt, sand, and gravel by slowing water can be expected on the inside of a bend.

The cutting action on the outsides of turns and the dropping of material on the insides can tend to make the bends more accentuated, forming series of horseshoe bends. Eventually, however, the river will cut all the way through the narrow end of each horseshoe, leaving a straight channel, and the process will start all over again.

The *flow* (the volume of water which is passing a point along the river in a unit of time) is another of the most important facts about a river, and it is the most variable of the major ones. Though the gradient of a river changes, the change is very slow, normally measurable in units of geologic time. The channels change a little more quickly, but the process is still so slow that people normally notice only small changes during their lifetimes. The flow, however, commonly changes dramatically from year to year, season to season, and hour to hour. The flow is influenced by the area that is drained, by various watershed characteristics, by rainfall, and often by human action. A river that is low and slow at three in the afternoon may be an impressive torrent at four because of a thunderstorm in the mountains above in the morning or because a power plant upstream was turned on at two. (Another way to look at these factors is to consider the flow to change with time and the gradient with distance, as one moves down- or upriver.)

The effects of the size of the channel, the gradient, and the flow are all intimately related. When a given flow of water enters a certain section of a river, the flow will be the same at every point down to the next significant tributary. The only loss of water will be from seepage and evaporation, which will be negligible with rapidly flowing rivers, and the only additions will be from streams and precipitation. If a dam is included in the section, the rule will not apply if the reservoir is being filled or emptied, but short of earthquakes, mudslides, and the like, the rule applies to any naturally flowing river. Time lags may have to be taken into account, particularly on long sections of a river, since a rise in the river due to rain or melting snow will travel down the river only as fast as the water is flowing.

Since the same amount of water must be flowing by each minute in a wide, deep stretch of the river as in a shallower and narrower spot a hundred yards downstream, the speed of the water has to be greater at the narrow shallows, and if there is another wide, deep section a little farther downstream, the water must slow down again. Where the water is going faster, the gradient must be greater, so the water is accelerated more by gravity. Similarly, where the water slows down again, the gradient must have dropped off also.

Depth, current speed, and width are interdependent. A narrow channel that is flowing slowly must be deep. A wide, quick-running channel must be shallow. So, as the kayaker sees quick water coming up at a wide passage, he looks for rocks and bars near the surface.

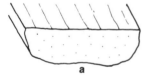 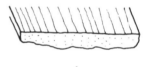

a   b   c

Relation of flow, gradient, width, and depth. The size of a river channel and its gradient change from one point to another, but the flow will remain the same between tributaries. Here three cross sections of the same river at different points are shown. At **a,** where the water is both broad and deep, it must be flowing slowest. For the same amount of water to flow past **b** in the same length of time, the current must be faster, and it follows that the gradient is steeper. At **c,** where the channel is shallow and narrow, the current must be fastest of the three, and the gradient the steepest.

At a narrow place in the river, part of the gradient on the surface may be built up by the water itself. When the water first reaches the narrows, it begins to pile up, because so much water is entering a narrow spot. As it builds up, the surface is higher above the level downstream, and the water flows more quickly down the steepened plane.

The river will normally be at a level of equilibrium through the channel, but when the flow changes, the course of the river may change radically. At high flow levels, the main part of the river may rise enough at a narrow point to be diverted into a different channel, while at low levels, this channel may be completely dry. The most obvious example is a river in flood spilling its banks and spreading out onto a huge, relatively level floodplain.

The flow of a river is measured in units of volume per unit time. The most common units in the United States are cubic feet per second, abbreviated c.f.s. This will change to cubic meters per second when the metric system becomes more widely used. Flow data on rivers are quite important. Although there are exceptions, rivers generally become more difficult (or interesting) to run as the flow increases. If you know the river or have information on it at a particular flow level, you will have a basis of comparison when you find out at what level the river is currently running. For example, if you know that a particular river was at about the limit of your level of competence when the flow was 3,000 c.f.s. and you find that it is currently carrying 6,000 c.f.s., you should probably postpone your trip.

The gradient is another objective piece of information that tells a great deal about the nature of a watercourse with which you are not familiar. More data are needed than with flow information, since any gradient is an average over a particular distance, and you need to know about individual stretches as well as longer runs. All rivers have variations in gradient from mile to mile, and some (known as pool-and-drop rivers) are steplike, alternating steep drops with relatively flat sections. Methods of calculating gradient are discussed later in this chapter. After you have run a few rivers, a record of their flow and gradient will give you some basis of comparison with rivers you have not run.

STANDING WAVES

The effects of curves in a river, obstructions, and variations in the steepness and speed of the water are numerous and subtle, and the beginner has to learn to recognize and anticipate as many as possible. He must develop a feeling for the effects they will have on his boat. A simple example has already been mentioned, that of water moving faster around the outside of a bend. Bends will be discussed in more detail later in this chapter.

One of the most important features of moving water is its momentum. When water accelerates in moving downhill, it picks up energy, just as a car coasting down a hill does. If a car moving downhill hits an immobile object large enough to stop it, a great deal of

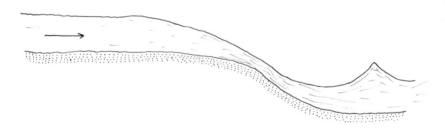

A standing wave results when the water in a river accelerates down a steep incline, and then is slowed when the slope flattens out below. The current bounces up off the bottom to form a permanent wave. Unlike the wave in an ocean, which moves while the water stays in the same place, a standing wave is stationary while the water moves by, losing some of the kinetic energy it gained in the drop before.

energy must be dissipated, and the effects are quite spectacular. The faster the car is going, the more noticeable the results will be. The energy is used up in sound waves, deforming metal, generating heat, and so forth. If the car instead hits a concrete wall angled at several degrees to the road, then the car will be deflected and the physical damage will be less. Another type of deflection occurs if the car is going down a steep hill and goes at full speed onto flat ground below—the springs will dip and rebound, and if the difference in slope and speed are large enough, the rebound may even bounce the car back up into the air. Since water is fluid, the effects of velocity changes are somewhat different, but the amounts of energy involved are large, and the dissipation can be dramatic and powerful.

In our example of a river with two wide, deep, slow sections separated by a narrow chute of faster water, the water must first crowd into the narrower section. Depending on the amount of water and the speeds involved, this may be hardly perceptible, or the water may pile up along the edges and pour turbulently into the center channel. In the latter case a V will form, with the sharp tongue of smoother water pointing downstream into the center of the channel. At the bottom of the chute, each particle of water must slow down again, which means that the energy it has picked up going down the chute must be dissipated. In the extreme case of a waterfall, analogous to the car hitting the obstacle, the energy will be dispersed by water rebounding in huge clouds of spray and foam. At the bottom of a normal chute, the water will bounce up as the car did while continuing in the same direction, fall down again, bounce again, and so on, forming a line of waves at the bottom of the chute, called *standing waves*. Large standing waves are also known as *haystacks*. The haystacks that will be found at the bottoms of chutes are using up the energy of the rapidly moving water that is just slowing down.

Let's consider what happens to the kayak coming down a chute. Even if the chute is mild and the standing waves at the bottom are small, the beginner will find that there is a strong tendency for his boat to turn broadside to the current, or *broach*. The reason is that

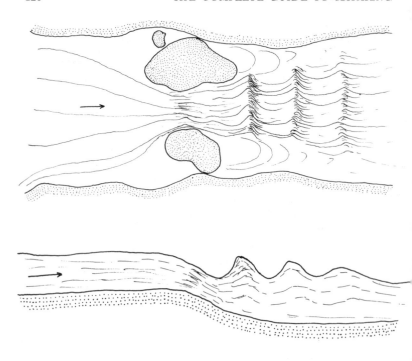

Two views of a chute formed by a channel that is constricted by boulders and drops somewhat. All the water moving down the river must squeeze between them and then drop into the pool below, so the current becomes very fast as it moves through the drop and then bounces up as it slows down below, forming a series of gradually diminishing waves called haystacks. These waves normally indicate good water depth below the chute. A large frothy area with no haystacks would be a sign of rocks with little water coverage below the chute. A kayaker entering a chute is shown on page 159.

when the boat comes into the slower water, its bow is suddenly slowed, both by the changing angle of the slope and by the drag of the slower water. Standing waves only accentuate this effect. The stern of the boat is still moving at a good clip, however. If the boat is going exactly straight, the momentum will tend to drive the bow un-

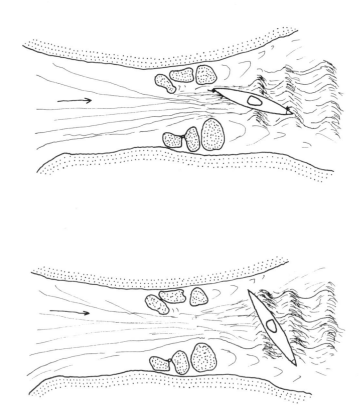

A kayak broaching in standing waves at the bottom of a chute. In the upper drawing, the kayak is just entering a set of haystacks at the bottom of a chute, out of which it is emerging at an angle. The stern is still in the fast water of the chute, while the bow is plunging into the slower water of the waves. Since the hull is at a slight angle, the current in the chute pushes against the exposed side, shoving it farther around, while the bow is being rapidly slowed and pushed in the other direction in the wave. As a result, the boat goes into the haystacks sideways, and the inexperienced boater is likely to lose balance and capsize.

derwater, into the pool or the first haystack. If the boat is turned to the current at all, however, the stern will tend to keep going as the bow is slowed, turning around the pivot point of the bow. As the boat's forward progress slows, the fast water next to the stern will also push on the side of the boat that is turning across the current, speeding up the broaching.

Since broaching for this reason occurs at the same place where haystacks are formed, the novice will find himself going broadside just as he enters the haystacks, and he has a good chance of tipping over. This sequence has been the source of the first moving water capsize for many a boater. Several tactics for meeting the situation are possible. The first is to be aware of the danger of broaching and to be particularly careful to enter the bottom of the chute with the boat pointing straight ahead. As the kayak enters the slower water, the paddler can either paddle hard forward, driving on through the haystacks, or brace downstream to keep his balance while riding the haystacks. Sneaking around the side and bracing downstream is a way of avoiding the biggest waves. The effects of both the broaching action and the haystacks may be reduced by hard backpaddling before exiting the chute, slowing the boat before it hits the slow water, and allowing a less plunging ride over the standing waves.

Standing waves also occur as more localized river phenomena. Where water is moving fast and flows over an obstacle higher than the rest of the river bottom, like a boulder, the water is piled up high behind and over the boulder in a *pillow*, and it then drops quickly down the other side, after which it slows, often forming a series of standing waves. Aside from the interest of such waves as a chance for a nice ride or as potential capsizers to be avoided, they are signals to the paddler of the presence of the boulder that caused them. The waves can be seen more clearly than the underwater object. Generally, when such waves are formed, there is a large enough pillow over the rock for a kayak to clear it. If the rock is barely beneath the surface, the downstream area will have a foamy turbulent spot and a few small choppy waves; the large regular haystacks are formed by boulders well beneath the surface.

EDDIES

Returning to our chute moving into a wide section of the river, if the widening is sudden, as when the bottom of the chute is formed by large boulders, then the momentum of the water coming out will carry the water some way past the exit of the chute in a widening fan of standing waves. The water on each side of the chute outlet is not being fed directly from above by this fast-flowing jet of water, but is instead pooled quietly behind the shelter of the boulders. At the boundary line between the pools and the jet of water coming from the chute, however, the moving water drags on the relatively quiet pools, so that the water there moves, too. Generally, small amounts of water are sheared off and carried downstream from the edge of the pool, and as the water level is lowered, the pool is refilled from the slower water farther downstream, where the energy of the current from the chute is already somewhat reduced. This causes a backward flow of water into the pools, which are known as *eddies*.

Eddies are common in fast water, particularly when there are many obstructions, drops, and changes in the width and depth of the river channel. Eddies form on the downstream sides of the inside corners of bends, on the downstream sides of obstructions in the middle of the river, and at many spots where a channel suddenly widens. The beginner will find them even trickier than the slack water at the bottom of the chute, because at the boundary of the eddy, the *eddyline*, there is a tremendous change in velocity. In rapids, for example, it would not be uncommon to find water moving downstream in a chute at over ten miles an hour and the water in an eddy behind a boulder moving upstream at a couple of miles per hour, so that over the space of less than a foot, there is a current differential of fifteen miles an hour. A kayaker crossing an eddyline unawares is likely to find the boat suddenly spun around and flipped over before he even knows that something is happening.

Eddies, however, provide for much of the kayaker's safety and a lot of his sport. Eddies are the rest spots in the middle of rushing

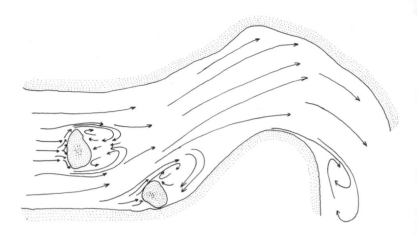

Typical eddy patterns. At the left is a midstream boulder. Water piles up on the upstream side, shoots past both edges, and then some of it flows back behind the boulder on the downstream side to fill the low place in the channel. This upstream current is an eddy, and the more powerful the main current, the longer and stronger the eddy will be. The boundary where the main current sweeps past the eddy, extending downstream from the edges of the boulder, is called an *eddyline*. Along the narrow border formed by the eddyline between the strong downstream movement and the main current and the upstream movement of the eddy currents, there is tremendous turbulence, as the main current shears water away from the eddy and carries it downriver. A midstream boulder will have two eddylines, one on either side. The ability to use the opposing currents found at an eddyline to advantage, rather than being thrown off balance by them, is the fundamental white-water paddling skill.

In the center is a boulder at one side of the river with a strong eddy behind it. To the right a weaker eddy is formed on the downstream inside corner of a river bend.

water, where the boater can get safely ashore or stop to take a good look at what is to come. Eddies can often be used to move upstream, and a skilled boater can work up some forbidding rapids by shifting from one eddy to another, dodging through the swift water between. The shearing action of the water along the eddyline can be used as a tool also, whipping the boat around quickly and effortlessly for the kayaker who knows how to use the current differential to advantage.

Eddies will be mentioned again and again in this chapter and after, and careful study of them will reward the beginner. The novice should learn to inspect every stretch of river for eddies both in advance and while running the river. A lot can be learned about them and other river phenomena by watching and experimenting with moving water elsewhere, in streams and rain gutters. Get a supply of rocks and build different combinations in a creek, and figure out how they would look on a larger scale from the point of view of a kayaker in a river.

Eddy circulation occurs in the vertical as well as the horizontal plane. Most eddies, in fact, have some movement in each plane. Vertical circulation is harder to detect, and it does not usually have so much effect on the boater, since he is generally confined to the water's surface. Some strong vertical eddies can be quite dangerous, however, and several types will be discussed separately.

RAPIDS

Rapids are sections of rivers where fast-moving water runs over a bed strewn with many rocks or boulders of various sizes. They range from easy spots where the water forms small riffles and where one has to maneuver around a few rocks here and there, to huge, powerful torrents of heavy water that can break a kayak like a matchstick. Most of the difficulties in running rivers are found in rapids, and they provide the most fun as well.

On day trips and practice river sessions, excursions are often made to rapids that run next to a road, so that the activity consists of running through the same rapids a number of times, perhaps with a car shuttle bringing the boaters back upriver. Kayakers love to play in rapids, moving back and forth between eddies, trying various ways of running chutes, maneuvering in the turbulence caused by obstructing boulders, and generally horsing around. Even on a long downriver trip, frequent stops are often made to "play" or "work" the rapids, moving back and forth through the turbulent waters until the possibilities have been exhausted.

Rapids normally give plenty of warning of their presence to kayakers coming down the river; the roar of the water crashing against the rocks allows plenty of time to look for a landing spot to scout the rapids from shore if they cannot be "read" from the boat. Scouting is always prudent, particularly for novices. Caution and advance knowledge of a river are important, however, because you occasionally find "silent rapids"—those where the river valley's acoustics prevent your hearing the rapids until you are already beyond the point of no return. This type of rapid can be quite hazardous if a boater blunders into it, because when he enters, he may be in the wrong position to run it safely, even if it is not beyond his ability.

Scouting a rapid simply involves landing at a safe spot above the difficult water, walking along the bank to find out how difficult and dangerous running the white water would be, and if a run is decided on, picking out and memorizing the best course. Do not run the rapid unless you are sure it is safe, and allow a wide margin of error for your own inexperience. Many factors should enter into the decision whether to go through or portage: the length, difficulty, and danger of the rapid itself; the character of the water below the rapid—whether it is a gentle pool where rescue would be easy or a stretch of fast water that might carry a swimmer and his boat down into the next rapid; the number of people in the party capable of carrying out a rescue in water of the difficulty present; the air and water temperature and the party's preparation for them; the remoteness of the area. *In case of doubt about the safety of the venture, portage or line the rapids.* (Portaging means carrying the kayaks around the rapids on land; lining means working them through with ropes.)

Generally, any party with relatively inexperienced members will also have experienced people who are capable of making judgments about the safety of running rapids. However, everyone should be concerned with party safety, and whereas the leader or leaders have the final say on matters of safety, each person should exercise his judgment. If you see hazards that the leader may not have noticed, you should point them out. It is also important to begin developing your own capacities and knowledge by watching the way the party is handled and acts.

Beginners should not be taken down any rapids where rescue is hard to manage. The actual danger of a rapid is related not only to the difficulty of running it. If no injury would be likely to result from a spill, if the party is well prepared for the water temperature and not excessively tired, and if rescue would be easy, running a difficult drop is simply good practice. No one learns to kayak well in white water without doing a reasonable amount of rolling and swimming. On the other hand, really dangerous situations can often develop in quite easy rapids when rescue is beyond the party's capacity or if someone is chilly, does not have adequate protection from the cold water, or is very tired. When the safety margin begins to narrow, it is time to portage.

The usual procedure with a party that includes novices is for some of the experienced members of the group to run the rapid first, showing the way and getting into position for rescue at the bottom of the drop. The less experienced paddlers then run the rapid one at a time, each making sure before he or she starts that the person ahead has cleared the difficulties and gotten into an eddy or slow water. This eliminates a situation where the rescuers have to choose among large numbers of swimmers, boats, and paddles bobbing about in the water, and it also reduces the likelihood of your boat (with or without you) running into the person who preceded you if he or she capsizes.

Techniques of rescue are discussed later in the chapter, but the first responsibility is always with the boater himself. The roll should be thoroughly learned before heading out on moving water. When you tip over, roll back up and go on. Don't panic and get out of the boat until your attempts (at least two) have really failed. You are safer in the kayak than out of it, you will save your experienced companions a lot of bother if you can get back up, and they will be a lot happier rescuing you if you have at least tried to right yourself. Finally, there is nothing quite so satisfying as your first successful recovery in real white water!

If you do have to eject, hang onto the paddle and the boat. As you pull your spray skirt grab loop with one hand, keep hold of the paddle with the other, and hold onto the boat with the first hand as you come out. As soon as you break water, get to the upstream side or end of the kayak, holding onto the grab loop, rescue handle, or painter. If at all possible, strike out for shore with a sidestroke as soon as you can. Even if you cannot get all the way there, the closer you get, the more likely it will be that a rescue boat can get you the rest of the way. Holding onto your equipment is important, because if you let go of things, the rescuers will have to decide which to get: you, your boat, or your paddle.

Don't turn the kayak back upright after you have gotten out of it. If you do, it will ship a lot of water, making it harder to tow, more subject to damage if it hits a rock, more dangerous to you, and harder to empty when you get to shore. It is essential that you *get on the upstream side of the boat*, if you are still in the rapids, or you may be pinned against a rock by a kayak under the full pressure of the current.

When "swimming" through a rapid, you will not be able to influence your path very much. Besides holding onto the paddle and boat and keeping your head out of water, you should get onto your back, with your feet pointing downstream to ward off obstacles. This is also the best position if you have lost your boat. You may be able to get into an eddy or some other safe spot, particularly if the water is not too deep, but if not, watch for your chance to strike out for shore, planning where you will swim as soon as you hit the calmer water below. Don't just flop around waiting for a rescue. The rescue boat will get to you as fast as it can; your job is to shorten the distance between yourself and the shoreline.

Having decided to run a rapid, you must memorize your intended course through it. This is one of the most important skills in white-water paddling. An expert looks at a complex rapid, picks out his course, and mentally goes through the entire sequence of movements and strokes he will have to make as he runs it. He may do this from the water or from shore. Scouting is much easier and safer from shore, particularly for beginners. One of the disadvantages of the kayak compared with other white-water craft is that the paddler is very low to the water and his visibility from the boat is poor. Therefore, the beginner must be particularly assiduous in trying to pick out his route in advance and commit it to memory, because he will be far less able than the expert to stop in small eddies on the way to look over the next drop. If resting places can be found that you think you can get into, be sure to use them, but plot the course beyond in case you miss. Watch the way your experienced companions run the rapid, and try to follow their route, unless, of course, they are deliberately playing the rapid. When you have scouted the route from shore, go back over it in your mind after you have gotten back in your boat, making sure you are orienting yourself correctly before you are committed.

Once you've scouted the rapid and determined that you still want to run it, you are ready to go. The entrance to the first chute is usually pointed out by the longest tongue of smooth water, its V pointing down into the rapids.

After you have entered the chute, *keep paddling*. Any paddling is better than none. If you become indecisive and hold your paddle out of the water, the boat is very unstable, and you will be dumped by the first crosscurrent, which will not be long in coming. Remember your course and try to hold it, duplicating as well as you can the maneuvers of the experts who preceded you, but not attempting strokes beyond your skill. Brace hard if you start to go

Lean downstream, so that the moving water cannot catch the chines of the boat and turn it over. Here a racer is turning and looking downstream at the approach for the next gate of a slalom.

over, and if you have turned broadside, brace downstream. *Do not lean upstream.* Use your draw to move over, and the water bouncing off the rocks will help carry you around them, but remember to keep paddling. If you capsize, don't panic—try to roll back up. This is the real test of how well you've learned to roll.

Once you have gotten through the rapid, one way or another, analyze your performance. Ask the experienced people with you what you did wrong, and watch other beginners come through, relating what you see them do to your own experience, so that you can do better next time. If the leader approves and you have time, you may want to portage your boat back up and run the rapid again to see if you can benefit from your experience.

FERRYING

Ferrying is one of the most basic river techniques, permitting the kayaker to cross fast-moving water in a controlled way. The instinctive action of the novice trying to cross the river is to point his bow at the spot on the opposite shore he wants to attain and to start paddling. It doesn't work very well. The kayak does indeed move toward the other bank, but in the meantime it is floating rapidly down the river, and if the reason for wanting to get to the other side was to portage around the rapid just below, this will be a disconcerting experience. Similarly, the beginner trying to avoid a rock or sweeper toward which the current is carrying him usually tries to change direction in his forward paddling somewhat and steer around

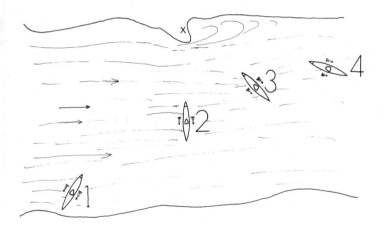

The *wrong* way to cross a fast current to reach a landing. The kayaker has noted some rapids below and wishes to reach the landing at X to inspect them. Aiming the bow at X, the boater paddles hard, but as progress is made, the current and the downstream component of the paddle strokes carry the boat beyond reach of the landing point and into the rapids.

the obstacle. Again, the technique is likely to be ineffective, because the current is moving rapidly in the unwanted direction, the kayak is floating the same way even faster, and the forward strokes simply speed the approach on a collision course, since the side component of the stroke is small.

The best tactic in these situations and many others is the ferry. Let's start with the problem of avoiding the rock. Suppose the paddler wants to pass to the right. If he points his bow somewhat off to the right and paddles hard forward, he will move to the right, but

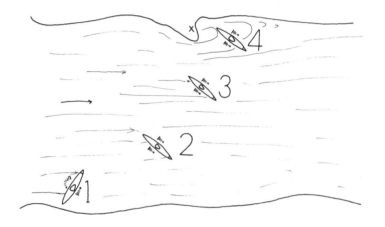

The *backward ferry* used to cross a fast current to reach a landing. The kayaker notes a landing across the river and turns the kayak with a back stroke (or back sweep) and a forward sweep so that the stern of the kayak is angled across the current. (If the boat had been pointed directly downstream to begin with, a single hard back stroke would have been enough.) Then, by maintaining the angle and continuing to paddle backward, the boater moves the kayak across the river losing little or no ground. Part of the force of the strokes pushes the kayak across, while part serves to counteract the downstream push of the current. At the same time, the boater can inspect the rapid below.

he will also add a lot of forward speed that will take him toward the
rock even faster. If instead he points his stern to the right (and
consequently the bow to the left, away from the desired direction of
travel) and backpaddles, he will also move to the right, but he will at
the same moment be slowing or stopping his forward motion toward
the rock, giving the side component enough time to be effective.
This is a back ferry, stern angled in the desired direction of travel,
with the paddler doing a backstroke against the current.

In the case of crossing the river above the rapid, your best tactic
is to point your bow upstream, angle it over toward the opposite
shore, and paddle forward. The main force of your paddling counteracts the action of gravity and the current, which are pulling the
boat downstream. The forward stroke keeps the kayak next to the
same spot on the bank, while the sideways component, combined
with the force of the current deflecting against the upstream side,
pushes the boat across the river.

Ferrying, then, is simply paddling against the current, but angling the upstream end of the boat in the direction that one wants to
go. In a back ferry, the stern is upstream and a backstroke is used,
and in a forward ferry, the bow heads upstream, and a normal
forward stroke is used. When the current is no stronger than the
stroke, a ferry gives the paddler complete control. He can cross
straight across the river at will. With a stronger current, the ferry is
still very useful, but some ground will often be lost in the crossing.
Both types of ferry are important and are resorted to frequently.
When the current is strong and it is important to lose as little
ground as possible, the forward ferry is naturally preferred, because
the forward stroke is stronger and can prevail against a faster current.

You can calculate the optimum angles for ferrying, but this is really largely a matter of practice. When the current is weaker than
the stroke, the paddler angles the upstream end of the boat over as
far as he can without beginning to lose ground. When the current is

A kayaker ferries across the fast water below a drop, paddling forward with his boat angled in the current. He is working across from one eddy to another. A forward ferry like this is more effective in fast water than a back ferry, making full use of the power of the forward stroke.

much faster than the paddler can move the boat, the kayak should be angled well over in the direction he wants to travel, since a small angle simply loses ground. In fast currents, a running (or paddling) start from an eddy gives the kayak a good head start, taking it a long way over before the kayak is really caught by the current. Other techniques for ferrying in fast currents are discussed later in the chapter.

The *forward ferry* used to make the same crossing. The boater begins by turning the bow instead of the stern upstream, using a back stroke (or back sweep) and a forward sweep. The ferry is then made by paddling forward with the bow angled upstream. The forward ferry is more powerful, because it uses the stronger forward paddle stroke, but it does require more time to turn the kayak upstream, if one is traveling bow first in the normal way.

FERRYING INTO AND OUT OF EDDIES

Proper use of eddies is the key to handling a kayak in rapidly moving water. Eddies provide rest spots, islands of calm in the midst of surrounding turbulence, from which the boater can survey the course below, and maneuvering room where the kayaker can prepare for problems downstream. Getting into and out of eddies is often harder than it looks, however, even in water that is not extremely rapid and turbulent.

The novice boater attempting to paddle directly into an eddy behind a rock as he comes down the river will often simply find himself spun out by the current, because he does not paddle hard enough. His bow enters the slack water of the eddy and is rapidly

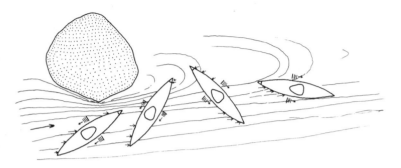

The problem of entering an eddy. The kayaker here tries to paddle directly into an eddy, but as soon as the bow crosses the eddyline, there is pressure on the bow from the eddy current on the downstream side, while the main current continues to push on the rest of the hull, so that the boat is swept around without ever forcing through the eddyline. If the currents were stronger, the kayak would also be flipped over by the sudden upstream pull of the eddy water under the hull.

slowed down, while the current pushes the rest of the boat around the pivot point of the bow, so that the paddler ends up going downstream backward and watching the eddy recede into the distance upstream. Learning this lesson, he approaches the next eddy stroking powerfully, so that his boat crosses the eddyline with a good deal of momentum, as it should. But the eddy has other surprises in store. As the kayak is driven across the eddyline, both the boat and the paddler have plenty of downstream momentum. The forward part of the hull is caught by the resistance of the upstream eddy flow, and the deck and paddler continue to move, falling into the water downstream.

Similar problems occur for the novice trying to get out of an eddy. If he paddles timidly into the current his bow will be caught and turned around back into the eddy. More forceful paddling will get enough of the hull out into the current to be grabbed from under-

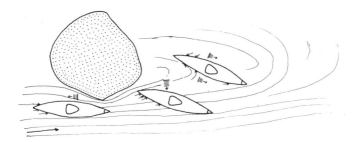

Setting into an eddy (ferrying in). One way to solve the problem of crossing the eddyline is shown here. The kayaker passes the rock that forms the eddy as closely as possible, making a stroke on the same side of the boat as the rock while passing it, in order to begin to turn the bow away from it. As the hull passes by, he draws the stern of the boat into the eddy, which also angles the kayak so that the main current works to push the boat farther into the eddy. Strong back strokes bring the kayak all the way into the eddy. Setting in is the easiest way to enter an eddy; its only problem is that it is too slow a method to be reliable in very powerful currents.

neath by the fast-moving water, pulling the boat out from under the kayaker and dumping him into the water upstream.

In crossing moderate eddylines, the paddler can use the current to his advantage by ferrying in and out. The paddler moving downstream brings his boat alongside the eddy, backpaddles, and points his stern toward the eddy. The ferry carries him into the eddy, and as the stern enters it, the moving water outside the eddy pushes the rest of the boat in. He can also turn the boat upstream above the eddy and forward ferry into it. The beginner should practice ferrying back and forth, using forward and back ferries between two eddies on opposite sides of a moderate stream or river.

When entering any eddy, it is important to hit the eddyline as high as possible. The only way to develop this skill is with lots of practice. Learning to anticipate the eddy from upstream and getting into position for it is one of the most important basic river-running skills. The farther down one gets, the harder it will be to catch the eddy. Small eddies in fast rivers require precise timing; a difference of six inches will prevent one from getting into an eddy behind a minor boulder in swift water.

To ferry out of an eddy, one can use either a forward or backward ferry, driving the upstream end of the boat hard into the current and then continuing to paddle hard as the current takes the kayak out into the river. Beginners should practice initially from low down in the eddy, where the current differential is weak. More efficient use of the eddyline, essential in fast water, requires hitting the eddyline high with a strong lean downstream and often a good brace, to prevent the current from catching the bottom of the kayak and turning the boat and paddler over. This ferrying technique will be discussed after the eddy turns. At first, however, with weak eddies, the novice should be able to ferry in and out easily to begin to develop a feeling for the turning effect at the eddyline.

EDDY TURNS

The good, conservative technique of ferrying into an eddy works well enough in easy water, but when currents become more powerful, it is simply not possible to backpaddle hard enough to swing the stern in behind a friendly rock as you hurtle by. More powerful action is needed, and the kayaker aims to drive the bow of the boat into the eddy at the highest possible point. The difficulty with this maneuver has already been mentioned: as the bottom of the boat is caught by the eddy current, the paddler will be spun over into the water. The remedy is to lean hard to the opposite side as the bow enters the eddy, tilting the boat and the body into the turn, just as a bicycle rider leans into a turn. And, as with the cyclist, the sharper the turn is, the stronger the lean must be. A timid kayaker going into a fast turn will meet the same fate as the timid cyclist; he will turn over.

Since the exact amount of lean required is hard to judge, particu-

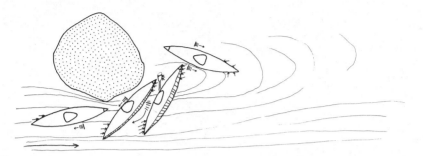

The eddy turn, the surest and most reliable way to enter an eddy. The kayaker passes the rock as closely as possible and drives the boat into the eddy as high as possible, turning the kayak with a sweep as it passes the rock, so that the bow crosses the eddyline at about a 45° angle. As the bow enters the eddy, the boater leans to the inside of the turn, to prevent the upstream eddy current from sweeping the hull out from under him. As soon as the first third of the hull is driven into the eddy, the paddler braces with a high brace on the paddle blade to the inside of the turn, in the eddy current. The paddle gives the kayaker a support to lean on and also serves as a pivot around which the boat turns, the opposing currents rapidly whipping it around and into the eddy. *The eddy turn is the most important maneuver in white-water paddling.*

larly for the beginner, a paddle brace or Duffek stroke is used on the inside of the turn, so that the kayaker can lean well over without having to worry about tipping too far. This brace has an even greater advantage; it becomes the pivot point around which the boat turns, reducing the skid of the turn and making it as positive as the crack of a whip.

The proper way to make an eddy turn is to drive into the eddy at the highest possible point at an angle of about 45° to the eddyline. At about the time that the first two or three feet of the bow have crossed into the slack water, reach into the eddy with a Duffek

A paddler in a slalom race making an eddy turn into the eddy behind the large boulder in midstream. He is leaning *into* the turn, and bracing with the paddle while also driving forward with it. If he had simply been paddling down the river for pleasure here, he would have driven the bow of the kayak into the eddy higher and been able to swing in easily with a simple high brace. Because he is racing, he first had to pass through the far gate (#26) and then make his eddy turn. He is also paddling for maximum speed.

stroke—a high draw with the leading edge of the blade tilted up at a sharp climbing angle—and lean over hard into the turn and onto the paddle. The boat will swing around into the eddy with the paddle acting as a pivot, and a slight draw will right you and the boat. The eddy turn is the most important maneuver in white-water kayaking and one of the most enjoyable.

Several mistakes are common among novices learning the eddy turn. The first, and the one which causes more upsets than any other, is timidity in leaning: a strong lean is vital, especially when

The same paddler making an eddy turn out of the eddy behind the boulder downstream with the main current. He drove the kayak into the current at the top of the eddy, through the nearer gate, and caught the current with his paddle in a high brace, again leaning *into* the turn and downstream.

entering powerful eddies. The lean is what prevents your tipping over in the violent crosscurrent of the eddyline. With a good lean, the kayak will whip around the paddle with effortless grace— without the lean, the same momentum will carry you over into the water, just as easily but with much less dignity. The body should lean well out over the water. The kayak, held firmly with the knees locked into their braces or pads, should lean, too, though not so much. The high brace is so strong a support that there is really no worry about leaning too far; the danger is always in not leaning far enough.

A second problem area is the correct angle of entry, especially in fast water. It is hard at first to judge the path that the kayak will take when you are paddling toward an eddy. If you close too slowly, the kayak goes low into the eddy, which makes for a less effective turn or a complete miss, and if you close too fast, the danger of hitting the obstacle causing the eddy forces you to turn back downstream, so that the bow enters the eddy almost parallel, making a good turn difficult. The answer, as usual, is practice aimed at the perfect entry: high at the very top of the eddy, with the bow entering it at approximately 45°.

Once the neophyte begins to concentrate on his lean and brace, perhaps having had the kayak pulled from under him a few times by the eddy, he is likely to start the Duffek stroke too soon, before the bow really enters the eddy. This error may cause a poor turn, or it may result in a bath, since the boater is leaning upstream while the whole boat is still in the current. The current is then tending to twist the hull of the kayak in the same direction as the lean, instead of away from it. The brace may save the unwary paddler, but if the current is strong or the brace weak, he will have a chance to practice his roll.

Just as critical as the turn into the eddy is the corresponding turn out of it. Here again, the kayaker uses the current differential to his advantage, instead of allowing it to unbalance him. The paddler, starting a few feet down to allow a buildup of momentum, drives forward through the eddyline as high as circumstances and nerve permit, again crossing the line at an angle of about 45°. As the bow pulls into the main current two or three feet, the paddler uses a Duffek stroke downstream and as far forward as he can easily reach, again leaning well into the turn. This presents the bottom of the boat to the fast current, so that it tends to turn the boat and paddler back up instead of turning them over. Remember that in all eddy crossings, *lean into the turn.* This is less instinctive with the turn into the current; the beginner often wants to lean upstream, but leaning against the current will guarantee an upset.

Several factors that are involved in both types of eddy turn should be understood. The lean itself has a number of functions. It is, first

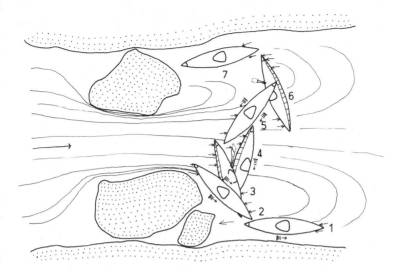

The S-turn, used to cross a fast chute. This is simply a combination of an eddy turn out of one eddy followed by one into the eddy on the opposite side of the chute. To make the eddy turn out, the kayaker paddles to the top of the eddy and drives into the current as hard as possible at about a 45° angle, leaning and bracing downstream. The force of the current on the paddle and the currents pushing in opposite directions on the two ends of the boat turn it downstream. As the other eddy is reached, the paddler rights the boat, drives the bow into the eddy with a couple of forward strokes, and braces on the opposite side to make an eddy turn in. One can go back and forth indefinitely between two eddies using S-turns and ferries.

of all, a lean against the capsizing action of the current you are entering. When a kayak is entering an eddy, the current in the eddy may not be strong, but even still water makes a strong current *relative* to the fast-moving hull. Second, the lean counteracts the centrifugal force created by the turn itself, which acts on the body and the boat. Since the greater part of the mass of the kayaker-boat combination is above the waterline, the centrifugal force pushes mainly from above the waterline, so it acts in the opposite direction from the force of the current against the hull, and the two forces produce a strong rotational torque that tends to flip the kayaker into the cold water on the outside of the turn. The tendency is counteracted by the tilting of boat and body. The lean also allows a long paddle reach, and it turns the boat up on its side where there is more pronounced rocker, enabling the kayak to turn with less applied force.

The action of the brace also has several components. Most important, the paddle grabs water with relative motion opposite to that of the kayak and the main current in which most of the kayak is floating. Thus, by simply planting the paddle, the kayaker creates a long lever—his body and arms—with forces acting on opposite directions at the two ends. The lever quickly rotates, and since the paddle has the firmer anchor, the kayak does most of the moving. The brace thus swings the kayak in from the current, preventing it from spinning back out, and holds it high in the eddy. The supporting stroke also gives the paddler something to lean on, so that the angle of the boat and his body do not have to be balanced perfectly against the force of the turn—any extra lean is compensated for with a pull on the paddle.

BRACING, FERRYING, AND SURFING
IN STRONG CURRENTS

In maneuvering through turbulent white water, balance is often hard to maintain. The current differential that occurs at any eddyline is only one of the most striking and useful of the sudden changes in the direction of flow of the water in a big rapid. Water travels horizontally in different directions, dives down under the general surface, and then wells up again and becomes frothy with air bubbles. Some of the specific types of white-water phenomena are discussed later, but the boater will encounter many variations as he runs down a river. The balance of the body in the boat is important, but as with the eddy turn, the paddle is vital in maintaining an upright position as the kayak is buffeted and twisted this way and that in white water. This is the reason for the earlier advice to keep paddling. As long as a paddle blade is in the water, it acts as an outrigger with which one can make necessary adjustments to balance.

Either a forward or backward stroke can be used for some support, and either can be shifted into a bracing stroke, but it is often preferable to ride through some sections of a rapid with a continuous brace downstream. As a general rule, one should not brace or lean upstream, since this allows water diving down from a wave or obstruction to catch the gunwale of the kayak and roll it under, and the brace may be too weak to counteract the tipping, because the paddle rests on water that is moving down. It is normally far better to lean and brace downstream. When possible, the kayaker anticipates the need for a brace. If he cuts diagonally downstream between two standing waves, he should expect the fast-moving water from the upstream wave to pull at the hull of his boat, tending to spin him into the water. The proper course is to *lean and brace downstream,* resting the paddle on the pillow of upwelling water forming the upstream side of the wave below him. Such a brace gives the paddler precise control of movement. By tilting the paddle blade at an angle, the kayak can be made to move in one direction or the other in the trough, because of the force of the moving water deflected from the blade. With a dip of the paddle into the wave, the kayak will be pulled over into the next trough. If, on the other hand, the paddler waits until the water catches the boat and starts to flip it, he will be forced to make a quick recovering brace upstream, an unbalancing move that upsets control of the kayak rather than contributing to it, and which in strong currents may not work. If water is diving down rapidly enough from the obstacle, this upstream brace may simply finish the job of dumping the boater into the water.

An anticipatory brace is thus always made on the opposite side from that toward which the currents would tend to roll the boat, while a recovering brace is made on the side toward which the kayak is being tipped. An anticipatory brace is preferred, and it leaves the paddler with good control of the kayak, rather than barely saving him from an upset.

Ferrying out of an eddy into a quick jet of water uses the same principles as the eddy turn into the current and the anticipatory lean and brace. The paddler drives the boat out of the eddy as high as possible, at a 45° angle, leaning well downstream and bracing to the side. The current will carry the kayak an amazing distance across the channel, usually into the next eddy, and practice in ferrying back and forth across such fast chutes of water is excellent training for white-water boating. The main difference between a downstream turn out of an eddy using a high brace and a ferry across the chute is simply the placement of the paddle in the water and the angle at which the blade is turned to the current. To turn downstream, the paddler should reach well forward, so that the blade catches the water well ahead of the center of the boat and drags the bow quickly downstream. With the ferry, the brace is back nearer the centerline of the boat, and the blade is angled to the current as the boat is, so that the pressure of the current tends to drive the boat and paddle across the channel.

In a fast chute there will normally be standing waves, and the kayaker should choose his point of entry from the eddy into the current to help send the kayak in the desired direction. For a turn downstream, you can aim the bow up onto the downstream side of a wave; as the turn is started the bow will slide readily off in the proper direction. For a ferry, on the other hand, it is best to drive the boat onto the upstream side of a wave. With a lean and a brace, the kayak will slide effortlessly along the sloping surface of the wave without losing any ground at all. The slope of the wave prevents gravity from pulling the boat downstream, and the pressure of the current against the paddle blade and the side of the boat push the hull across the channel.

A good boater can often cross a chute in this way without even putting his paddle in the water after driving out of the eddy. He simply heads the boat in the right direction and leans downstream strongly enough to resist the turning force of the current on the

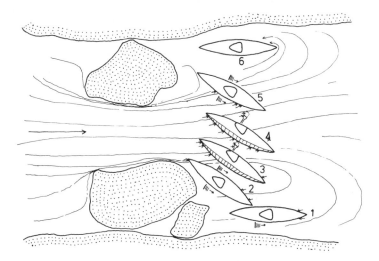

Ferrying across a fast chute. An alternative method of crossing a chute to the S-turn is a ferry, which is performed similarly. The bow is again driven into the main current from high in the eddy, at a slightly smaller angle. If there are standing waves, the boater takes advantage of them by entering at a point that will enable him to ride across on the upstream side of a wave, and so lose less momentum. The kayaker must lean downstream as the current is entered to avoid being turned over, and he may paddle forward a few strokes to gain speed. The beginner should use a downstream brace, though the ferry can be performed without one. The paddle is placed farther back than with the S-turn, so that it does not tend to turn the bow, and it is angled more to the current. The force of the current against the angled hull sweeps the boat across before it really is dragged much downstream. As the eddy on the far side is entered, the kayaker rights the boat and paddles forward, if necessary, to finish getting into the eddy. Ferrying back and forth in chutes is a favorite white-water sport.

hull. Beginners will want the additional security of the brace. Regardless of whether you brace or not, you must lean downstream. The force of a strong current as the boat leaves an eddy will flip the unwary novice over before he even realizes what is happening.

Ferrying back and forth along the upstream side of a big standing wave is often called *surfing*, since it is similar to riding a wave in ocean surf. If the wave is high enough or has a surface current running back down it, a good kayaker can often ride back and forth along the upstream side of the wave without even entering an eddy, swinging his stern back around toward the center of the channel as he reaches the end of the wave, and changing his lean and brace to bring him back the other way. A good sense of balance and precise timing and control of the kayak are required.

Ferrying, surfing, and bracing turns can all be accomplished from either side, backward and forward. Stern-first control is far trickier than bow-first, and the beginner will want to be sure of himself with forward ferries in fast water before attempting the same maneuvers backward. The ability to control the boat and the angle of your braces is invaluable, however, so back ferries in fast water should eventually be tried. Learn stern-first eddy turns first, since they require less precise leans and paddle control than ferries.

HOLES, ROLLERS, AND STOPPERS

When large amounts of water flow over a submerged boulder or outcrop, the high velocity of the drop on the downstream side may carry the water in the vertical current well down below the surface on the far side, so that instead of traveling up the slope of the first haystack below, the main current going over the obstacle dives below the surface and emerges farther downstream. The spot behind the rock where the current is going down into the river is called a *hole*. The surface current on the upstream side of the first standing wave may also flow back into the hole, and the backward-flowing water may be very frothy from turbulence. Such a standing wave is called a *roller*. A long roller may be a *stopper:* if a boat is caught behind it, particularly if it has broached to the current, it may become trapped in the trough upstream from the wave. Since the upstream side of the wave slopes and the surface current is reversed, the boat will only go over it if it has good forward momentum or is driven over with a paddle. A stopper may be difficult to paddle over, because the aerated froth on the surface is not very dense and gives little purchase for the paddle. As a boat broaches, the swift current from upstream will tend to catch the gunwale and begin rolling it, and the boat will not float out downstream, because it is trapped behind the stopper.

Holes and rollers come in many sizes and varieties. Small holes are favorite playing spots for kayakers. One can paddle into the hole, get the bow of the kayak in it, and sit on the roller behind, holding the boat on the upstream slope while balancing or bracing. A deep stroke or a reaching brace downstream carries the boat off when one tires of the game. In a somewhat larger hole, experienced paddlers can also play, with some risk of being "eaten" by the hole and spat out downstream. Large holes, however, can be very dangerous, breaking up boats and giving kayakers a nasty shaking up and dous-

A kayaker surfing in the waves below a fast chute. The bow of the boat, facing upstream, is buried in the trough. If the wave and hole were big enough, the bow might drive deep enough to either spit the boat out backwards or flip it over in an ender.

ing in the process. The possibility of a big hole that must be avoided is one of the reasons why rapids should be scouted if they are not known or completely visible from the river upstream, particularly in heavy water.

"Stopper" is a loosely used term, in that it may refer to a wave that will stop a boat for a few seconds before floating it out to the side or to one of the truly dangerous types of standing waves. A very large roller may give the boater an unpleasant thrashing before tossing him out without really being a stopper. A true stopper is more likely to be formed by a drop-off stretching at about the same level across the river for some distance, so that a long and regular roller is formed downstream. The long standing wave below is a hydraulic jump, a slope facing upstream over which it is hard to drive a boat, and one that is so long that the kayak and possibly the boater may have difficulty escaping. With most holes and rollers, a boater may turn over a few times, but he will finally float out. With a long stopper, a person or a kayak will simply keep turning over in the same place in the current indefinitely.

A really big stopper can even continuously roll a kayak end over end, although hydraulic jumps of this size occur only in very big water. The hydraulic jump on such a stopper may extend many yards downstream, with the aerated water of the "white eddy" flowing back in great sheets into the hole. This type of hydraulic jump is a killer. More commonly, a boat will roll on its side, and a kayaker with a life jacket will float partway up the standing wave, drop down and submerge in the hole, and come up again in a few seconds to repeat the sequence.

Most of the dangerous stoppers are formed by man-made obstacles in the river, because natural barriers are rarely continuous and regular enough to form a really long hydraulic jump. Dams or weirs are the most common stopper-causing obstructions, so it can be very dangerous to run even a low dam, particularly without inspecting the water beyond first. The stopper formed by a dam need not be very large to be dangerous, particularly for inexperi-

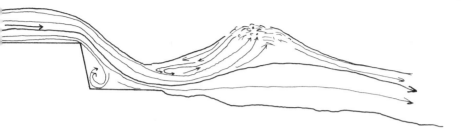

A keeper or reversal, one of the most dangerous river hazards. The drawing
shows a typical hydraulic where water runs over a man-made dam or shelf.
The main current flows *under* the surface, and a standing wave of aerated
water is formed with a surface current flowing *upstream* into the trough.
Floating objects like boats and swimmers are often trapped in this trough.
Even quite small and innocuous-looking dams and keepers can trap a kayaker, flip the boat, and drown the swimmer in the recirculating water. Man-
made shelves and dams, which often form perfect waves across the width of
the river, are the most dangerous.

enced paddlers. The novice may look at the hydraulic jump beyond
a dam, thinking it inconsequential compared with some boiling
white water he has been through, only to find himself trapped in the
trough behind the standing wave. But stoppers of this kind can also
be formed by shelves in a natural rock formation, where long, regular layers of rock may be broken off in straight ledges that run all the
way across a river bed.

When coming into holes and stoppers unawares, the first tactic to
try is to keep the boat in line with the current and paddle through
as hard as possible, taking deep strokes, particularly if the surface is
foamy. A deep stroke will be more likely to catch the current moving downstream below the surface, and it will certainly reach water
denser than the surface froth. Quick, decisive paddling is vital; if the
paddler hesitates until he is in the trough, he will probably broach.
If the boat does begin to broach, the paddler must immediately lean

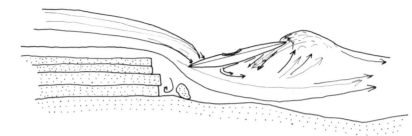

A kayak which has just entered a keeper formed by a natural ledge. The boater will have a hard time driving over the reversal, because the boat is going uphill, the water is flowing back, and the foam gives poor grip for the paddle. The current beating down on the stern may cause the boat to flip end over end. Typically, the kayak will turn across the current and only a strong downstream brace reaching down into the main current below the reversal will save the kayaker from capsizing. Staying with the boat is still best, even after capsizing, since the kayak and the paddler together are more likely to wash out than the two separately.

and brace downstream to avoid having the current roll the boat. A deep draw into the standing wave downstream will often catch water that will pull the boat over the hydraulic jump, particularly if it is small enough that the kayaker can reach over the stopper to get the paddle into the main current.

If the kayaker cannot pull out over the stopper, angling the bracing blade may carry the kayak down the trough in either direction, depending on the angle. Usually a way out can be found on one end of the standing wave, where the jump will at least be weaker. Care must be taken to maintain a strong lean downstream the whole time.

If the boat rolls, the paddler should roll back up on the downstream side. In this direction, the current will assist the roll. A few seconds' hesitation underwater may result in the underwater current's pulling on the body and dragging it out of the stopper, particularly if both arms are stretched straight below the head, holding the paddle as deep as possible. If not, try drawing deep as you begin to roll up to try to catch the deep current. If you bail out of the boat in a shallow stopper, you may be able to kick off the bottom over the standing wave. Otherwise, try swimming to the end of the wave to get around if you can. Be alert to the efforts of your companions to help, particularly if you have stationed someone on shore with a throwing line before trying to run the stopper. Finally, you can try

Paddling in heavy water. The kayaker is angled upstream and ferrying to avoid the huge hole, a stopper, which is behind him and extends over to the left of the photograph.

diving as deep as possible to get into the downstream current. In a big hole in heavy water, there will be too much turbulence for any of these schemes to have much meaning, after you are out of the boat. Fortunately, the current will usually carry a swimmer out.

A small stopper treated with proper respect is a good place to play. You can surf along it with the nose of the boat in the bottom of the trough and the stern angled up on the wave, using a high brace in

A hole, which, depending on the size of the dip, the skill of the paddler, and whether one is approaching or looking back, is very scary or a lot of fun. The hole is formed as the water moves over a submerged object, accelerating on the downhill side, and forming a turbulent standing wave with a reversal flow on the downstream side. Holes are like keepers, but because the main current flows on both sides, they will normally spit out a boat or swimmer after a short time. A hole can be hard to see from above and has only one downstream wave, rather than a series of haystacks. Its turbulence may also hide other rocks. Large holes can be quite dangerous.

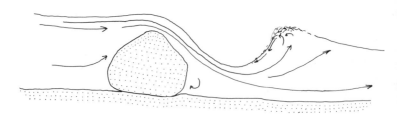

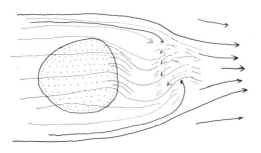

the stopper to carry the boat back and forth. Bringing the boat high up on the wave and driving bow-first into the trough can catch the bow in the downstream current, and if the boater throws his body forward at this moment, the boat will flip into the water end over end. This is an "ender," after which you simply roll back up to go on with something else. Enders are good fun to do deliberately with a strong boat, but unintentional ones are rather disconcerting.

READING WATER

Some of the standard patterns of fast water have been described in this chapter. The kayaker must constantly study these patterns in actual rivers, so that he can recognize them from his sitting position upstream and know what to expect. White-water kayaking requires a continuous development of a sense of water patterns and an instinctive set of physical reactions to deal with them. When he sees a big hole, the paddler must immediately move the boat away. When he notes an eddy before a concealed drop, he must pull into the slack water without hesitation to avoid being swept into the rapid below before having a chance to inspect it.

The first sign of the deep channel has already been mentioned: the long, smooth V of water pointing downstream. A sequence of haystacks below also indicates deep water flowing over the obstruction that formed them. On the other hand, a single foamy spot indicates that the obstruction above it is near the surface, and the boat will probably strike it if it runs straight for the turbulent place.

A rock sticking out of the water will have a pillow of water piled up on it which will help the boater to clear the rock, since this water is itself bouncing off the obstruction and will tend to push the hull of a kayak away from the rock. Draw away from the obstruction as hard as you can, and the cushion will finish the job. The occasional rock sticking up out of fast water with no cushion is undercut and dangerous: the current will tend to sweep a boat under the overhanging lip.

A rock that is just slightly submerged under the water presents the most difficult problem of detection. Uusally there is no pillow

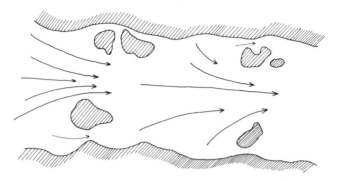

The main channel of a river forms V's where it flows between constrictions. The point of a V will thus indicate the main channel, where the water is likely to be deepest and least obstructed. "Following the V" will usually keep the boater out of the shallows, but it is no substitute for scouting.

behind the rock. A spot of smooth water in the midst of more turbulent surroundings, a slight V with the point upstream, a hump in the water, or a single spot of turbulence that is not followed by a series of standing waves may mark a rock that is only slightly submerged. Avoiding such rocks must depend completely on the actions of the paddler, because the current does not bounce off them and will not tend to deflect the hull of the boat away from collision courses.

More deeply submerged rocks will form a series of standing waves downstream. The presence of the standing waves generally indicates that there is enough water coming down the channel above them so that a kayak will not run aground, but remember that a hole may be concealed between the obstacle and the standing waves. If you run over a drop above a hole in error, remember to keep paddling as you head into the hole—beginners tend to become suddenly transfixed in horror as they go over the hump above and down into the hole, but this is precisely the point where you must paddle hard forward, with deep strokes.

This series of drawings shows the pattern of the water flow over the same rock at various levels of runoff. Note that a reasonably fast current is assumed; in slow-moving water there may be no hint of a rock just below the surface.

a shows the pattern when the top of the boulder is well out of the water, which piles up somewhat on the upstream side and forms an eddy below the rock, the length of which depends on the current.

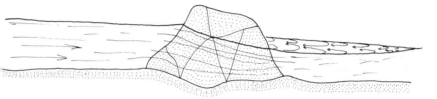

b illustrates what happens when the water just covers the boulder, now a "sleeper" which is hard to see and too shallowly covered to allow a kayak to pass over. The single, frothy wave below, if it can be spotted, signals that the rock upstream is only thinly covered.

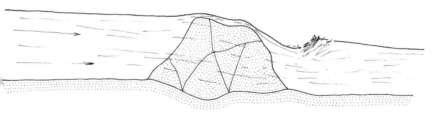

c shows the rock with a deeper and heavier flow, forming a *hole* on the downstream side. There is now enough clearance over the boulder to carry a boat over; the reversal wave beyond guarantees the paddler an exciting ride—or a terrifying one.

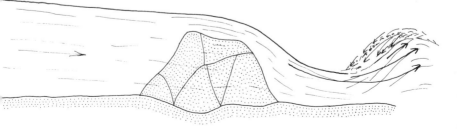

d illustrates a still higher water level, with the rock well covered and a series of standing waves or haystacks formed below it.

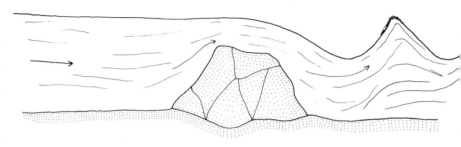

e pictures high enough water to completely wash out most of the surface turbulence caused by this boulder, which probably will not even be noticed by the kayaker.

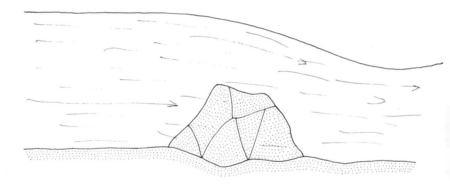

There will often be a small standing wave above the hole, and the presence of such a wave with big haystacks or a single breaking wave visible below should alert you to possible trouble in between. The first haystacks below a hole will be breaking, always in the same place. In heavy water, when large series of haystacks are the rule, one large breaker with no big standing waves below is a sign of a hole—so is a stationary breaker where other whitecaps are moving about in complex patterns.

An area of small choppy waves to the side of a line of big regular ones indicates a shallow area filled with small rocks and slower current. Such an area provides a route where you will be less likely to be carried rapidly into trouble, but where you will probably scrape the bottom of your boat.

Remember that scouting the rapid will give you a far better perspective on its nature than the view from the water. Holes will no longer be concealed by the drops above them. Barely submerged rocks that are hidden from upstream are easily visible from below. A good run can be planned and serious dangers evaluated in advance.

In bends, the fastest and deepest channel will be on the outside, but you should anticipate possible sweepers and obstructions when trees might be undercut on the bank. Undercutting of rock is also possible, so that at certain levels, the river may sweep under ledges

Running a chute. The kayaker is starting in the smooth tongue of water that generally marks the main channel. Note that to the left the water is dropping first over a shallowly covered ledge which would certainly scrape the bottom of the boat if it went that way and might hang it up. In the center of the photograph are a couple of holes. They are not terribly large, but the froth can cover sharp subsidiary rocks.

overhanging the river by only a foot or two. Water sweeping rapidly around a sharp bend may form an undertow on the outside of the bend, and even if it does not, the kayaker must be careful to avoid being swept out against the bank.

The easiest way to go around a fast corner with the main current is to *set around* the bend, simply angling the boat to the current and ferrying toward the inside of the turn. With a back ferry, the normal method, the bow would be pointed toward the outside of the turn at a greater angle than the current, and backpaddling would keep the boat moving around the bend on the inside. A faster trip around the bend can be had by staying in the main channel, heading the bow to the inside of the bend, and paddling hard to overcome centrifugal force as the current sweeps the boat around the curve. The angle of the bow can be adjusted so that most of the force of paddling is directed downriver, with just enough offset to keep the kayak from being carried to the outside of the bend.

RESCUES

Like the paddler's first line of defense against upsets, the Eskimo roll, rescues must be practiced in advance and mastered before they can be relied on. The rescue skills of the whole party are important, including the ability of the rescuers to coordinate with one another. Although experienced party leaders have to be responsible for beginners, the sooner every paddler begins to develop rescue techniques and a knowledge of his limitations, the stronger the groups of which he is a member will be.

The basic rules for self-rescue have already been mentioned in this chapter. If you cannot roll and have to bail out, try to keep hold of the boat and paddle, get to the upstream end of the boat, which is left floating cockpit-down, and swim for shore or the nearest eddy. If you have to swim through a difficult rapid first, stay on the upstream end of the kayak and try to go through on your back, feet-first. The same position is assumed if the boat is lost. The rescue techniques considered here are for swift water. Other methods that can be used in flat-water conditions are discussed in Chapter 6. They may be appropriate in calm sections of a river, but they cannot be relied on in fast water.

The most common river-rescue technique is to assist a swimming boater, one who has his kayak and paddle in tow. The rescuer emerges from the eddy where he has stationed himself downstream from a rapid, paddles ahead of the swimmer, and swings his stern within reach of the person in the water. The swimmer gets hold of the grab loop and is towed to safety. *The person in the water must keep swimming,* particularly if the water is swift and another rapid is coming. Towing a person and his boat, together with a paddle that is probably held perpendicular to the direction of travel, is a slow business. The more help the swimmer can give, the more likely he is to get out before being swept into the next rapid. If shore is some distance away, an eddy along the way may be a better choice of destination. It will at least provide a rest stop. Only practice will enable the rescuer to judge whether he can make it to safety before drifting into the next drop. If not, the best course may be to ferry the swimmer and his boat into the safest channel to swim the next rapid, instead of trying to get to shore or to an eddy that is too far away. In any case, the drag of the swimmer and boat will quickly pull the stern of the rescue boat downstream, so an upstream ferry is the normal rescue method.

If a paddler becomes separated from his boat, his paddle, or both, first priority must always be given to the safety of the swimmer. Circumstances vary, and rescuers are always called on to make spot judgments. In a situation where there is a long, calm stretch, where the water is not too cold for the clothing worn by the swimmer, and where he is obviously going to get to shore without difficulty, the rescuer may go to pick up the loose boat instead, but whenever there is any doubt, equipment should be ignored until the people are safe. Many other situations are possible. With several rescuers, some go after the paddler and others make for the equipment, but

they must understand each other's intentions. In some circumstances, less competent boaters may help, but in general, they
should stay in safe spots while the rescue is carried out, lest they
overturn, too, complicating the situation for the rescuers. The importance of practice cannot be overemphasized, and it should include working together in advance if a team is expecting to handle
emergencies in difficult water.

Towing a boater who is capable of holding onto the grab loop of a
boat is comparatively simple, although not nearly as easy as it
sounds. Rescue of equipment, or, if a serious error has been made,
an unconscious boater, is far more difficult. Paddling a boat requires
both hands, so neither is free to hold onto anything else. Improvised
solutions are possible in easy rescue situations, but more difficult
problems require some preparation. The simplest item to rescue is a
paddle. You can usually pick one up from the water, align it with
your own, and paddle with both until an eddy can be reached and a
better solution arranged. This is much simpler if both paddles have
the same twist. Paddlers with small hands will have trouble in either
case. If there is a spare paddle holder or other fitting on the deck,
the paddle can often be attached to that. A holder with a snap or
Velcro closure that can be attached to the shaft but will easily come
loose if necessary can be put on the strap of the spray skirt or on the
deck in front of the cockpit so that the paddle can be towed alongside, but all these arrangements have to be figured out in advance.

To bring a boat ashore without a rescue line, you can get downstream and try to push it across the current, ferrying, but this is
tricky. It is easier with a couple of rescuers working on one boat, but
this is a poor solution in wide rivers. A painter instead of a grab loop
makes the job far simpler. The painter is grabbed and held in the
teeth, while the rescuer makes for shore. To reduce the strain, the
painter can be wrapped a couple of times around the upper arm and
then held between the teeth. *Never tie the boat to be rescued to
yourself or your equipment,* lest it carry you irrevocably into difficulties downstream or catch on a rock. The towing line must always

be held so that it can be instantly released if trouble develops.

A substitute for a painter on the boat being rescued is a line carried by the rescuer with a climber's snap-link or carabiner on one end. This can be clipped to a grab loop or used to form a quick slip-loop around a victim's chest. It is then used like a painter to tow the boat or person being rescued to shore or to an eddy. Such a line can be carried tucked into the spray skirt or wet suit so it can be grabbed easily with one hand. If a person is being towed, it is obviously important to keep the victim's head out of water, if he is breathing. If he is not, artificial respiration must be started within a few minutes of the accident that caused stoppage of breathing. This may require pulling into an eddy or beaching on a rock where you can stand, so that resuscitation can be started quickly.

SAFETY

Safety on rivers is a party responsibility. General attitude and constant care over small items are really the most important safety precautions. Most serious problems that occur on a river are the result of a buildup of seemingly small violations of safety principles, rather than of single dramatic mistakes. Very few good boaters take serious risks, and if they do, those risks are usually carefully calculated and not undergone lightly. Many of the greatest hazards in kayaking are subtle ones. An inexperienced kayaker who dies as the result of a spill in a rapid is not likely to have become a fatality as a result of mutilation among the rocks. He will probably succumb instead to the effects of cold water on his unprotected body, to drowning because of failure to wear a life jacket, or, most often, to a combination of these and similar factors.

The basic safety principles begin with adequate preparation, whether on long tours of several weeks or an afternoon paddle in a local creek. The most important rule for the beginner is to paddle with boaters who have enough experience to handle rescues in the water being undertaken. You may be able to enjoy a safe trip on easy water with other neophytes, but any water difficult enough to provide a real challenge will require more experienced help. If you have to teach yourself and still maintain a good safety margin, resign yourself to slow progress.

Boating alone is inherently far more dangerous than boating with others. The best safety rule is probably *never* to boat alone. It is vital to adhere to this rule except in situations where your safety margin is very wide. Thus, it may be safe to work in a warm river by the road, a river that is easy by your standards and has calm water below where you could swim to safety after an upset, but do not do it unless you are absolutely sure it is safe (and have enough experience to make the judgment). Similarly, you should not boat in water beyond your level of competence, unless there are more advanced kayakers along who are aware of your ability and able to assist you in case of trouble.

Personal safety requires wearing a wet suit if the water is at all cold. (See the detailed recommendations in Chapter 2.) Other warm clothing, including wool clothes and wind protection, must be carried when air temperatures are cold enough (or might become cold enough) to require them. Extra dry clothing must be conveniently available on shore, or, more often, it must be carried in a watertight stowage bag in the boat. The importance of warm clothing cannot be overemphasized. Cold water can kill an unprotected swimmer in a few minutes or disable him so that he drowns. Even after getting to shore, he may quickly die from exposure without dry clothes and active rewarming of his body by companions. (Note the fate of the solo paddler in such a situation.) Dry clothes and fire-building materials suitable for getting a blaze going even in the rain should be carried by each paddler when cold weather is a possibility. Fifty- or sixty-degree temperatures may constitute cold weather for a boater exposed to the breeze after a dunking in frigid water. The cool air, the wind-chill factor, and evaporative cooling will rapidly sap the remaining warmth from the body of a kayaker who has taken a swim without a wet suit.

It is also important to remember the insidious effects of cold on others. If you see one of your companions shivering or displaying blue lips or other signs of cold, you must take steps to warm him. His judgment and kayaking ability may soon be affected, causing an upset, and his chilled body may then be unable to cope with even moderately cold water. Remember that with strenuous physical activity, blood sugar can be exhausted, causing people to become dangerously cold even in very mild weather.

An adequate life vest is another essential for personal safety in white water. The reasons for wearing a vest even if you are a good swimmer have been discussed in an earlier chapter and will not be repeated here. A boater without a life vest can endanger his whole party if he requires rescue after trying to swim down a foamy rapid—his buoyancy will simply not be enough to allow him to breathe.

A helmet is necessary in any rapids that are not straightforward for the individual involved, and it should be considered essential for any kayaker in any powerful white water. No matter how reliable a kayaker's roll may be, or how strong a boater and swimmer he is, if his head hits a rock and he is knocked unconscious, his life will be in danger. In considering whether a helmet should be worn, remember that the best kayakers turn over occasionally, intentionally or otherwise, and that there may be a rock under the surface. The safest course is to wear a helmet in any white water.

Good flotation for the boat should always be used in white water. The kayak will be less likely to become damaged in an upset, will be less of a hazard to others, and will be easier to rescue, if it cannot fill with water. Good flotation bags, tied into the boat if they could possibly pop out, or other flotation arrangements, such as bulkheads, are essential. Grab loops that can be easily caught are also necessary if you should have to rescue the boat. On a wilderness river being able to save a boat is a safety factor.

The most important factor affecting a party's safety is its preparation for the run. Such preparation includes individual competence, proper equipment, both long-term and recent training, group cohesiveness, and homework regarding the particular river to be run. Preparation for a spring training session on a local river paralleling a road may involve no more than a quick check by each person of his equipment and a few stops along the road for visual inspection of the rapids. Preparation for a long tour may involve months of work getting information, building equipment, and paddling together.

Tours for beginners have to be carefully chosen for their suitability. Long rapids and those with poor runouts are obviously bad choices until a paddler has developed some competence on moving water. Even experienced hands who have run a particular rapid themselves should inspect it specifically for the level of ability of the people with them. A drop that may not even catch the conscious attention of an expert, and hence will not be remembered, may be both terrifying and dangerous to a novice. The beginner should work at length on flat-water practice and a strong roll before he attempts white water, both for personal safety and out of consideration for those going with him. If you go on a trip with experienced boaters, make sure that they have a clear feeling for your level of experience before you leave, as a matter both of courtesy and of safety.

An iron safety rule which cannot be repeated too often is to *inspect any rapid before running it or getting in a position from which you cannot avoid running it. If the rapid cannot be seen from the river above, get to the shore and scout it.* Ignoring this rule regularly will get you in serious trouble one day. That is how people manage to paddle over waterfalls and dams—you might be lucky for years, but sooner or later the odds will catch up with you. Inspection is important on many rivers, even if someone in the group has run the rapids before, particularly if heavy runoff has occurred since—a logjam might have built up right across the only channel. Logjams are a particular hazard because the current normally flows underneath them, and sharp branches may be sticking out in all directions to injure the boater who is above water or snag the one being swept underwater.

The normal rule for a group running a river is for the most experienced paddler to take the lead and another of the better paddlers to come down last, as "sweep." As a general rule, no one passes the lead boat or falls behind the sweep. No exceptions should be made without permission of the leader, and never where the river is difficult. A large group may break into several smaller ones, but the same rules are followed within these. Each boater is responsible for maintaining contact with the kayak behind. Thus, if you run around a fast corner, you should pull into the first eddy and wait until you see the following boat before starting downstream again. This prevents the group from getting split up, losing someone, or having a member capsize without anyone's knowing. It allows each paddler to see the course being followed in rapids. When the leader pulls into an eddy above a rapid to scout it or give instructions on running it, everyone pulls in, not passing without permission.

Frequently, if there is a wide divergence of ability in a group, the leader will either have some members portage or line a difficult passage while others run it, or will station rescuers in slack water below the rapid before less experienced members run it. Where there are particular hazards, rope throwers may be stationed below the rapids, or some members may portage them to provide a rescue team, portaging back up to run the pitch themselves after others have passed safely. In any tricky situations, a boat should not start into the drop until the preceding one has completed it; this avoids having to worry about more than one rescue at a time.

Throwing lines are useful in some situations, with throwers stationed below a rapid in advance. They may be particularly helpful if a stopper is being run. Polypropylene rope, which floats, is best for throwing lines; a large knot is tied in the end to weight it. Practice with throwing should be acquired in advance of need. At a stopper, the rope is thrown beyond the victim so it can be caught. For a swimmer floating downstream, throw the line across the channel a little below the person—he will overtake it. If someone is stranded on a rock, obviously the line is thrown across the current above the boulder so that it will be carried down. Take care that the end of the line is secured on the shore, so that the force of the current will not simply pull it through your hands. To control the line once it is thrown, sit down and run it around behind your waist, and belay it with the opposite hand. Belaying means braking the rope with one or both hands after it has been run around the waist, a tree, or some other object to multiply the frictional force that can be exerted on the rope. In general throwing lines may be helpful on small rivers where the main channel is usually close to shore. They are rarely of any use on large rivers.

Safety is often influenced by aspects of a trip that may at first glance seem unrelated. On a long trip when the weather turns bad, the camping skill and equipment of each member of the party will influence his physical and mental well-being in a way that is bound to affect performance on the river. In really harsh situations hypothermia—dangerous chilling of the body core—can result when someone comes off the river and does not have the equipment and skill to get himself dry and warm. A good deal of camping experience is required to keep insulation dry on a rainy river trip. It follows that on a long trip, other skills and gear have to be considered besides those strictly related to boating.

Both the leader and each member of a party must take responsibility for safety, and this involves careful evaluation of the strength of each person and of the group as a whole. The individual's foremost responsibility is honesty with himself and others about his experience and capabilities. Be sure you understand your own ability and that the leader understands it as well. If you con yourself onto a trip that is beyond your abilities, at best you will make the trip an ordeal for yourself and everyone else, and at worst you may lose your boat or your life. Touring conditions vary a lot. Having run one rapid of a given difficulty with a safe, easy run-out does not mean you are ready for long sequences of the same level, particularly in wilderness conditions with cold water and a loaded boat.

The leader is responsible for making sure that each member of the party is capable and properly equipped for making the trip safely. This means checking boating ability with a jaundiced eye and also understanding other skills that may be necessary, particularly camping, rescue, and first aid skills. A strong boater who has never camped away from a car may be a weak party member for a two-week wilderness trip. The leader must be particularly careful in screening people for long and serious river cruises. It is vital that he be sure that each prospective member has suitable experience and knows the difficulty of the trip and the equipment that will be needed. Besides the consideration of safety, one inadequately prepared member can ruin a trip for everyone else.

Remember that a river that curves a few miles away from the road in a deep canyon could make rescue very difficult, even though casual examination might lead one to think otherwise, since the tour is a short one, beginning and ending at the road.

First aid supplies should be carried on all river trips. On tours where the party is away from the road, at least two fairly complete first aid kits must be carried, and at least two members of the group should be experienced in first aid in wilderness conditions. Redundancy is an important safety principle on longer tours. A single first aider may be the person injured, and the only first aid kit may be in the kayak that is lost. First aid training, too, requires a lot of advance preparation.

One first aid kit should be carried by the last kayak, so that it is always quickly available. Every member of the party should know elementary first aid, including mouth-to-mouth artificial respiration and how to stop severe bleeding.

Repair kits for boats and a knowledge of how to use them are important on long tours. Getting stranded with a boat that has a large hole in the hull is poor form on a river with an 80-mile walk-out.

Finally, it is important to remember that overall party strength is the most basic and subtle factor in river safety. It is comprised of many separate parts, ranging from individual skill and conditioning to group morale and solidarity. A group of intermediate paddlers might be quite safe on a river with many rapids of moderate difficulty but good run-outs, provided they also stick together and portage when necessary. Experts might be able to get a group of beginners happily through the same river, but not if they resented having to wait at every bend and dip, either because the beginners came under false pretenses or because the experts took on the responsibility without really thinking. A blend of good attitudes and good judgment is the common key both to safety and to fun on the river.

RIVER RATING

It is convenient to be able to rate the difficulty of both river sections and individual rapids objectively, so that a competent boater who has never run a particular river will know what to expect. "Moderate rapids," "difficult drop," and "tricky maneuvering" are such subjective terms that they mean little unless you have kayaked many times with the user, so that you know not only his boating ability, but his penchant for exaggeration or understatement.

A number of rating systems are in use in North America, and all of them leave something to be desired. It is difficult to rate a river objectively, because there are many factors involved. Kayakers not only vary in their abilities, but some are better at some types of boating than others. A paddler who is an expert at weaving through tight passages in small rivers may be thoroughly intimidated by his first encounter with easy big water, and the converse is equally possible. Different boats and styles of paddling are most suitable for different situations. Rivers are rated by boaters who use other kinds of craft than kayaks. A passage may appear quite different on a cold, nasty day when you are not really in good physical or mental condition from the way it seems on a beautiful, sunny afternoon when you feel able to do anything. It is difficult to balance various factors: how do you rate a very hard but completely safe maneuver compared to a fairly easy move that is potentially dangerous because of the conse-

quences of failure? Should remoteness, which increases the
seriousness of a rapid, be reflected in the rating? The questions are
endless. Finally, rivers vary depending on the flow. How can you
rate a river just run without knowing the effects of greater or lesser
amounts of water?

Still, despite many problems, an imperfect rating system is better
than none at all, since it permits the communication of important information, which can be supplemented by verbal descriptions and
qualifications. The most widely used system is an international one,
which rates difficulty by three letters and six Roman numerals. A
description of each level of difficulty follows.

Class A   Lakes, ponds, and flat sections of rivers flowing very
slowly, generally at no more than a mile or two per
hour.

Class B   Smooth water flowing somewhat faster, but less than full
backpaddling speed, so that backward ferries can easily
be made without losing ground.

Class C   Smooth water flowing faster than backpaddling speed,
perhaps with sharp bends requiring some care and occasional maneuvering around obstacles.

Class I   Easy rapids. Riffles and small, regular waves. Passages
are clear, easy to find, and require only elementary
maneuvering to enter. Obstacles are easily seen and
avoided. Sharp bends are simple to negotiate.

Class II   Rapids with some eddies, turbulence, and waves of up
to 3 feet high. Obstacles may require some maneuver-
ing, and there may be some holes and a few obstructions in the main channel. Rescues easy. Moderate current and frequent eddies permit stops in many places.
Channel is straightforward and readily recognized.

Class III   More difficult rapids, requiring a good deal of maneuvering around obstacles. Scouting may be required to
find the correct route. Some eddies may be strong, and
fairly powerful holes and turbulence may be encountered if the optimum route is missed. Waves of up to 5
feet. Small falls. Rescue not too difficult for competent
parties. Eddies may be small and hard to get into, but
there are stopping places beyond all danger spots. Class
III covers a multitude of situations, having perhaps the
widest range of difficulty of any rating.

Class IV   Difficult rapids, challenging for strong boaters with considerable experience. High, irregular waves, powerful
eddies, and strong crosscurrents will be encountered,
along with difficult maneuvering. Obstructions in the
main channel. Scouting is generally mandatory, and
strong teams are required to make successful rescue
reasonably likely. Big drops, falls, and holes. Rest spots
and landings often irregularly spaced and fairly difficult
to enter.

Class V   Extremely difficult rapids which are treated with respect even by the teams of experts who are capable of
running them. Long, continuous, turbulent white water
with irregular and powerful waves, crosscurrents, eddies, white eddies, and holes. Best course may be difficult to pick out even from shore, and a perfect run will
still require encountering severe turbulence directly.
Rescues very difficult. Extremely hazardous for any but
a practiced team of well-equipped experts.

Class VI   The limit of navigability for the very best boaters running in ideal conditions. All the above difficulties extended to their limit. Cannot be attempted without
some risk to life, even by a team of experts.

As with other aspects of white-water kayaking, learning to rate a river, or even make a first approximation, requires considerable experience. To the novice, a class II rapid is likely to look terrifying. Even ratings made by experts have to be taken with a grain of salt. Ratings where the river flow is unstated are normally taken to apply to ideal conditions for running the river, but they may simply indicate the conditions when a particular paddler ran the river. If you have gotten the rating verbally, you should discuss it with the person who has run the river; additional information will not only help give you more detail, but it will give you an idea of the accuracy and precision of the person you are talking to. Some excellent paddlers do not have very good memories for rivers they have run, and others may simply not take much note of rapids that are well below their abilities.

Though the international rating system is supposed to be uniform, there are definitely regional variations in its use. Some variations are due to differences in rivers: problems that are common in one part of North America will tend to be underrated by the locals, whereas someone coming from an area with another type of difficulty predominating will take some time to get used to new paddling situations. Thus, big water hydraulics might be held in more awe by one used to smaller intricate rivers, whereas those used to heavy water phenomena may tend to underrate them. In addition to such natural inconsistencies in rating, however, rivers may be differently rated simply because of inadequate communication or because of ego-boosting among local hotshots. Underrating of rapids can imply: "We wouldn't call that trivial drop a class IV; there's nothing to it. Standards must be pretty low in your area." Such competitiveness is in poor taste, and it defeats the whole purpose of a rating system, because it lowers the quality of communication. You should be aware that it occasionally exists, however, and take it into account.

A really good written guide to a river will state the flow to which a rating applies, and the best guides may give ratings at several flow levels. They will also give a lot of specific information besides flow levels and numerical ratings.

Big water. The boater is coming up out of a hole. There is another immediately ahead of him and a monster in the background. This sort of water demonstrates the difficulties of rating. It is not technically difficult, since there are no intricate rock gardens, but it is very powerful and could be extremely dangerous.

Beginners should be extremely cautious in using ratings. Ratings are very useful tools, but neither a rating nor a description can be used like a cookbook to get down a river safely. Having successfully pulled through one class III rapid does not mean that one can successfully negotiate, or even safely attempt, any class III rapid. It certainly does not mean that one is qualified for an extended trip on a class III river.

In general, the beginner who has practiced his strokes well on flat water and mastered the principles of the simple ferry can safely run class I water and attempt class II. It is assumed, of course, that experienced paddlers will be along to perform rescues. It is easy at the beginning to lose boat and paddle in quite elementary water, until the reflexes of holding onto equipment are developed. The apt boater who works hard at eddy turns and more difficult ferrying techniques will soon find himself moderately competent in class II water and ready to try easy class III. Progress is slower from that point, however, and no rapid of class III or higher should be attempted lightly. Long class III runs in cold water and with big holes and drops can provide challenges for a long time. Before he can really consider himself a class III boater, the neophyte must develop a thorough command of eddy turns in difficult situations, ferrying across fast chutes, surfing on rollers, reading water accurately, rolling reliably on either side in turbulent water, and performing rescues without a hitch in easy class III water. This will take a lot of paddling, and by the time the goal has been honestly reached, the kayaker will be able to judge future progress himself.

PLANNING RIVER CRUISES

The first step in planning any white-water tour is to find out as much as possible about the river. Most often this is done by word-of-mouth, particularly for short day trips; but on longer, more remote tours, it may involve months of planning. Word-of-mouth information has to be carefully evaluated; it is only as good as the source and your interrogation of him. The things that you find out can be checked carefully (and should be) if the tour runs along a road, but when it does not, the consequences of erroneous or misunderstood data have to be kept uppermost in the mind.

It is particularly important to find out if there are any rapids that are very long or otherwise badly arranged for rescues; if there are any "silent" rapids or pitches without good stopping places above; if there are any rapids that cannot be portaged should they turn out to be beyond the ability of the party; at what levels the river is safe and at what levels it is low enough to require many carries; whether it is difficult to walk out in case a boat is lost or damaged.

Some of the details of using maps and other information sources are considered in the discussion on camping in Chapter 6, but they can be just as important on short trips, particularly when the river bends away from the road. Even a small section where the river is invisible can be dangerous—it often is. If there is a stretch of rough, deep sheer-sided gorge, it is just that place that the road is most likely to bypass and that, in any case, is likely to be impossible to see from the car because of the steep walls that conceal it. Do not be complacent about unknown rivers or about rivers for which information is sketchy and third-hand. Inspect everything possible beforehand, ask as many people and read as many accounts as possible, and always stop and scout when a section ahead cannot be seen. Remember, too, that logjams can appear after flooding, and new boulders can fall from cliffs or be washed down side streams, so that even a river you have run personally will not necessarily be the same the next time down.

The responsibilities of leaders and party members have been discussed already in this chapter, but they must not be overlooked in planning, particularly on trips with novices along. The leader has to make sure that the party is competent, and members have to make sure that the leader knows their capacities. If someone who is leading a white-water trip is not interested in your ability, perhaps you should think twice about going.

Proper equipment and safety gear must be standard on all white-water trips. Unless you are going every weekend and have developed a foolproof mental list, it is best to use a checklist before every trip. It is rather frustrating to drive a few hundred miles to a river and find you have left your spray skirt at home. A checklist is found on page 306.

6
Touring on Lakes and the Ocean

Kayaking on large bodies of water seems generally simpler than river cruising, if only because it tends to look less intimidating. This observation is not always true, of course, if you compare a placid stream or sluggish river to booming rocky surf. Still, water that looks frightening is more often seen in rivers. As a rule, touring on large bodies of "flat water" *is* easier than river running, so the first impression here is accurate. The sea should never be underestimated, however, for its dangers are likely to be far more subtle than those of a boiling rapid, and the kayaker caught out of his depth is probably more likely to meet with serious consequences than the river cruiser. Even large lakes can get the overconfident boater into trouble.

Ocean touring along the coast has seen only a little development in North America, though it is quite popular in Britain. This is ironic, because the kayak was originally developed as a seagoing craft, mainly in North America, and it is admirably suited for exploring on coastal waters. Many dwellers along the east and west coasts, who drive hundreds of miles to get to rivers and curse the brief season, have an unlimited field for kayaking much nearer home in the Atlantic and Pacific Oceans. Lake touring in kayaks can also be very enjoyable, and it is usually feasible both earlier and later in the season than river running.

The variety of kayaking available on large bodies of water is at least as great as on rivers. At one end of the spectrum, paddling may be done on lakes near shore on calm days, so that there is no real

Paddling on flat water has its own beauties and rewards.

problem with either wind or large waves. Much coastal touring in protected bays and inlets is similar. Kayaking becomes much more challenging when the possibility of wind, waves, and tides are added, as one goes farther from shore, takes longer trips, or goes out on days when there is a stiff breeze. At the other end of the spectrum, riding surf is as thrilling and challenging a game as whitewater paddling.

FLAT-WATER PADDLING

On genuine flat water, with only slight waves or none at all, paddling is simple enough unless the wind comes up. The boater simply points his kayak in the direction he wants to go and paddles ahead. Even in the directionally unstable slalom kayak, the practiced paddler can keep a fairly straight course, but he will have to work harder and will go more slowly than companions who have longer touring boats with some keel. It is in this sort of paddling that most of the currently manufactured foldboats excel, although even they will be slower and less lively than a modern, narrower fiber glass touring kayak.

A rudder assembly can be of some help in paddling of this sort, and some kayaks have rudders available for them, which are operated with a foot bar through a system of ropes and pulleys. Unfortunately, a rudder makes the most difference with a slalom kayak, and it is not likely that one will be available for a slalom boat. A reasonably ingenious boater can make his own.

Steering is not really the main problem for the kayaker with a slalom boat, however, for he can maneuver the boat altogether too well. What is really lacking is a keel, which, because it runs the length of the boat, gives more directional stability than a rudder. A good improvised keel can be made to lend directional stability to a slalom kayak on flat water by running a length of rope down the center of the bottom of the hull. With a little thought, the grab loops can generally serve as anchors for the rope, which must be pulled tight and run straight down the center of the hull, with any knots above the normal waterline. Material such as polypropylene, which does not stretch when wet, is best. The rope needs to be anchored right along the centerline, and a few pieces of boat tape will do this job as well as anything. With such an improvised keel the paddler of a slalom boat will still not be able to stay abreast of his companions in touring boats on flat water, but he will waste far less energy in keeping his kayak going in a straight line.

Wind is far less of a problem for the kayaker than it is for the canoeist, since the bows and deck of the kayak are much lower in the water and are more rounded. Even so, a stiff wind makes steering difficult and can complicate the problem of holding a course, particularly when it begins to whip up waves, as it will on any large body of water.

PADDLING IN THE WIND

As long as the waves do not become too large, the effects of the wind are not too difficult to manage. If you are paddling straight into the wind, your progress will be significantly slowed, of course, and the bow of the boat will tend to be caught by the wind and slued off to one side or the other, so that constant small corrections need to be made in the course, normally by incorporating some sweep stroke when paddling on one side. The main trick to learn in this type of paddling is to make the corrections without breaking the normal paddling rhythm. Leaning forward tends to lower the wind resistance presented by the body and also to lower the bow somewhat, so that it is caught less by the wind.

In paddling at an angle to the wind, you eventually get a balance in your stroke, putting just enough sweep in the side opposite the wind to keep the boat going in a constant direction. This can sometimes be done by shifting the grip on the paddle, so that one side is projecting out a bit farther from the hull. It is important to remember also, in plotting your course, that the wind will have an effect like the current in a river ferry. It will press against the side of the hull angled toward it, pushing the kayak to the opposite side. This motion is often imperceptible to the paddler, except by observing points along the shore or islands in the water. By lining up two points to provide a reference line, you can tell if the wind is carrying the boat significantly off course. If heading toward a single point, a compass bearing can be taken, and if the bearing begins to shift, then the kayak is being carried sideways.

Paddling across the wind in light waves causes few problems. The kayak can be expected to drift with the wind, and this should be anticipated. It may be particularly important to be alert to such drift if you are traveling along a rocky coast with an onshore wind, to avoid being carried dangerously close to shore without noticing. A strong wind, especially a gusty one, may also cause occasional balance problems by catching the raised blade of the paddle from the side, forcing the paddler to brace against the blade in the water to avoid capsizing.

Running before the wind is simplicity itself when there are no large waves, since the wind is helping the paddler along. The stern is rarely high enough to be pushed aside and drive the kayak off course, unless the boat has been loaded incorrectly. Even if it is high, course corrections with the paddle are simple enough. The main thing to be cautious about when running with the wind is the fact that waves are likely to become larger with time and as you approach the lee shore (the one toward which the wind is blowing).

WAVES

The main problem facing the kayaker on large bodies of water is the action of waves, and this is particularly true on the sea. Waves are produced by the wind blowing over the surface of the water. On lakes of moderate size, waves are usually quite simple, and their relationship to the wind that caused them is clear. The direction of the two will be the same, and the waves can simply be expected to

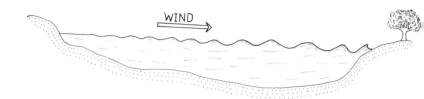

Waves are formed by wind sweeping across a body of water. Barring wind shifts, sheltering bars, and the like, the waves become progressively bigger, so that large breakers may occur on the leeward shore, though the water on the windward side is quite calm.

come up awhile after the wind begins to blow, with an amplitude that is clearly related to the strength of the wind.

On really large bodies of water, particularly on the ocean, things may be more complex, since waves can travel a long way from their point of origin. They will meet other waves coming from other directions, and winds blowing against them or at angles to them. On the sea, tides and currents may run with the waves or at various angles to them, causing complicated effects. Large waves, in particular, can present a welcome challenge or a potential danger to the kayaker.

Although the water that makes up a wave is in motion, the motion is cyclical; the water moves up and down and back and forth, but in the end it stays in the same place, while the wave moves on. Some net motion may occur if the waterline on a beach is being driven up by a storm or if there is a current or tidal motion in addition to the waves, but essentially the water remains in the same place. The situation is just the reverse of what frequently occurs in a river, where the water is moving and a standing wave is stationary.

The skills generally needed to ride sea waves smoothly in a kayak are not very different from those required in a river. Basic paddling skills need to be learned thoroughly before you wander off onto large bodies of water. Many novices get into trouble on lakes and coastal waters, however, because the waters look placid and easy, so they are tempted to get off far from shore before mastering fundamental techniques. If wind and waves then come up, or if a capsize occurs, particularly if the kayaker is alone, problems may be much greater than expected.

In deep water, waves are generally long, and the rise and fall are gentle enough that even very large waves can be paddled over with ease. Slalom kayaks will have more of an irritating tendency to be pushed around off course than less sensitive boats, first in one direction and then another, but in really steep waves, they are easy to balance, and once off course, they are easier to turn back on. An attempt should be made to keep paddling at a steady rate, though progress will vary as one crosses each wave: climbing up the front of the wave, sliding down the back, and then wallowing in the trough. Course corrections are most easily made on top of the waves, both because visibility is best from there and because the ends of the boat are free of the water and easy to turn. A general course is not hard to keep, however, since the kayak stays at a fairly constant angle to the waves.

Waves of increasing size can create unforeseen difficulties in keeping a party organized. The group may suddenly find that several members have disappeared from view. Because of the low position of the kayaker on the surface of the water, waves need not get very high before two paddlers in adjacent troughs are invisible to each other. When the waves become higher still, a kayaker in a trough cannot even be seen from a crest a couple of waves away. Initially, this situation is not serious, although when it happens it can cause momentary alarm. It requires very careful efforts to keep the party close together. With a small group, everyone simply needs to stay close and to keep aware of the locations of all other members, but with a large party, four kayaks should maintain positions at the outside of the party, and kayakers should also pair off to keep track of one another. A party spread out in high seas can easily lose track of one member, and the situation can rapidly become serious if he should capsize or panic.

Waves begin to *feel bottom* and break when they reach a certain *critical depth*, related to the height of the waves. Thus, they may not break over a bar well out from shore except when they rise over a certain height. On a steep beach like that shown here, the waves will rear up and break very suddenly. A more gradual beach is better for surfing.

A wave begins to "feel bottom" and break when the depth of the water over which it is moving is reduced to approximately one and one-quarter times the height of the wave. Then the long deep water waves curl over, forming walls of water as they roll into shore, and the tops go crashing down, the resulting froth moves on up the beach and dissipates its energy, and then slides back under the next wave as it breaks. Surf and breakers can form a superb playground for the kayaker, but they can be very dangerous as well. Large waves can usually be ridden fairly easily in deep water, but breakers are a different matter. Riding them takes more skill and can be deadly with really big waves and rocky coastlines.

The fact that waves break when they reach a certain depth of water related to their own size has many important consequences for the boater, particularly in the ocean. You may launch easily from a protected spot on a beach and paddle over a sandbar a quarter-mile out without even noticing it. On return, however, you may find that because the waves are a bit higher or the tide lower, there is now a line of breakers at the sandbar and that there is no easy way through. Only careful, long-term study of the wave action will begin to teach you all its tricks. In the area where you paddle, study the waves under many different conditions. On some beaches, when the tide is at particular levels, the breakers coming into the beach may actually get larger when the height of the waves at sea goes down, because the smaller waves can go over shallows at some distance from the shore without breaking, whereas the larger ones break on the bar and only secondary surf reaches the beach.

Waves can change direction and be modified when they cross reefs and bars or go past obstructions. When two groups of waves meet, they combine in ways that can be very confusing to the paddler on the water's surface. Where the crest of one wave coincides with the trough of another, the two will cancel, and if they are of approximately equal height they will nullify each other completely, leaving a flat section of water. On the other hand, when the crests and troughs coincide, they will form much higher waves. Two waveforms meeting each other at an angle can thus form patterns with

Wave refraction may occur behind a large rock or small island, around which the waveforms bend. There is a calm protected spot just behind this rock, but beyond that there are some huge breakers where the waves coming from both sides add together.

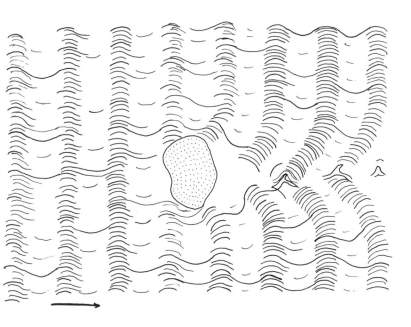

lines of calm and lines of high waves alternating. If the bottom is not deep, the high waves may even break, adding to the confusion.

An example of this type of problem is often found behind a large rock some distance out from the beach. The beginner may well seek shelter behind the rock from the waves moving in toward the shore, only to find that the waves bend around the obstruction, converging behind it and forming a choppy area with some extremely large crests where the refracted waveforms converge.

Waves can also be reflected from surfaces, and this is particularly common along breakwaters and cliffs, where the water remains fairly deep right up to the obstruction. Waves striking such an obstacle at an angle can form a line of gigantic waves parallel to the breakwater where the incoming sea waves and the reflected waves add together. Nearby a line of calm water can often be found, where the two sets cancel each other out.

The way in which waves break when they come into shore depends on the height of the waves, the depth of water, and the form of the beach. In general, a beach that slopes down slowly will cause waves to break gently some way out and roll on in toward the beach,

Wave reflection off a breakwater that the waves strike at an angle. Lines of great breakers and lines of cancellation occur at intervals out from the breakwater.

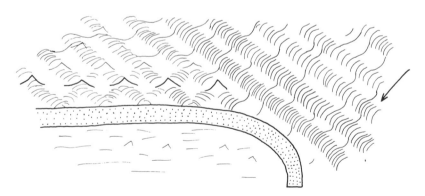

dissipating their energy gradually. A beach that drops off rapidly results in waves that come nearly all the way in before reaching water that is shallow enough to make them feel bottom and break. Such surf will rear up suddenly right near the shore and come down with a great crash against the beach. Suddenly breaking surf like this also indicates that there is probably a severe undertow.

There are many variations. Some beaches have gentle breaking at low tide and very sudden breaking at high tide; some have rapid breaking along a reef some distance out at low tide and gentle breaking on the beach itself at high tide. The kayaker must become fully aware of the characteristics of the beach before launching his boat.

Wind can also affect waves that have already been formed. A wind blowing with the wave motion will tend to enlarge it. This is readily apparent when one is crossing a lake before the wind or paddling along an inlet with the wind blowing across. Waves will be nonexistent along the windward shore, and they will become larger and larger as you paddle across, until they break, sometimes with terrifying force, on the opposite side.

A wind blowing against the waves will eventually stop their motion, but the first effect is to make the waves shorter and choppier and the leading sides much steeper. This can cause real problems with high waves in deep water, for the kayaker finds himself driving into vertical walls of water when traveling with the wind, or being overtaken by them when paddling with the waves. Driving through such waves can be really exhausting, and the problem should be anticipated when possible and shelter sought.

TIDES AND CURRENTS

Ocean tides and the currents that are caused by them create many complex patterns, particularly around coastal inlets, bays, islands, and the mouths of rivers emptying into the sea. These water movements can be used to advantage by the kayaker who pays care-

ful attention to them, or they can bring the unobservant to grief.
Tides are caused by the gravitational pull of the sun and the moon
on the oceans. This gravitational attraction pulls out a bulge of water
on the surface of the sea, which moves around with the rotation of
the earth, with the main tidal influence being caused by the moon.
High tides occur when the moon is overhead and when it is on the
opposite side of the earth. There are thus approximately two high
tides and two low ones each day.

The highest high tides and the lowest low tides occur when the
sun and the moon lie along the same line with the earth, so that
their gravitational pull combines. These are called *spring tides*, and
they occur when the moon is full and when it is new. The smallest
tidal variation coincides with the half-moon, when the sun and
moon are not in line, and this is called a *neap tide*. The difference in
height between low and high water is about one and one-half times
larger during spring tides than during neap tides.

Tides also vary over longer periods, because the moon's orbit
around the earth is not circular but elliptical, so the moon is sometimes closer and sometimes farther away. Tides are higher when the
moon is closer to earth. When the closest passage of the moon corresponds to a spring tide, the tidal variation will be considerably
greater than normal.

The actual height of the tide along a particular beach, harbor, or
estuary will depend not only on the factors just mentioned but on
the shape of the coastline and inlets. Tidal tables are available in
most coastal areas to show the times of high and low tide and the
variation that is expected. Consultation with local fishermen or other
boaters can be helpful in finding out about local tidal movements
too. Some strangely shaped inlets can cause weird tidal action, am-
plifying normal tidal movements or causing very sudden ones. For
example, at the mouths of some rivers the tide comes in as a large
breaking wave. More commonly, extremely fast currents can be expected at certain times through narrow channels which carry the
tidal flow into and out of large bays. If the kayaker wants to get out

to sea rapidly, sometimes riding such a current can be a fast and pleasant way to cover a lot of distance at breakneck speed with no effort—providing he is sure that dangerous turbulence is not waiting around the bend. On the other hand, if the boater wanted to travel across the same channel, he should make the trip at slack tide, the period between the movement of water in and out. The length of the period of slack tide will vary from place to place, but it will be longest at neap tides and shortest during spring tides.

It is also important to remember that the height of tides is greatly affected by storms and winds. A big storm offshore coinciding with a high spring tide can raise the water a truly phenomenal amount, with big waves adding to the effect. On the other hand, a strong wind blowing off the land may reduce the tide as well as flatten the waves. Tide tables are accurate only in the absence of storms and strong winds, including those far out at sea.

The moving water in tidal races, channels, and estuaries produces the same general effects as a river, except that the flow reverses four times a day. The paddler should expect eddies to form behind obstructions and where the channel widens, together with all other typical moving water phenomena. These patterns can be complicated by the action of incoming waves as one comes out into the unprotected ocean.

A *tidal rip* may occur along a shore or beach, most frequently when the tide is going out. What happens is that much of the water being brought in with the waves moves back out to sea in narrow channels. Tidal rips usually occur where a large bar or reef a little out from the waterline allows water to build up in a deeper channel that runs parallel to the shore, so that water first runs parallel to the beach and then on out to sea in a channel, flattening the waves somewhat as it goes. Such a rip can provide a fast ride out through the surf. It is usually quite narrow, and when the kayaker exits from it, he may need to lean into the turn to prevent capsizing when he hits the stationary water to the side.

The importance of studying and understanding the tides and currents around any coastal area where you plan to kayak cannot be overemphasized. Many complicated factors related to tidal movement affect the kayaker, but even at the simplest level the whole planning of a trip often revolves around the tides. Trying to fight your way into a large harbor through a narrow channel against an outrushing tide is completely futile, and even the strongest paddler will become rapidly exhausted without making any headway. Since the stability of the kayak depends on the paddler, you cannot afford to get overtired when paddling on the ocean. More subtle currents farther out to sea can carry the unsuspecting kayaker far off course.

NAVIGATION

Trips on lakes and the ocean present the kayaker with far more of a challenge to route-finding skills than river running. On a river, the main uses of a map are to help keep track of progress and to enable one to anticipate rapids. The river runner cannot really get lost, except in the sense of missing a take-out or plunging into a set of rapids head-on when he planned to portage. If the boater can simply manage to keep going downstream or heading back up, he is certain to find a recognizable landmark without having to look too far.

Out on open water, or even along a coast, however, things are not nearly so easy. If you are out of sight of the shore, either because you went too far out or because of fog or storm, there are obviously no landmarks to recognize. Even in sight of islands or the coast, you quickly find that recognizing particular landmarks from the water is quite a different matter from on land, especially from the two- or two-and-one-half-foot vantage point you get sitting in a kayak.

Both a compass and adequate maps or charts are the normal requisites for a start at finding your way systematically. The best way to learn to read maps and charts is to use them while working around familiar areas close to shore. The charts used by other coastal traffic are usually the most useful to the kayaker, because they concentrate on features that are recognizable from the water, particularly islands, shoals, signal lights, buoys, and points. A compass can be used to confirm a position by taking bearings on landmarks, and can thus enable the boater to determine progress, to maintain a particular course, and to paddle in the general direction of land during conditions of poor visibility.

Maps and charts have to be sealed in a waterproof case; a "ziplock" plastic bag, which is closed with a mating groove and ridge arrangement, works well for the purpose. Sections of charts can be sealed in individual zip-locks, and the one in use can be slipped under another sheet of plastic held to the deck with boat tape. The compass should be tied either to the body or to clothing or secured somehow to the deck of the boat in such a way that it can be removed to make sightings.

Keeping constant track of your progress is the surest way of not getting lost. It is a lot easier to locate a particular spit of land on the chart if you know that you passed a certain inlet three-quarters of an hour earlier. Trying to identify an island in a complicated lake can be virtually impossible once you have lost track of your location.

The effects of wind and sea currents on the movement of a group of boats can be quite significant without being immediately noticeable. With wind and waves on either a lake or the sea, you can at least anticipate the direction of drift, but with tidal currents, you may be completely unaware of your course unless periodic checks are made. The simplest way to keep track of your position is to make periodic sightings on islands, buoys, or points on land. To maintain a particular course, try to find two objects that line up in the direction you want to go. By keeping them lined up, you will know you are headed in the right direction. With only one object on land, a compass bearing can be taken and checked periodically so that corrections can be made if you are drifting to one side or the other. To check progress along the course, make a sighting between two objects (or a compass bearing on one) at a good angle to your direction of travel, preferably at right angles. If you should find after a reasonable amount of time that you are not making progress along your

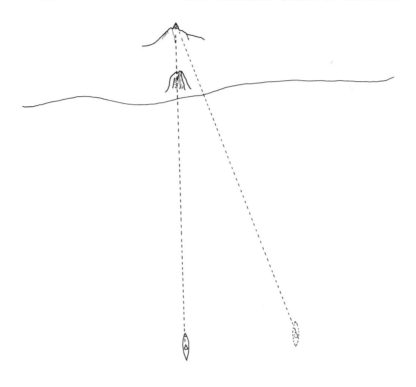

Lining up two distant objects is a useful way to maintain a course or to judge whether wind and waves are causing drifting. Simply paddling toward one distant object is much less accurate, because drifting to one side may not be noticed until a lot of error has accumulated. With two landmarks lined up, drifting to one side will show up immediately when the objects go out of line, as shown in the drawing.

course, or are even being carried backward, then you will have to revise your plans.

Practice basic map and compass reading before getting out either on large bodies of water or complex chains of lakes with many islands and bends.

SURFING

Riding surf in a kayak can be as exciting and involved as running difficult white water. The kayak is a superb craft for surfing, because the paddle gives the boater a great deal of control and can be used for leans just as in a river rapid. The kayaker can slide down the surface of a big wave, do a few pirouettes, and then pull back over the top before the break. Enders, both intentional and accidental, are common. In fact, kayak surfing has become a specialized branch of the sport that can only be introduced here.

Slalom kayaks work well enough for moderate surfing, although specialized surfing kayaks have been made to improve control and widen the range of what can be safely attempted. These are short, shallow boats with wide, upturned bows and cockpits fairly far back. Some surfers using slalom boats fit attachments called wave-breakers to their bows to reduce their tendency to dive.

Careful inspection of the beach is vital for the surfer. The coastal paddler is concerned only with one launch and one landing, in between which he gets well away from the region of breaking surf, but the surfer will be spending hours playing in the shallows. An unnoticed little group of rocks just under the curling waves can destroy his boat, or, if he happens to hit it upside down, can do a good deal of damage to him personally. The whole beach should be carefully checked at several tide levels before much surfing is done there, and danger areas should be noted. Watch for rocks, particularly old breakwaters that have been largely covered with sand. Note where you would be carried by waves coming from different directions and the location of any spots along the beach where a quick drop-off causes waves to break too quickly.

Start off by practicing with small waves 1 to 3 feet high. Learn to launch the kayak in surf, to catch the waves and steer the boat in them, to draw the boat up over the wave tops, and to roll in the surf. When the boat is set parallel to the wave crests, it is easy to roll up with the wave action, on the seaward side. In large waves it is virtually impossible to roll the other way. If you are confronted when paddling out by the wall of a large wave that is just breaking or about to break, turning over deliberately and allowing the wave to pass before rolling back up is often the easiest way through. Your body will catch the water inside the wave and keep the kayak from taking off. If the wave is really big, it may even turn you upright, end over end, so that you end up facing the shore trying to figure out what happened.

Launching in surf can be tricky, because when waves are coming in, you do not have time to step into the boat on the water, fiddle with the spray skirt, and then get moving. Normally there is a pattern in the waves that you should notice while you are watching them before launching: a group of large waves will roll in, followed by a number of smaller ones that do not send water so high up the beach. Wait until a big group has passed, pull your boat down where the water is coming up a couple of inches deep after a smaller wave breaks, and get in and adjust your spray skirt. You should be ready by the time the next group of larger waves comes. In between waves lean forward to get both hands on the sand (one holding the paddle) and hunch yourself and the boat forward. A couple of waves later, you should be afloat, and you then have to start paddling hard, straight out through the surf, until you are beyond the break line. The bigger the waves, the more important it is to paddle straight on through without hesitation.

Get some practice out beyond the break line, rolling, catching waves, and bracing on wave faces. To catch a wave, simply start paddling as its crest approaches from behind, so that the kayak is up to speed before the crest passes it. Then use the paddle as a rudder to the rear to keep the bow pointed straight into the shore. The boat will coast down the front of the wave. When the slope gets too steep, give the paddle a flick to turn the kayak off to one side or the other, and do a high brace leaning well into the wave. The situation is like that in a river when you are bracing downstream, because the kayak is moving down the face of the wave, and the water is moving up. A timid lean or a lean toward the shore will flip you and the boat over. Lean into the wave, toward the open ocean, and brace. A little experimenting will give you a feeling for the proper blade angle and paddle position alongside the boat to maneuver the way you want to. Bracing toward the stern keeps the boat headed at a downward angle. As the paddle is moved by the centerline and toward the bow, the bow will tend to be pulled up the wave. A good surfer can pirouette on a big wave, turning the bow straight up and then shifting his balance and bracing blade to slide over on the other side of his boat. Digging the paddle well into the wave with a blade angle straight across will cause the boat to rise up over the crest before the break, so that you can paddle out and catch another wave. On small waves in early practice, you can reach right over the crest to plant the paddle in the down-flowing water behind and draw the kayak over the top.

Doing an ender (also called *pearling*) is easy in the surf, sometimes a little too easy. Make sure that the water is deep enough, lest you plow the bow into the ground or roll over onto your head. Simply head the kayak down the front of a steeply sloping wave and

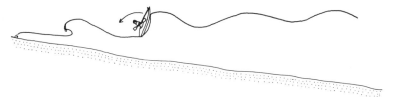

A kayaker pearling in the surf. By paddling straight down the front of a breaking wave, the kayaker has driven the nose of the boat deep into the water, and the kayak will easily turn end over end, especially if the kayaker leans forward. This maneuver is great fun, but it should be done only in a kayak with a strong front deck and in water deep enough so that there is no danger of the bow or your head hitting bottom.

paddle into the trough. As the bow digs into the trough, lean forward and watch the world turn. Wait a little while after going into the water to allow the wave to pass, and then roll back up. With big waves and a little skill, one can do an ender in this way and have the wave flip the boat back up. Backwards end over ends are even easier, once you get up the nerve; lean backward at the critical moment to speed the flip. Backward leans during forward enders prolong the upright position of the boat and drive the bow farther into the water; lean forward until you feel you know what you are doing.

The hazard with enders in surf is getting into water that is too shallow and pearling either intentionally or not. If the boat is apparently going to flip, it is better to lean way forward and get it over with; the forward lean also puts the spine and head in a safe position. The beginner's instinctive response is to lean back to try to balance the boat, driving the bow down, often into the sand, and flipping the boat higher, harder, and farther into shore. As the bow drives into sand, foot braces may well break out under the strain, tending to wedge the paddler down into the boat. Remember also that tremendous pressure is put on the bow of a boat in an ender, because of the increasing water pressure as it is driven down several feet under the surface. Surfing boats should be strong. Don't take your special lightweight slalom racing boat out into the big waves.

Safety considerations are vital in surfing. Even small surf is dissipating tremendous amounts of energy, and the kayaker who ignores this fact is in for trouble. A life jacket should always be worn in the surf, and wet suits are very important in cold water. A helmet will help prevent your being knocked silly against the hard sand if you wipe out in a wave, and hence will leave you able to do something about getting yourself and your equipment out of the water intact. If you should happen to be carried into some rocks head-first, a helmet will probably save your life. The best surfers can suffer mishaps, and having someone else around to help can prevent a minor accident from turning into a fatality. Finally, and most important, never surf with a kayak around swimmers. A kayak hurtling through the surf is a fearsome instrument of the grim reaper. Swimmers are bound to get in your way if they are in the vicinity, so the best thing to do is to find a section of beach that is isolated. You can often paddle down to a spot that is not readily accessible from the road. A lot of the best surfing can be had off-season when the water is too cold for swimmers. When the weather gets chilly, just put on your wet suit and you'll have no trouble finding an unused beach.

SAFETY IN DEEP WATER

Most of the safety margin of the kayaker in deep water, whether touring in lakes of medium size, along the coasts of larger lakes or the ocean, or making a trip out of sight of land, must come from advance planning, thought, and preparation. The stability of all the narrower types of kayaks is wholly dependent on the paddler. Going any distance into deep water in a slalom boat or a similarly tippy kayak without mastering the Eskimo roll simply doesn't make sense. Even those who paddle the wider touring boats should practice the techniques they plan to use in case of a capsize, either by learning to roll these large boats or by working on rescue techniques, preferably both. Remember that rolling a boat in heavy waves with a full load of gear is a little different from righting an empty kayak in a swimming pool.

Wet suits and life vests are even more important on large bodies of water than in river touring, when conditions warrant them. Cold water will sap the strength of an inadequately protected swimmer with frightening speed, no matter how strong he or she is. If a party is several miles from shore in cold weather, even a successful roll can leave a boater in serious trouble if he's not wearing a wet suit. A life jacket will allow a person who has fallen out of his boat in rough water to concentrate on self-rescue or his companions to take care of his boat without having to worry about him, since he will not have to waste a lot of energy staying up. A helmet is necessary only in surf, but if the launching or landing areas have rough surf, even people out for a tour may want to bring helmets. Flotation in boats is essential for deep water, so that in case of a capsize the amount of water that can get into the boat will be as small as possible. All equipment, dry bags, and flotation should be secured to the boat so that nothing will be lost in case of a capsize. Normally there should be at least one spare paddle in the party.

Adequate food, water, and spare clothing have to be carried on open-water trips. It is easy to underestimate the amount of energy that is used up during hard paddling, and energy reserves must be maintained, since you never know when an emergency may occur, particularly on the ocean. A common mistake is to paddle hard for the better part of a day, using up all the body's supply of available blood sugar, and to become suddenly hypothermic as chilly weather and exhaustion hit at the same time in the afternoon. Eating through the day is important to prevent both hypothermia and exhaustion, and the leaders of trips should make sure that everyone eats and is adequately dressed. The person who most needs all the extra energy supply he can get is generally the one who will put off eating and putting on extra clothes. Both of these actions take effort, and they tend to be neglected just when they are really important, when the weather is raw and adverse conditions have required a larger effort than everyone expected.

Dehydration can be a real problem particularly on salt-water trips and on trips in lakes where the water is unsafe to drink. Paddling is hard work, and considerable liquid can be lost in perspiration and evaporation from the lungs. Carry enough water, and make sure that everyone drinks. Hypothermia can affect a dehydrated person more quickly than it can one who has had sufficient water.

SELF-RESCUE

It cannot be overemphasized that the Eskimo roll is the most important form of self-rescue for the paddler of the normal narrow kayak. A roll that only works some of the time may be more dangerous than none at all, because it may persuade the paddler that he has a safety factor, when it is really illusory. For serious trips in deep water, a reliable roll can provide almost complete security. Without a good roll, the neophyte must be very cautious about undertaking trips far from shore or going on coastal tours where landings cannot be made at will, as along cliffy shores or those where the surf may rise to dangerous levels. The other types of self-rescue discussed here should be considered as extra back-up procedures, which would not normally be used by the competent boater except in practice sessions. They can be very useful to the paddler of a wider touring boat which is difficult to roll, providing security when this type of craft is taken out in rough water.

If the kayaker has to bail out, he should remember to leave the boat turned upside down, so that little water will be shipped. It is difficult at best to empty out a kayak in deep water. The small cockpit that works so well to keep water out as long as the paddler stays with his boat works just as effectively to keep the water in, once it is there.

There are two basic techniques for self-rescue if you have left the boat in deep water and are without the help of another kayak. *To do any good, they must be practiced in advance.* Repeated failures in a real situation of difficulty are simply likely to exhaust you without reuniting you with your kayak, particularly since ejection from the boat is most likely to occur when you are tired and cold, and when there are waves and a stiff breeze, rather than on calm, sunny days.

The better method, providing it can be accomplished, involves getting back into the boat and righting the kayak with a normal Eskimo roll. This sounds very difficult, but it is not really too hard with some advance practice, providing your spray skirt is not very difficult to fit. An example of the sort of situation that might demand this action would be a capsize after losing a paddle. If a hands-only roll is unsuccessful and there is not another boater nearby to assist, the kayaker is forced to bail out. He may be able to swim with the boat to recover his paddle, or failing this, get out his spare.

After catching your breath and getting organized, the method is simply to dive underwater, swing upside down into the boat, attach the spray skirt, and roll back up. The two trickiest problems are managing the paddle and getting the spray skirt around the coaming. It is a great advantage in this and other deep-water situations to have a piece of shock cord on the deck under which the paddle can be slipped, a wrist loop on the paddle, or some similar arrangement to secure the paddle. Otherwise it may have to be held in the hand while you struggle with the rest of the procedure. Some boaters leave the paddle floating beside the boat while they duck underwater, grabbing it from underwater as they begin their rolls, but this risks losing it, particularly in big waves. Getting the spray skirt on is mostly a matter of practice and patience. Most kayakers really can hold their breaths long enough to manage this, but they will never manage to do so in case of need unless they have tried it a few times in advance. Clearly, to use this method, you must have a very good roll, which gives you the confidence to keep struggling with the spray skirt, knowing that you can roll right up as soon as it is on the coaming. It is also helpful to practice leaning up above the water for breath once you are positioned in the boat, a trick that can usually be managed and that gives extra time to work with the skirt.

A second method of self-rescue is to remove the skirt from around the waist, attach it to the boat, hold the waist opening closed, and turn the kayak upright. It is even better to slip out of the waist opening when leaving the boat, so the skirt remains on the coaming. Once the kayak is upright, the difficult part of the operation begins. Slide up onto the rear deck with a kick of the legs and a pull on the grab loop or painter, getting astride the stern of the boat with the legs wide apart for stability and the body hunched forward. Without a painter extending along the deck between the two grab loops, many people find it impossible to get far enough forward to grasp the coaming, a good reason to tie a painter along the deck for deep-water touring. Slide along the deck, keeping the body low and trying to retain your balance until the hips can be dropped into the cockpit. You must then wriggle awkwardly back into the spray skirt, which must usually be released from the cockpit first and put on over the head. It is easier to put on the spray skirt in the water after the boat is upright, but this is risky because if you make a mistake and capsize while boarding, a lot of water will be shipped. Without plenty of advance practice or the steadying influence of two other boats, one on each side with paddles stretched across the empty craft, there is little chance of performing this operation successfully with a narrow kayak. The roll is better. With the wider, stable touring boats like most foldboats, however, this method works very well.

With two-person kayaks, entry into the righted kayak should be made by beginning with one person on either side of the boat, behind the cockpit. The forward hands of each hold the rear of the coaming, and the other two hands are locked across the rear deck, while one person gets astride the rear deck. The boater in the water can then hold the spray skirts closed in case of upset while the active partner slides up the deck and into the cockpit. The paddler in the boat can then keep the kayak steady with paddle braces while the second person climbs in along the rear or the front deck.

A boat that is partially swamped can be entered much more easily than one that is floating high in the water. The difficulties arise after you are in, because the boat will be very sluggish and tippy until the water has been emptied. A really large sponge tied to the seat and tucked under it will be invaluable in this situation, because with it the boat can be emptied fairly quickly, providing the water is not too rough. High waves will sweep into the boat and make bailing impossible, however.

RESCUING OTHERS

With a group of kayakers who avoid becoming separated, there will normally be assistance available in case of a capsize. There are a number of distinct rescue problems that may arise, so practicing for them in advance requires quite a bit of time. As with self-rescue, advance practice is essential to develop the individual skills required, and good teamwork has to be worked out, too.

The simplest form of rescue is assisting another boater who has lost his paddle to roll up. A lot of practice is required to make this a useful skill, because only long practice will induce enough confidence in each member of the party to ensure their staying docilely upside down in the water, waiting for help.

The capsized kayaker who has lost his paddle must first attract the attention of his companions. This is done by reaching up out of the water with the hands and banging on the upturned bottom of the boat. The capsized boater then holds both hands out of the water, one on either side, so that he can be approached quickly by the nearest companion. The rescuer must bring the bow of his boat into the hand of the upside-down boater, quickly but gently, so that if the capsized person raises his head for air, he will not be struck by the end of the kayak. When he feels the bow, the capsized person reaches up, grabs it with both hands, and rolls upright. With practice, all this can be done quite quickly, but practice at leaning forward, getting the head out of water, and breathing will allow the underwater kayaker to keep a much more balanced outlook while he is awaiting rescue. Though loss of a paddle should be quite rare, the difficulty of emptying boats and reentering them from deep water makes practice of this procedure well worth the trouble. Put bumpers on the boats and helmets on heads before practicing this technique.

If the capsized boater ejects from his kayak, rescue problems become more difficult, particularly if the exit was done in an awkward way so that a good deal of water was shipped. This is where adequate flotation in the kayak makes a lot of difference, because it will limit the amount of water that can get into the hull.

If the exit is controlled, the capsized boater may be able to prevent much water from entering the kayak by leaving the spray skirt on the cockpit and squirming out through the waist hole. The kayak can then be turned over while the waist hole is held closed, and the skirt can be donned again before the swimmer gets back into the boat.

To help the swimmer back into the kayak, the rescuer must simply stabilize the empty boat. This makes reentry fairly easy, because the person in the water can get in from the side, with the cockpit rim to grab onto and without the balance problems associated with trying to enter a free-floating kayak. The rescuer normally holds both paddles and pulls the two kayaks together, but pointing in opposite directions; he then leans all the way across the forward deck of the other boat just in front of the cockpit, resting his chest right on the deck, dropping his lower arm over the far gunwale, and holding onto the cockpit rim with the other hand. The position is very stable, providing the weight of the upper body rests right on the deck of the other boat. The paddles can be held with the hand that is across the deck, secured by wrist loops, or slipped into a shock cord or Velcro retainer on either deck. The swimmer can now pull and swim himself up into the cockpit, hauling himself farther by reaching over to the cockpit rim of the rescuing boat, and finally getting himself arranged and the spray skirt on while the boat is still held stable. This operation is solid even in big waves. It is far more reliable than any self-rescue method other than rolling.

If any water has been shipped, the person who has just been rescued can bail the boat out with his sponge before putting the spray skirt back on. If there are large waves, this can be done while the kayak is still being held by the rescuer. If much water has been shipped, it is preferable to try to empty the boat before the kayaker gets back in.

The simplest way to empty a boat that has been partly filled with water is for two rescuing kayaks to pull parallel to one another, facing in the same direction, with both paddles held together across the front decks to form a bridge. The bow of the kayak to be emptied is raised onto the bridge and shot up as quickly as possible, the two rescuers pulling on the grab loop, and the swimming boater pushing from the water while holding to the bow of one of the rescuers. The kayak is pulled up as swiftly as the boaters can manage so as to prevent more water from entering as the cockpit comes out of the water. The upside-down kayak is pushed up until the center is about on the paddle shafts, and the lower end is then slowly lifted to dump the water, the rescuers pushing down on the upper hull, and the person in the water doing most of the work by lifting the lower end up, while keeping hold of the bow of one of the rescue boats. This lift should be made slowly, to avoid damaging the kayak being rescued, allowing the water to drain out gradually.

Once the boat is out of the water, it can be seesawed back and forth a couple of times to get the last water out. The rescuers then flip it over, slide it into the water, and the swimmer either gets in with the assistance of the two paddle shafts, or one of the rescuers leans over to brace the boat so that he can enter from the side, as previously described.

If there are only two kayaks in the party, or only one rescuer is available for some other reason, the boat can still be emptied, but the procedure is more difficult, requires more practice, and is less reliable in rough water. If the boat is floating fairly high and has a deck line (a rope length running from one end to the other over the deck, usually tied to the grab loops) the rescuer brings his boat up next to the bow of the capsized kayak and perpendicular to it. He grabs the tie-in at the bow and pulls the overturned boat quickly up across his own forward deck until the cockpit rests on it and the rescued boat is balanced across the deck of the rescuer. This must be done quickly and smoothly, for the overturned boat will begin to fill with water if a pause occurs when the cockpit is half out of the water. The pull is accomplished by hauling on the deck line and grabbing the cockpit as it comes up. The assurance needed to manage this in rough water can only be achieved with practice. Once the boat is up on the deck, it is rocked back and forth a few times to empty it of water. The first rock is a continuation of the motion that pulls the boat up, using the inertia of the water, boat, and body to dump most of the water out of the boat. When the rescued boat is empty, it is flipped over and slid off to the other side, bow to the rear of the rescuer, who then flops over onto the deck of the rescued kayak and has a rest while holding it for the swimmer to enter, as described earlier.

Several comments about this technique are necessary. It is important to practice extensively before using it in a real rescue situation, since the first attempt will probably fill the boat to be emptied with even more water, capsize the rescuer, or both. The deck of the rescuing boat must be quite strong, or it will collapse under the weight of the other boat and the water that fills it. Advance practice will allow the potential rescuer to judge what his deck will stand. Depending on the coamings of the two boats, there is often a catching problem as the boat that is upside down slides up toward the balance point, and it must be lifted a little to get it on over. Finally, there is no point in even trying this method unless the capsized craft is floating quite high, since it will be impossible to finish pulling it up onto the deck if there is much water inside—the stern will simply drop deep into the water, and even more water may flow into the cockpit opening. It is worth starting at the bow end, since there is more flotation at the rear of the boat, and some of the extra water in the bow will flow out of the boat as the initial lift is made.

When there is too much water in the boat for this technique to be used, it is still possible to empty the capsized craft with only one rescuing boat, but the method is tricky and imposes even more strain on the deck of the rescuing kayak. The rescuer paddles his boat around until his bow is up against the center of the overturned craft and perpendicular to it; he maintains a light pressure by easy forward paddling. The boater in the water gets on the opposite side of his kayak, reaches under the deck of his boat with both hands to grab the loop on the bow of the other boat, and pushes his kayak up onto the deck of the rescuing craft, so that the bow of the rescuer sticks into the cockpit of the capsized boat. The swimmer then levers his own kayak up onto the rescuer's bow, quickly at first to prevent more water from entering, and then slowly as the water pours out. Finally, it is possible to push the rescued boat right up on the deck of the rescuing kayak, far enough so that the rescuer can reach out and grab the coaming. The capsized craft will now have tipped down into the water at one end, the remaining water having poured into that half of the boat. The swimmer can work around to the opposite side, reach up and get the grab loop, and *slowly* pull the raised end down to empty the other half of his boat. (The swimmer has a lot of leverage, and if he pulls too quickly, he will probably break his rescuer's deck—this may prompt a slower rescue at some future date.)

Though this method of rescue can be quite effective and should be thoroughly practiced, it should be used only rarely. Well-practiced rescue techniques among deep-water boaters indicate competence and strong preparation, but their actual use means that basics like the Eskimo roll have been neglected. If a choice had to be made, a group having good rolls and poor rescue techniques would have to be considered safer than one with lots of rescuers but too many members who have not bothered to learn fundamental skills.

All the rescue methods which use a second boat for stability can be used easily by those paddling in wide touring foldboats, but these kayaks do not have adequate strength for rescue methods that lift boats with any significant amount of water to empty. Both the rescued craft and that of the rescuer undergo considerable strain. It is better to close the spray deck of the foldboat, turn it over, and bail it out with a sponge than to attempt to empty it on the deck of another kayak and break a frame in the process.

7

Camping and Wilderness Travel with the Kayak

Much of the emphasis in this book is on extended trips and tours, using the kayak as a wilderness craft. Others may disagree, but my feeling is that the best kayaking is always found along wilderness waterways. Whether you are paddling along quiet chains of lakes, dropping down difficult white-water runs, or surfing on a beach along the coast, the pleasures and challenges are sweeter when the roads are left behind and the party is camping in unspoiled country.

The skills of wilderness kayak travel can be broken down into a number of separate areas. Some are related directly to other kayaking techniques and their adaptation to long trips away from civilization, and some have much in common with the methods used by any lightweight wilderness traveler. Many of the necessary kayaking skills have been discussed in other chapters, since there is no radical dividing line which separates wilderness kayaking from similar boating in a less remote setting. There is a difference, however.

Aside from the pleasures of minimal pollution, fascinating wildlife, and other attractions in boating away from roads and from people other than your companions, wilderness kayaking has a seriousness which is not present in roadside river running, lake touring from a picnic ground, or surfing near the car. Whether you are riding coastal waves or drawing madly to miss an undercut boulder in a class IV rapid, there are some fundamental differences between a situation near the car and one eighty miles from the nearest human habitation. A boater who has some awareness of what he is doing will be a lot more cautious about running into a big hole when the walk-out is one hundred miles than he will when it is one hundred yards. Losing a boat is a sad thing at any time, but the plucking at the heartstrings as one drives home in a warm car is nothing compared to the despair you feel as you stand shivering on a beach, with nothing but what you are wearing, scores of miles of trackless forest between you and any human habitation. The necessity of relying on one's own skill and judgment for comfort and safety is one of the many attractions of wilderness travel of all kinds, and of wilderness kayaking in particular.

Proper preparation in all respects is the key ingredient for enjoyable wilderness trekking. This means that each member of the group and the party as a whole have to be ready for the trip. Fundamental kayaking skills and rescue techniques have to be practiced. Individual paddlers must be skillful enough that they do not endanger themselves and other members of the group because they are incompetent to negotiate the rapids and surf that are expected. Innumerable trips have become miserable ordeals because of members who simply were not ready for them. Even more critical is the overall strength of the party. Some class III rivers can be safely run with a few paddlers who are barely competent to paddle rapids of this level of difficulty, providing there are a number of strong kayakers along who do not mind being slowed up. A group without the strong members could run into serious difficulties on the same river, in all probability losing at least a few boats. Not all class III rivers could be run safely even by the first party, if the rapids were continuous and the penalties for taking the wrong route through a rapid were severe. As a general rule, unless the river and the skills of the various paddlers are well known, the minimum level of competence on a multiday wilderness trip should be higher than the hardest conditions expected. Running one class IV rapid does not prepare a river runner for a two-week run on a class IV river, unless it is known that all the difficult rapids can be portaged, and the group is prepared to give the less proficient members time to do so. Similarly, one trip on a calm lake does not give someone the skill to

The approach to a rapid has a special excitement on a wilderness trip many miles from the nearest road or assistance.

handle possible heavy winds and 6-foot waves on a big lake, nor does a single experience in surf permit the assumption that a boater will be able to land a loaded kayak on a difficult beach.

Competence in wilderness camping can be quite important on extended trips, particularly in difficult areas or seasons. Of course, such experience may be gained in other wilderness activities, like mountaineering or backpacking, but don't underestimate its importance. Some people without much camping experience can certainly be accommodated on wilderness river trips, but they may need some watching by other members of the party, particularly in equipment selection and in difficult conditions during the trip. It is surprisingly easy for experienced outdoorspeople to forget how difficult some of the most basic camping skills can be for the beginner. Hopping over wet talus, building fires in the rain, or keeping clothes dry may be second nature to the longtime wilderness traveler, but to the novice camper they can be insuperable obstacles. Pacing yourself, knowing when you are becoming dangerously tired or cold, remembering to eat or put on warm clothes, are habits that are developed with experience. Even a strong boater who has not spent much time in the wilderness is liable to try to run that last hard rapid of the day without realizing that he has become barely functional from fatigue, hunger, or cold. These are the situations which cause accidents, and in the wilderness accidents are dangerous.

Physical conditioning is another important aspect of advance preparation. The need for conditioning may vary with the trip, but even good boaters often allow themselves to become soft during the winter and then undertake trips early in the season that are simply beyond their endurance level. Ocean coastal trips can be particularly demanding—no amount of good technique will enable the kayaker to fight a headwind, a strong current, or an oncoming sea for hours on end if muscles have become weak and flabby from disuse. Be honest with yourself and your companions in this matter. Experienced leaders expect to have to screen out overambitious beginners, but on really difficult trips, poor conditioning can be just as hazardous to your companions as weak kayaking skills.

SUPPORTED AND UNSUPPORTED TRIPS

There are normally few decisions to make about logistics on coastal tours or trips on lakes or mixed lakes and rivers. Each boater carries his personal gear and a reasonable share of the group equipment. On river trips, however, there are two distinct ways of organizing a trip. Parties of kayakers may simply plan on carrying all their equipment in their boats from the put-in to the take-out, or the group may include some rafts to carry the bulk of the gear, leaving the kayaks largely unencumbered with food and equipment.

One technique of wilderness kayaking is to carry all the necessary food and equipment in the kayaks. One advantage of this method is the ability to move quickly when the river slows down, as in this section of the canyons of the Yampa River.

This decision is quite important. Virtually every aspect of a kayak river run is influenced by the presence of rafts in the group or the lack of them. Even the level of experience required of members of the group is affected. A person whose competence to run the rapids on the river might be questionable can often be included on a supported trip. His camping gear and dry clothes will be carried on a raft, making his boat more easily maneuvered and lessening the possibility of equipment loss if he should capsize in a rapid. Loss of his boat would not create nearly the problem that it would on an unsupported trip, because he could ride out on a raft.

On a raft-supported river trip it is possible to carry equipment and food with far less attention to weight and bulk than is necessary on jaunts using only kayaks. With most equipment carried in the raft, rapids may be run that one would hesitate to attempt with all essential gear in the kayak. The kayaks float higher and are more maneuverable. Nonpaddling passengers can be carried in rafts, so a river trip can be a family affair even though not all members kayak.

Kayaks can be of some help to rafters, too, providing the paddlers are competent. Kayaks provide a safety factor in case a rescue is needed, since kayaks can be maneuvered and worked upstream, while a raft moves downriver with the inevitability of the progression of the seasons. Kayaks can move ahead and work back and forth across the river to find landing sites or campgrounds, warning the rafts beforehand of the need to get into the proper channel or next to the correct bank.

Raft-supported trips have their complications as well. A whole different set of personnel is added to the trip, with different kinds of knowledge, different equipment, and different qualifications. Portaging rafts and their contents around rapids which are too difficult, too intricate, or too low is a nuisance at best and is sometimes impossible with a big raft and a difficult portage. Rafters have a slow time on sections of flat water over which a kayak can glide easily, particularly when there is an upstream wind. (It is an iron law, observed by generations of river runners, that all winds that blow

Another possibility for wilderness river running is to travel with a raft, allowing more hedonistic camping but requiring more complicated logistics and sometimes a lot of waiting when the river slows down. The kayaker here is on a week-long trip with raft support in the lower canyons of the Rio Grande.

while boats are on the water blow upstream.) In general, rafts and kayaks simply move differently, so keeping the party together on a mixed trip can be a nuisance.

There are some aesthetic attractions to unsupported trips on which everything is carried in the kayak. The main advantage is logistical simplicity, especially when trips are planned on the spur of the moment. It is easy enough to arrange a trip with a number of other kayakers with whom you have paddled before, each bringing his own gear, with some central planning of food and repair kits. Coordinating a supported trip is far more complicated.

As a practical matter, until you have met some rafters, perhaps on trips taken with a club, you will probably make unsupported trips regardless of preference. For anyone doing much wilderness kayaking, however, it is worth observing and learning everything possible about rafts and rafting, since you will eventually become involved with some trips that include rafts. Rafts can be considerably more dangerous than kayaks in luring the incompetent into places where they have no business. A kayak has the virtue of dumping out the foolhardy beginner while he is still in fairly easy water, whereas the raft will float him into real difficulties first.

EQUIPMENT

Most camping equipment used on kayak tours is similar to that carried by other lightweight campers. On raft-supported trips, the kayaker may be able to indulge himself by not having to worry so much about weight and bulk, though this will depend a lot on the number and size of the rafts along and how many people they are carrying. It is important to find out the exact situation in advance and to make sure that everyone on the trip understands it. Raft owners may have enough waterproof containers to stow whatever gear they are carrying for kayakers, but this should not be assumed. A useful and durable waterproof container for stowing gear in a raft is a military surplus delousing bag, which is made of black rubberized fabric. Delousers are available in surplus stores, can be sealed at the top, and will carry reasonable gear for one person. For a completely safe watertight container, get a large, heavy plastic bag to go inside the delouser and tie it off three times.

The *clothing* necessary will depend on the season and the trip, of course, but it is prudent to anticipate the most severe weather that can be reasonably expected rather than the most pleasant. Cool nights can be expected even in the desert and are almost certain in the mountains in the spring. In cold weather, the joy of getting out of a wet suit and into dry, warm clothes is indescribable, and so is the misery of not having any. Essentially, this means that a minimum of two sets of clothes will be necessary, one for use on the river and one in camp. Two sets are adequate, but wet river clothes may have to be put on in the morning if conditions are not good for drying. If chilly weather is anticipated, one set of clothing should be of a material that retains some insulating qualities when wet, such as wool or items filled with polyester batts.

One pair of *shoes* will be standard boating sneakers—the holier, the better. If side trips are planned in rugged country, the second pair should be reasonably sturdy hiking boots. Some people like to carry moccasins for lounging around camp, but these should be carried in addition to hiking boots when hiking boots are needed. It is important to consider the possible hike-out when choosing footwear. A fifty-mile cross-country walk in moccasins or boating sneakers over ground strewn with cactus, sharp rocks, or snowfields is not a pleasant prospect for most civilized feet. Heavy wool socks suitable for hiking should be carried along with hiking boots. Coastal campers will also normally want some kind of dry walking shoes in addition to their boating sneakers.

Raingear of some kind should normally be carried to be used with dry camping clothes. Some boaters bring a poncho to serve as both shelter and rain garment, but this has a number of disadvantages, since a single piece of equipment cannot be used to protect a sleeping bag and a person at the same time except when the person is in the bag. Ponchos, rain suits, and cagoules (long waterproof parkas) all have advantages; the main thing is to have one of them. The boater has a hard enough time keeping things dry as it is, and he needs all the help he can get.

In hot weather, clothing that provides sun protection may be essential. The kayaker often has no way to find shelter from the sun's rays, so that sunburn and heat exhaustion can be a real problem. A lightweight white cotton shirt and a hat to be worn when the helmet is not in use should be taken on many trips. A kerchief or a handkerchief can be used to shield the neck. Those with sensitive skin should have shirts with long sleeves and consider carrying cotton gloves in case of burning problems.

Sleeping bags need to be lightweight and easily compressible, particularly if they are carried in the kayaks. For most river trips, really warm bags are not necessary, since temperatures below freezing are not the rule. Those normally termed "three-season bags" by backpacking suppliers are more than adequate for most people on most trips. In fact, they are often too warm.

A *sleeping bag cover* in the form of a large envelope made of coated nylon cloth on the bottom and uncoated material on the top makes a helpful supplement. It keeps the bag clean and serves as a ground cloth. It makes the bag warmer when the camper sleeps inside the bag, but it can also be used to sleep in by itself when the weather is very warm. When temperatures are intermediate, you can sleep inside the cover with the sleeping bag used as a mattress or blanket.

Down bags are the most widely used, partly because they are standard among backpackers and mountaineers, and for years there was no suitable commercially available substitute. Down sleeping bags do give the most warmth for a given weight and are the most compressible. If you own a down bag or are buying one for another purpose, it will do very nicely for kayaking, providing you are very careful to keep it dry. Good quality down bags (the only kind worth buying) are quite expensive, however, and they are useless if they get wet, requiring a great deal of time to dry. *Lightweight sleeping bags insulated with batts of polyester fiber* (such as Du Pont Fiberfill II and Celanese PolarGuard) have become available in the past few years and are ideal for kayaking, since they are not only lightweight, but also warm enough for kayak trips and can be stuffed to reasonable size. Even when it is wet, polyester insulation does not collapse as down does, so that some insulation is still provided, and polyester insulation is easily dried. Polyester bags are also a good bit cheaper than down ones, so they are definitely recommended to anyone buying a sleeping bag primarily for kayaking.

Regardless of the type of sleeping bag that is used, a *foam pad* or an *air mattress* should be taken to provide a comfortable bed and insulation from the ground. Kayakers are bound to end up occasionally in rather rough campsites, and a ground bed makes these tolerable. Besides, sleeping bags provide little insulation from the cold ground, although polyester bags are somewhat better than down in this respect, so the money, weight, and bulk of the sleeping bag is partly wasted unless a ground bed is taken too. Closed-cell foam pads ⅜ inch thick are economical and provide good insulation without taking up too much space, but they make the least comfortable beds. Air mattresses of good quality are expensive. They take up the least space of any of the ground beds, but they are colder than

Wilderness trips require a conservative approach to boating equipment. In cold weather and cold water, the boater cannot rely on a warm car or cabin at the bottom of the rapid. This boater, 75 miles from the nearest road, has on a full wet suit and a Grand Canyon vest.

the others and most people find them less comfortable than poly-urethane foam pads. The latter give good insulation and are very comfortable, but they are moderately expensive because they have to be covered to keep moisture out and to protect them from tearing. Thickness of 1 inch is minimal, of 1½ inches is comfortable, and of 2 inches is luxurious. In any case, pads that are 3½ to 4 feet long are usually adequate since clothing and other equipment can be used for a pillow and to pad the feet.

Unless the trip is in the far north during periods of continuous light, *flashlights* or *headlamps* should be carried by each member of the party, along with adequate replacements for bulbs and batteries. I prefer a headlamp with a separate battery case, because it leaves the hands free for anything from cooking to scrambling over rocks. Many boaters prefer waterproof flashlights, however. The number of spare batteries that needs to be taken will depend on the length and style of the trip (will you be cooking in the dark frequently?), the life of a set of batteries in your flashlight with the size bulb you are using, and similar considerations. Be sure that your batteries are fresh; many on the shelves of stores are not, particularly in little country shops near rivers. Regular carbon-zinc batteries are the shortest-lived, particularly under continuous use, and they go bad most quickly on the shelf. Alkaline batteries are better in all these respects but are more expensive.

Carbide lamps can be handy for light around camp at night, but they should supplement battery-powered lamps rather than replace them. Carbide lamps produce lots of light, and the fuel is cheap and lightweight, but they cannot be turned on and off at will, so they are best used when light is needed for long periods. Carbide lamps burn acetylene gas, which is produced by dripping water into fresh carbide pellets in the bottom of the lamp. A new charge of carbide is put into the bottom, which is then screwed on, and water is poured into the top until it is about two-thirds full. The regulator is opened full for a few seconds and then closed down to produce a steady drip. (The rate of flow at various settings can be checked beforehand with the bottom off the lamp.) Acetylene gas should then come out of the jet and can be smelled or tasted with the tip of the tongue. The hand is cupped over the reflector to allow the gas to collect, and the sparking wheel is rotated with the heel of the hand to light the gas. The drip is regulated to produce the right size jet. Note that carbide lamps do not respond immediately to increased water flow. The drip rate should be increased slowly, because if the lower compartment gets flooded, water and goo will be pushed by the pressure in all directions. Carbide lamps need to be kept impeccably clean, and some practice should be considered mandatory at home, since they are cranky devices when not properly treated. Spent carbide should be buried or carried in a separate container, not dumped on the ground. Lamps should be emptied as soon as they are turned off to keep them clean. Once a charge of carbide is partially used, it will probably not retain any acetylene after being allowed to sit for any length of time.

Shelters vary with the training and preferences of the campers and with the nature of the trip. Carrying a *tent* is the surest way of guaranteeing reasonable comfort, especially for less experienced campers. Unless the trip is supported by large rafts, though, tents should be compact and lightweight. Those made of nylon are the normal choice; those constructed of heavy canvas are generally unsuitable. Larger tents are less versatile, but they allow lots of living space for each person. The best tents for kayaking are either made with breathable nylon and have a waterproof nylon fly (a cover made to be pitched over the main tent), or they are open structures through which the air can circulate, perhaps with insect netting covering the openings. Examples of the latter are lean-to tents that are open at the front and small two-man mosquito-netting tents equipped with a fly that pitches over the top. Most of the tents suitable for kayak camping are made for backpackers and mountaineers. The best ones are expensive.

Many experienced kayak campers prefer simpler shelters, since severe wind and cold are not likely on boating trips. A *tube tent,* made either of plastic or of coated nylon, is one such shelter. A tube tent is simply a tubular section of material about 10 feet long and 9 feet wide when spread flat on the ground (12 feet wide for two people). A line running through it can be tied to paddles, trees, bushes, rocks, or poles to hold the tube up. It is kept on the ground by the weight of the occupant and his equipment. Plastic tube tents will last a reasonable length of time, considering their price, if they are treated carefully. A few spring clothespins can be used for partial closing of the ends in strong wind.

Tarpaulins, sheets of coated nylon or plastic, are more versatile than tube tents and have less of a condensation problem on the inside, but they may require more imagination to pitch. Tarps are best made of coated nylon, since there is more direct strain on the material when they are pitched than there is in tube tents, making plastic tarps rather short-lived. Tarps used for shelter normally have many grommets and tie tabs attached, so that they can be pitched in a number of ways. Various special clamping devices are available for plastic sheets and other tarps that lack sufficient ties, but you can improvise by putting a small stone at the desired point and tying it off with a piece of parachute cord.

Mosquito netting is worthwhile in many areas to ensure a decent night's sleep. If you do not have a closed tent with mosquito bars on the doors and vents, carry pieces of netting large enough to drape over your sleeping bag and pitch up over your head. In many ways a mosquito bar of this type is better than a closed tent, since it can be used to sleep outside on warm nights and fewer bugs can get in before you bed down.

If a *ground cloth* is not already a part of your shelter or sleeping bag cover, one should be carried. A poncho may double for a ground cloth, though many prefer cheap plastic sheeting for this purpose.

Many other small items are included in the checklist on page 306. Some, like matches in a watertight case, a candle or chemical firestarter, a pocket knife, water bottles, and map and compass, should be considered essential survival gear. Practice in their use before you need them is essential. Learning first aid, fire building, route finding, and other basic outdoor skills should never be left to someone else. Other items listed, like insect repellent, are self-explanatory and should be taken if there is a chance they will be needed.

COOKING EQUIPMENT

The amount and type of cooking equipment taken will depend on the nature of the trip, the type of food used, and the number of people along. Raft-supported trips, particularly large ones, often carry big stoves and pots, grills, and other items to permit cooking for many people. Obviously, big pots are required to cook for large numbers, and where stoves are necessary, they must be of comparable size. Such items are unwieldy, and they are generally avoided on trips where all the gear is carried in the kayaks. Cooking in groups of about four is generally most convenient in these cases. Preferences for cooking utensils vary, but three pots will do nicely for a group of four, two of them with a capacity of perhaps 2½ to 3 quarts and the third of the same size or smaller. A lid that will serve as a frying pan is standard, but if you plan to catch and fry small fish, it is worth carrying a lightweight steel frying pan, preferably coated with Teflon. A spatula is normally carried with the frying pan. Other utensils may include pot holders and a large spoon. Each person normally brings a spoon, a cup, and a bowl. When cooking over fires, it is convenient to have separate lightweight bags for each pan, so that the pans can be nested without being cleaned of soot.

For extensive cooking over fires, it is handy to have a small wire mesh grill on which to rest pots. It should be large enough to hold a couple of pans, but small enough to fit easily in the kayak. The grill should be carried in a bag for neatness and to prevent its puncturing a float bag.

A stove is a necessity on many kayak trips today. On truly wild rivers there is nearly always enough fallen dead wood and driftwood so that one can build fires without doing environmental damage or leaving too much evidence of one's passage. Truly wild rivers are rare today, however, for most rivers are dammed, even though there may be wilderness sections. Dammed rivers do not normally flood, so there is less driftwood, and the remains of fires are usually preserved for years. Some recommendations on making fires without leaving a mess are included later in this chapter, but where there is not enough deadfall and driftwood, particularly at designated campsites, it is important to carry a stove. There is no excuse for breaking off standing wood, dead or not, to build fires. In these days of increased river use and diminishing unspoiled river mileage, every paddler has an obligation both to preserve the environment at his campsites with minimal damage and to leave as little sign of his passage as possible. Often this means carrying a stove.

On some trips a stove is required or advisable for other reasons. Some desert rivers have little or no available wood for considerable distances, especially when there are extensive gorges. Stoves can be convenient when the weather is very wet and fire building difficult.

Lightweight stoves of the type suitable for carrying in a kayak. On the left is a Primus stove using standard propane cylinders, in the center a very light pumped stove burning white gasoline made by Mountain Safety Research, and on the right is a Primus self-pressurizing white gas stove with a special cooking stand and windscreen.

At heavily wooded campsites in dry, windy weather, the fire hazard may be too great to risk building campfires. Beaches along ocean coasts often have little or no wood.

The usual lightweight backpacking stoves serve well enough for cooking. Some campers prefer the convenience of butane or propane-fueled models. White gas or naphtha is cheaper and more readily available. The most efficient small stoves are pumped models, but self-pressurized types are quite satisfactory if you learn their quirks before using them on a trip. The amount of fuel needed varies with the type of food used and the cooking habits of the party, but a cup of fuel per day for each cooking group is generous for most circumstances, unless extensive purification of water by boiling is anticipated. For luxury cooking, two small stoves can be carried for a cooking group, enabling the chef to have two burners available without carrying a large stove. Canned heat is generally worthwhile only as an emergency cooking device.

CARRYING YOUR EQUIPMENT

One of the biggest problems faced by the touring kayaker is carrying his gear without losing it, getting it wet, or spending half his trip packing and unpacking it. Unfortunately, most of the stow bags that are readily available are as much of a hindrance as a help. They tend to be too thin, so they are easily punctured and will no longer hold air. Others are simply designed badly, at least for the kayaker, because they will not fit his boat.

Because of the small volume of most kayaks, flotation and storage have to be combined, unless a trip is raft-supported. The best way to do this is to have flotation bags that will fill all the available space in the boat, which can be opened and loaded with gear and then closed and inflated so that gear is kept dry and water is excluded from the entire volume of the stow bags. Such stow bags can be built of a fairly heavy-duty airtight material, or a lighter material can be used and the bag can be covered with another sack that is intended to protect it from abrasion. Either method will work, but the kayaker should remember that equipment inside the bag may be as likely to puncture it as objects outside. Sand, grit, and various abrasive materials should be cleaned from camping gear as much as possible, but such things invariably get into storage bags on a wilderness trip.

The stowage bags that are commonly sold are often too small to fit larger volume touring boats. It is much better for such a bag to be a little oversized, since it does not have to be inflated fully. Large rectangular bags fit kayaks poorly.

One solution to the problem of getting good flotation bags that can be used to store gear is to make your own. A method for doing so is described in Chapter 10.

Stow bags are generally made after the same pattern as flotation bags: one large bag fills the whole stern section behind the seat and another occupies the bow ahead of the foot braces. Additional small bags which tie into the boat may be put just behind the seat and in the area between the legs. Another good pattern is to have two bags the size of the bow bag and another rectangular bag made to fill the extra volume in the stern just behind the seat. This is a convenient arrangement, because the rectangular stern bag can be used for items that need to be easily accessible. It can also be used for those things that are carried in the boat on a raft-supported trip, while the other two bags would then be used strictly for flotation.

The large storage bags are usually loaded after they are in the boat. A few items are put in the end section of the bag, it is pushed down into the end of the boat, and the other baggage is put in. The bag is then sealed, normally with two sections of PVC (polyvinyl chloride) pipe, one of which is cut open along the side so it can be snapped over the other, with the open end of the bag sealed between the pipes. Another system, which is better but less readily available, uses a flap to hold down the rolled opening tunnel. The bag is blown up to fill the end of the boat. Normally the bag can be blown tight, since the air will subsequently contract somewhat when

A river camp on the banks of the Yampa. These campers have brought a tent, to avoid using the more cramped shelter of a tarp. After a day of boating, warm, dry clothes are welcome protection from the evening's chill. Fires are not permitted in undesignated campsites like this one in Dinosaur National Monument, so small stoves must be carried, along with a portable latrine, but all gear on this trip was carried in the kayaks.

the boat is put in the cool water. However, if the kayak will be left for some time in the hot sun, where the air may expand because of the heat, the bag should not be fully inflated, lest a seam break or the pipe pop off.

Care should be taken to avoid puncturing the stow bags with sharp-edged equipment. Damage can also be caused by placing hard items inside it so that they can shift back and forth and wear through the bag. Using small storage bags, particularly for equipment like stoves, utensils, and tin cans, will help prevent damage to the flotation bag.

The heaviest equipment should be stored as close as possible to the center of the boat. The end of the kayak has to be turned farther and faster than the center, so adding weight at the bow or stern has a far more detrimental effect on maneuverability than adding weight near the middle. Lightweight items like foam pads and clothing bags can be pushed into the ends of the bags before they are put into the boat, packages of medium weight like sleeping bags can be put in next, and the heaviest items are packed last. One should also make an effort to balance the weight loaded into the bow and the stern, or the handling will be seriously affected. A low bow will tend to make the kayak dive into standing waves and holes, while a heavy stern will tend to make the boat hard to turn quickly into eddies. Clearly, the things that need to be readily accessible, such as lunch and spare clothes, have to be near the opening of the stow bag, or, better, in a small auxiliary bag.

Things that need to be kept dry should be in separate watertight sacks, particularly the sleeping bag. Even if the main flotation bag is perfectly waterproof, some wet things are bound to be put in, especially after a rain, and the moisture will permeate other equipment, unless it is kept in separate sacks. Heavy plastic bags sealed with rubber bands can be used for this purpose.

Storage bags need to be secured to the boat if there is any possibility of their escaping. Full flotation bags normally are tight enough when inflated to stay in by themselves, although with the bow bag this may depend on the type of foot braces in the boat. Any smaller bags will definitely have to be tied in, so they should be provided with loops or grommets to permit this. Smaller bags intended for storing heavy objects like cameras are safest if they are inflatable or have separate flotation attached, so that they can be retrieved if they are separated from the kayak.

Cameras are a problem to carry, because one would like to have them always available to take photographs, often right in the middle of a rapid, yet they need to be fully protected both from the water and from impact. To complicate matters, they are expensive and they will not float. The only really good solution is to buy a waterproof camera, the carrying strap of which can be threaded through the life jacket so that it is almost impossible to lose. The lens of such a camera can be washed just before a shot is taken, so that even the water-spot problem on the lens is eliminated. With a normal camera, however, any answer will have major drawbacks.

A normal camera can be put in a watertight container inside one of the flotation-storage bags. This method will prevent its loss or damage as long as the boat is not lost, but it will also guarantee that no pictures will be taken on the water. The camera will be somewhat more accessible if it is put in a special small watertight camera bag or an ammunition case (available at surplus stores) tied to the seat and kept just in front of it, permitting occasional shots when one is on calm water and has the time and inclination to pull up the spray skirt, open the container, take the picture, put the camera back in, and put the spray skirt back on. Few pictures will be taken on the river, but the camera will be completely protected.

A light camera container can be carried around the neck and secured through the life vest. This is not as safe as carrying the camera in the boat, since any carrier that can be opened with reasonable ease can take in water and be damaged during a swim in the rapids. On the other hand, the camera is readily available whenever one can be sure of not capsizing for a minute or so, and loss is quite unlikely.

Spare paddles are another problem. Ideally, they should be immediately available and yet out of the way. The traditional method is to carry the spare, separated into two halves to be joined with a ferrule, fastened to the front deck with shock cord or in some other arrangement that will allow it to be grabbed if needed. However, it is questionable whether this accessibility is worth the price of water-catching protrusions on the deck, which can also hang up on rocks when the kayak is floating upside down in the water. Most boaters these days carry the spare inside the boat, paying the penalty of not being able to grab it quickly. Only a take-apart paddle will fit inside the boat.

FOOD AND COOKING

Cooking is much simpler these days than it used to be for river runners and coastal tourers, as it is for all lightweight wilderness travelers. Besides the expensive prepackaged meals that are available at backpacking stores, there is a great variety of dehydrated foods available in any supermarket. The kayak camper can thus carry a couple of weeks' worth of food in his boat without much trouble or sense of deprivation at meal times.

Raft-supported trips often carry a lot of canned food, and this does have some advantages. Canned foods are easy to cook, meals are quickly planned and packaged before the trip, and costs are kept at a reasonable level. There is no storage problem on the river, since cans are already protected from water damage. Most campers prefer to mix the canned goods with other foods, but there are good reasons for using quite a few cans when the weight and bulk are not prohibitive. Canned fruit can be particularly pleasant on an extended trip.

If cans are taken, they are normally put in one large bag of net, burlap, or woven plastic fibers, which is tied into the raft. There is no need to protect the cans from water, but the labels should all be torn off in advance and the cans labeled with a waterproof marker.

The labels will otherwise turn into a soggy, gluey mess, but will not remain attached to the cans they started with. Another bag made of tough fibers should be brought to carry the burned and crushed empty cans—the bag must be tough to protect hands and raft fabric from sharp edges. Plastic garbage bags are poor for this purpose.

Kayakers carrying the food in their own boats should keep canned items to a minimum, perhaps using a few types of canned meat and fish to go into casserole-type dishes, but concentrating on dehydrated foods and others that do not require heavy packaging and that do not contain large quantitites of water. Generally, if the food selection is moderately well planned, concentrating on low-moisture items, 1½ to 2½ pounds of food per day will be needed for each person. Many types of dishes can be prepared, like fried hashes and patties, omelets or scrambled eggs, or even turnovers. I once managed a tolerable *quiche Lorraine* with a reflector oven. The staple method for food preparation on trips, however, is the one-pot meal boiled over the fire or stove. It is simply a stew or casserole-type meal which combines a number of ingredients into a tasty, easily packaged, and easily cooked supper.

Most one-pot meals have starch bases, and many starches are available in the neighborhood supermarket: noodles; spaghetti; macaroni; brown or white rice, regular or quick-cooking; dried potatoes, mashed, hashed, diced, or sliced; bulgur wheat, which has been crushed and parboiled, and is cooked like rice. To this base are added various combinations of vegetables, meat, meat-substitute, fish, cheese, flavorings, spices, and even dumplings. One-pot meals are particularly handy for beginners, because they are easier to plan and do not require a lot of juggling amid the unfamiliar complications of the outdoor kitchen.

One-pot meals can be made from scratch or bought ready-made, or the camper can begin with a packaged type and make additions to it. There is a variety of such meals sold at the grocery store, and these simply need to be repackaged to make them suitable for use on the river or along the coast. Whenever you buy prepackaged meals either in backpacking stores or in the supermarket, exercise caution in deciding how many campers can be fed, particularly if they had had a strenuous day of paddling. The people who write the labels for such foods seem to have a very rich fantasy life. Four-person packages are sometimes thin fare for two, and I have seen suppers of 1 ounce of food per person allegedly containing a full evening meal, yet actually representing about $1/24$ of a rather modest daily caloric requirement.

Protein, flavor, and texture in one-pot meals are usually contributed by meat, fish, cheese, and substitutes for these, though nutritionally adequate and tasty dishes can be made without them. Cheese is used frequently, but the moister cheeses will keep only for a few days in hot weather. The drier cheeses like Parmesan and Romano give lots of flavor and lots of protein for the weight, and they will also keep for long periods without refrigeration. Other possible ingredients include dried beef, jerky, freeze-dried meats, canned tuna, dried codfish or other dried fish, powdered eggs, and various soy meat-substitutes. Tuna, although it is canned, tastes good and goes a long way. Dried fish is frequently neglected, but it is cheap and an excellent source of flavorful protein. Dried beef works well, but it is expensive; it should be repackaged in plastic before the trip. Both freeze-dried meats and soy substitutes make good dishes with proper flavorings; they do tend to be somewhat bland without good sauces.

Many dried vegetables can be used, though they usually have to be purchased from specialty houses unless you dry your own. Dried vegetable soups are one source. The cheapest way to obtain dried vegetables is to buy in bulk from one of the dried food suppliers and then repackage in desired quantities. Dried onions are readily available in stores and make an excellent addition to many one-pot meals. Dried peas and beans are cheap, easy to get, and a good source of protein. They require a little extra effort to use, since they will take too long to cook unless they are allowed to soak during the day for a meal that evening. (A small, lightweight pressure cooker is ideal both for soaking and for cooking them.) Soaking helps some other dried vegetables like corn, too. Try carrying a few fresh treats like tomatoes and avocados in Tupperware containers to eat after a couple of days, and then use the container to rehydrate dried foods.

Many herbs and spices will improve the flavor of one-pot meals. If you are in a hurry or are feeling low on imagination, the dried, packaged sauces and soups can be added to suitable one-pot meals to provide lots of flavor.

Soups can be very pleasant at the beginning of the meal, particularly during chilly weather. They can be ready 15 or 20 minutes after you get into camp if you have them stored in a handy place, and people can sip at them while they are getting other chores done and the cook is getting organized for the rest of the meal. They are also a good way to stretch meals a bit if you have a large cooking group for the size of the pots or if some meals are a bit skimpy.

Desserts are a matter of personal preference. Some people never bother, while others take elaborate measures to cook up puddings or baked deserts. Cookies can be packed inside pots and make a good quick dessert.

Have plenty of drinks available, and find out in advance what people like. Some have to have coffee, while others can't stand it. In general, tea seems to be drunk more outdoors than at home, while coffee is wanted less. A pot of boiling water and a variety of instant drinks promote good cheer, particularly on cold evenings. Tea bags, instant coffee, bouillon, instant hot chocolate, and a number of others are popular. Hot Jello as a drink is pleasant when the weather is cold. Carry adequate supplies of additives after inquiring what people use (sugar and nondairy creamers or the equivalents).

Baked items make a nice change, once in a while. If you are building fires, a reflector oven is easy to learn to use. Just keep the fire built up in front of it and move it closer or farther away to regulate the heat. Things bake quite quickly with a reflector oven. If you're not an experienced outdoor cook, have one person concentrate on the reflector oven, or use it on a lazy afternoon, when lots of other things aren't distracting you. Hot breads can be made without an oven, too. Either carry Bisquick, or make up your own biscuit mix for a fraction of the cost. Add water to the mix, stir, and bake by dropping spoonfuls into a frying pan or twisting some on a stick and baking over the fire. You can make sweet buns just by adding various ingredients, dabs of brown sugar and raisins, for example. Bisquick mixture can be used for dumplings by dropping spoonfuls into the top of a stew and covering for ten minutes or so after they are in. Watch out—they expand.

Cold lunches are the norm, although brewing up a pot of hot soup is sometimes worthwhile on a raw day. Durable bread or canned crackers, cheese, salami, peanut butter, jam, nuts, candy, and dried fruit make good lunches.

Breakfast preferences vary a good deal. Elaborate cooked breakfasts are very time-consuming, but some people are miserable without them. Others would rather have an uncooked breakfast of granola or some other cold cereal, bread and jam, or an "instant breakfast," so that they can get right on the river or out hiking without having to cook and wash pots and pans. Many compromise by having hot water for drinks and instant hot cereals, but not doing any real cooking. People tend to be far more narrow-minded and cranky about breakfast preferences than other meals, so whoever plans meals should be sure to inquire in detail about who wants what. Those who are convinced that they cannot survive the morning without a cup of coffee and a plate of eggs will not be pleased with a glass of imitation orange juice, a bowl of Grape Nuts, and a pat on the head.

Planning meals can be done in a number of ways, depending on the type of trip, its size, and the participants. One or two people can plan all the food for the whole group, but this is a big job. If the party is small or is broken into small cooking groups, suppers and breakfasts are most easily planned within these groups. For a small group, the division of labor can be arranged in many ways, depending on the experience and preferences of each member. Often a party of experienced people divides the responsibility evenly, taking care of cost distribution at the same time. For a cooking group of four on an eight-day river trip, for example, each person would be responsible for two breakfasts and two suppers. Condiments, seasonings, and drinks are normally all carried in one batch, and each person might be responsible for certain of these: drinks, salt, pepper, sugar, honey, and so on. Lunches are often handled individually, since preferences vary, packing is simplified on a trip that is not raft-supported, and each person has his own lunch taken care of even if the party is large and breaks into smaller groups on the river that do not coincide with the cooking parties. On other trips one person may take responsibility for planning all the food, while his or her companions handle other chores, such as obtaining maps or washing dishes.

Organization on coming into camp at night is partly dependent on efficient arrangement in the morning. Cooking gear, the evening's supper, and the bag containing seasonings and drinks should all be packed where they can be easily retrieved. Hunting around in the back of a flotation bag for supper after getting into camp late is unpleasant for both the hunter and the others waiting for the meal. It is that much worse if the flashlight is down in there with the meal. Similarly, if you are having creamed codfish, and the fish needs to be soaked for the day, you must remember in the morning to put the fish and water in the soaking container.

All food should be packaged at home in an organized way. Different people have different systems, but the simplest is to pack everything in plastic bags, with each meal sealed in its own bag. Include directions on cooking times, amounts of water, and the like; don't rely on memory unless you have cooked the same meal many times before. Regular plastic bags and rubber bands can be used, but the neatest method is to use a heavier plastic sheeting and to seal it with an iron. Press out as much air as possible before sealing. If each person is responsible for a few meals, each will carry the ones he or she made; otherwise they may be put in breakfast, lunch, and dinner sacks, or into bags divided by days. Obviously, the weight and bulk of food and community gear should be evenly distributed among boats.

PICKING A CAMPSITE

The choice of a campsite may in some cases be made for the kayaker, since on some heavily used wilderness rivers, campsites are now assigned. In this case, the party has only to keep organized enough to spend the desired length of time on the river, neither hurrying past play spots only to reach camp for lunch, nor getting out on the river late in the morning and dawdling along so that the group does not get into camp until after dark.

Whether campsites are assigned or freely chosen, the group should have worked out a rough schedule in advance on the map, so that approximately the right number of miles are covered each day. It is usually best to camp at least a couple of hours before dark, and, depending on the nature of the river, to start looking for a campsite an hour or so before you want to stop. Then you can call a halt when a good one is found. Pushing on toward dark often results in poor campsites or worse. When a river has a lot of people on it, so that the best campsites are in demand, you find the nicest spots by getting up early and camping early.

The landing spot is the first consideration in choosing a site, particularly when rafts are along on the trip. If the river is fast, kayaks should go ahead when it is time to start looking for a place to camp, so that the people on the raft can be given plenty of warning to get on the correct side of the river. Take note of the size of eddy and type of beach that the rafts on your trip need; a raft simply cannot get into the tiny eddies that a kayak can, and it will be a nuisance or an impossibility to get the raft up on the shore without a beach or bar. An unsupported kayak group can often get a good campsite on a heavily used river by choosing a place where rafts cannot land. Be sure that the less experienced kayakers can land, however.

The ideal campsite has a beach onto which the boats can be pulled, well above the level to which the river might rise overnight, and a sandy or grassy spot large enough to accommodate the party, or several spots within reasonable distance. It has potable water and firewood available, and enough conveniently placed rocks, logs, and trees around for cooking and pitching shelters. There should be enough space and cover so that a latrine area can be found that will not pollute the river and will provide suitable privacy. Finally, of course, there should be a side canyon to explore and a few nearby play spots for those who have not yet had enough boating that day. In fact, since this is the ideal campsite, we may as well specify a hot spring big enough to soak in, too (not an unreasonable provision along some western rivers).

Unfortunately, the ideal campsite often has another attribute. It is frequently the one you pass up at three in the afternoon because there are so many good spots that you know there will be another in half an hour—which, of course, there aren't.

ORGANIZATION IN CAMP

In most respects organizing matters in camp is like organizing things anywhere else—different people have different preferences, and being able to do things the way you want to is what wilderness travel is all about. Some prefer loosely arranged trips, particularly when a number of experienced campers are out together. Obviously, everyone should do his or her share. It is often necessary to assign tasks to beginners who do not know how to set up a camp and who will otherwise stand around helplessly, feeling left out. Community chores can either be rotated or left to particular people through the whole trip, providing no one gets stuck doing things he doesn't like all the time. Large groups will have to be more organized than small ones, particularly if cooking is done centrally.

The first priority after getting everyone landed is to make sure that boats and equipment are completely secure. On a wilderness boating trip loss of even small items of equipment can be quite serious. Waves, tide, wind, and rising water must all be considered in making sure that all equipment is safe. Wet suits, spray skirts, and even boats can be blown into the water by the wind. The lapping of waves against a kayak or raft that is pulled half out of the water can float it off. Incoming tides and rivers rising because of rain, melting snow, or opened dams high up in the watershed can come many feet up a beach to float boats away. Boats should be carried to a clearly safe place, tied up, or both. If no other ties are available, a pole, a paddle, or a rock can be buried in a trench in the sand, with a line tied around it. This is called a deadman anchor. Other important equipment should not be left lying about where it might be blown off by a gust of wind, and experienced boaters may have to remind beginning wilderness travelers of this. A lost wet suit or spray skirt can endanger an entire party.

Normally, the next priority is to get food and cooking utensils out and to hunt up firewood so that the meal can be started. If rain threatens, setting up shelters has priority. Or if there is enough time to allow an exploratory trip up a side canyon, then supper can wait. In addition, in chilly weather, it's nice to get wet clothing out to dry early, so that wet suits, underwear, and boating sneakers don't have to be put on frozen the next morning.

If you are inexperienced at lightweight camping, it is worth spending some time in advance of the kayak trip practicing setting up your shelter, building fires, and starting stoves. Even with fire starters, getting a blaze going when it has been raining can be very difficult, and this is usually when a fire is really needed. Small self-pressurized gasoline stoves are easy to operate once you know how, but try them first at home (outside the house).

Fallen deadwood and driftwood that is high enough above the waterline to be dried out well are the best sources of firewood. A walk up a side canyon is often productive. Build fires on sand, where the traces can later be eradicated. Ashes should be buried or put in the river. If rocks are used to build a fireplace, covering them with sand or mineral soil will prevent fire scars. If there is already a fireplace or fire-scarred rocks, use them. Carbon blacking will last about as long as the human race, or possibly longer. Never build fires on humus or forest duff, since coals can burrow down into the ground and smolder for weeks. If surrounding woods, grassland, or marsh are dry, keep the fire down low, and if there is also a wind, use the stove instead. Don't leave the fire unattended, and before you depart, put it out and clean it up. Leave the campsite looking as pristine as you found it.

WATER

Water will be no problem when the river itself is potable. Unfortunately, there are few rivers left in the country which are safe to drink without treatment. When it is at all doubtful whether water is safe, it is best to assume that it is not, particularly on extended wilderness trips, since kayaking with a severe intestinal upset can be practically impossible.

When the main river is not trustworthy, side streams and springs are often a source of good water, and it may be worthwhile to bring some larger containers, so that drinking water can be carried. On raft-supported trips, 5-gallon collapsible water carriers can be used. For all-kayak parties, smaller collapsible jugs or ½-gallon and 1-gallon bleach bottles make good containers.

Springs are generally safe, providing there is no evidence of fouling at the spring itself and if it seems clear that the water has traveled some distance underground. A stream that flows underground for a few hundred feet can be easily distinguished from a true spring. Side streams may be much purer than the main river or far more polluted; the river runner has to make his own judgment after looking at the country and the maps. If cattle or sheep are grazed on land above the river, then side streams may well be very polluted, particularly when they drain large areas.

The most reliable method of water purification is to boil it. Boiling for 20 minutes will ensure the destruction of any disease-carrying organisms, and it is definitely the recommended method of water purification wherever substantial danger seems likely. Cooking water is no problem, since it is sterilized during the cooking.

In most kayaking situations, chemical purification methods are satisfactory. The fastest and cheapest technique is to carry a small bottle of liquid chlorine bleach and an eyedropper. Add ten drops of bleach per gallon, or three per quart, shake the water, and wait 20 to 30 minutes before using. Leave the cap of the container loose when shaking, so that treated water will run over the mouth of the bottle. One should be able to smell the chlorine after the waiting period, a guarantee that there is free chlorine present in the water; otherwise more bleach should be added. When water is murky, the debris floating in the water tends to bind organisms, making them more difficult to destroy, so the amount of bleach should be doubled in the case of cloudy, smelly, or otherwise very suspect water. Very murky or muddy water can be filtered through cloth before purification. If a lot of silty or muddy water is anticipated, nylon floss, sold in tropical fish supply stores and chemical supply houses, can be bought and used to filter the water.

Halazone tablets liberate chlorine gas, and they are used like bleach. Add two per quart of water if the water is clear and odorless; add four or five if the water is more suspect. Wait 30 minutes, shaking the bottle with the cap loose after the tablets have dissolved. Globaline tablets, which liberate iodine gas instead of chlorine, are slightly more effective and are used in the same way as Halazone, but they give the water a taste even more unpleasant than chlorine.

Water which smells or has a bad taste can often be made more palatable by boiling it 20 minutes with charcoal obtained from the fire. The charcoal can then be filtered out by pouring the water through a bandanna or some other piece of cloth.

Kayakers along the coastal waters of the sea have a more substantial water problem than river runners, and they should be sure to carry adequate fresh water supplies unless they are sure of streams along the way. Rivers entering the sea will be salty for some distance up, and they may well contain dangerous industrial pollutants as well. Fresh water can sometimes be found where rain water is trapped in rock pools. Digging in sand beaches above the water line will sometimes yield fresh or only mildly brackish water since the fresh water stays above the salt, but be sure to purify it if there are beach houses around. Ocean water can be used for cooking, of course.

PLANNING NOTES

Many considerations already mentioned in previous chapters are particularly important to parties on longer tours. The competence of individuals and especially of the party as a whole is critical for group safety on a long tour, in case of accident or unexpectedly difficult conditions. In organizing a tour, it is important to consider kayaking skill and outdoor experience. It is just as important to have members who are personally compatible, especially if the trip is to be long or difficult.

Everyone should have similar feelings about the objectives of the trip in terms of the miles to be covered in a day and attitudes about side trips, early starts, and the like. No formal discussion of this sort of thing is usually necessary, but it should be brought up to make sure that different members of the group do not have wildly different conceptions of the trip, which might later cause hard feelings. Some understandings about leadership are also important in large groups, parties composed of members with widely different levels of experience, and those made up of people who do not know one another well.

Information about rivers needs to be obtained from as many sources as possible, well in advance of the proposed trip, particularly in the case of an unknown or relatively difficult river. Where permits are required, planning may have to be started a year in advance. On river trips, be sure to ascertain the flow levels for which the information you have applies, what gauging stations or agencies have figures, and how to check on the flow level before the trip begins. It is vital in planning trips to develop a critical eye and ear for all reports about rivers or coastal areas. Any report is dubious unless it contains considerable detail about the route itself, water level, the type of craft used by the writer or person you are speaking with, and some comparison with a river you have paddled or a rating using some widely known scale. On coastal tours, information about currents, tides, and beaches, together with beacons, buoys, or other landmarks, is essential.

Equipment, food, and transportation all have to be arranged a reasonable time in advance of the trip. If a river is regulated closely by some official agency, find out in detail what equipment requirements they may have, and recheck this just in advance of the trip, preferably in writing; then carry the letter with you. It is currently fashionable among the powers-that-be to regulate amateur boaters "for their own good." Since nearly all of the regulators are concerned with safety on power boats or 35-foot pontoons (big commercial rafts), and know essentially nothing about kayaks, these regulations are often capricious at best. It is particularly important to find out the *exact* requirements for life vests and spare paddles. Make advance inquiries about doubtful roads and all other details that may be required for the shuttle.

SHUTTLES

Most kayak trips start at one place and end at another, so it is nearly always necessary to arrange a car shuttle. Typically, all the drivers go to the put-in, and while the passengers stay to arrange the gear and get things ready all the cars are driven around to the take-out, and then one of these cars brings the drivers back to the put-in. Shuttles may be only 30 miles, or they may be many hundred. Sometimes the driving is shorter than the river miles, but often it is considerably longer. It may be over good roads or bad, easy or difficult to find.

So many strategies can be used to manage a shuttle that it would be pointless to try to discuss them in much detail. Easy shuttles can be managed in any number of ways without really making much difference, but long shuttles can consume lots of time, effort, gas, and automobile wear, so on long ones or those near distant rivers or lakes, it is important to plan things well in advance. A shuttle done completely by the kayakers always requires at least two vehicles, though a group of four boaters can generally manage to get to the river with one car. Thus, if the river is a thousand miles from your home, figuring another way to manage the shuttle will save putting a couple of thousand miles on one car.

It is often possible to arrange for local drivers to ferry your automobiles to the take-out point for a reasonable fee. Since back and forth driving between the put-in and take-out can be saved, this may even turn out to be cheaper than doing all the work yourselves. If there are possibilities of vandalism or theft near the river, you may be able to arrange for the shuttle drivers to drive your cars to their homes and then to the take-out at a prearranged time. This strategy is sometimes cheaper, too, because the shuttle drivers do not have to provide their own transportation to or from the river. You pick them up in town before driving to the put-in and drive them back after taking out. This requires a rigid schedule, of course. Another possibility is to have a local driver pick you up at a prearranged time in a truck, ferrying you back to your cars.

There are a number of considerations that you should take into account when planning a shuttle. Costs have to be shared; figure out the equitable way of doing this before the trip so that everyone is satisfied. Some shuttle roads may require trucks or four-wheel-drive vehicles, particularly after a rain, so give road condition some thought in planning the shuttle. Be wary of leaving the cars at the bottom of a steep clay slope or similar spot that would be impossible to get up after wet weather.

Buses, hitchhiking, bicycles, and motorbikes can be helpful in managing some shuttles—for example, when you want to leave your cars with someone who will keep an eye on them. Local people willing to act as shuttle drivers obviously must be reliable, and it is surprising how many there are. Many guidebooks mention local contacts; otherwise, some polite letters or phone calls to residents of nearby towns can be productive. There are often many residents in such towns who can use a little extra cash. Arrange the terms in advance, and try to pay at least part of the shuttle fee after delivery of the car.

8

An Introduction to Slalom and Downriver Racing

Tastes vary among kayakers, as in any group. With kayakers, racing, probably more than any other facet of the sport, inspires fierce advocates and equally fierce detractors. There are many boaters for whom kayaking *means* racing—kayaking is, for them, essentially a competitive activity. The rest of their boating is a training program designed to bring them to peak ability for the racing season. Those of the school who enjoy an occasional river tour consider it incidental to their main paddling pleasure, white-water racing.

Noncompetitors are likely to be equally vociferous about their lack of interest in or positive dislike of racing and the mentality associated with it. Some of the best river runners in the country are proud to claim that they have never been in a race and intend to maintain the record. A fair number of boaters not only do not like to race, but feel that the racing mentality is bad for what is at its root a wilderness sport. Where racing fans feel that the competitive frame of mind is a positive influence, detractors believe it to be detrimental to any real fellowship, promoting instead a kind of elitism, and pandering to commercialization of the sport.

Between the racers and antiracers, there are a good many kayakers who either enjoy both racing and touring as different activities, each pleasant and worthwhile in its own right, or who see racing as good training for other aspects of the sport. But whatever the virtues of racing for advanced kayakers interested mainly in white-water touring, slalom paddling is excellent training for the advanced beginner and intermediate boater wishing to hone his skills at pad-

243

dling in rapids. Slalom racing demands precise control of the kayak, and this is just what is needed by the kayaker who wants to progress to greater control of his boat in difficult rapids.

THE SLALOM

The white-water slalom, patterned after the skier's slalom race, is designed to test the ability of the boater to maneuver quickly and with perfect control through a rapid. A series of gates, perhaps twenty or thirty of them, each consisting of two poles, are suspended over a white-water course about ⅜ to ½ mile long. Some gates in sequence are ten yards apart, while others are right next to each other. They are hung in such a way as to require accurate maneuvering in the middle of the rapids, as the kayaker descends, occasionally calling for upstream or backward paddling. The object is to travel downstream from the start to the finish line, passing through each gate in the manner indicated, with no mistakes, and as quickly as possible. A competitor's score is the time taken to complete the course in seconds, plus penalty points assessed for errors in running the course. Each racer is allowed two runs, with the better score counted.

The gates are suspended over the water with cable or nylon line, so that the bottoms of the poles are as close to the water as possible without touching. One pole is striped red and white and must be kept to the paddler's left while the gate is being negotiated; the other pole is striped green and white and must be kept to the racer's right. If the gate is labeled *R*, it must be negotiated stern first; otherwise, the competitor paddles through bow first. No part of the boat, the kayaker, or the paddle may touch either pole without a penalty.

The gates are numbered and are negotiated in order. The number faces the side from which the racer must enter. In international competition, the opposite side is also numbered, with a red *X* over the number, but in local races, the reverse-side number is often not shown.

A racer in a typical slalom situation. The gate in the center (#4) is a standard gate and is to be negotiated forward. The current flows from the right side of the photograph to the left. The paddler has passed through the gate, turned below it, and is positioning himself for a reverse gate below.

To complete the course, the kayaker must cross the finish line right side up, without having had to leave his boat. Eskimo rolling in the race is not penalized, except within a gate, but bailing out of the boat disqualifies the run.

PENALTIES

The following penalties are assessed against the competitor for errors made on individual gates, and they are added to his time in seconds for completing the course:

10 points—If the gate is negotiated in the proper direction with the boat oriented the right way, but one pole is touched on the inside by the paddler's body, paddle, or boat. Multiple touches on the inside of the same pole count the same as one touch.

20 points—If the gate is correctly negotiated, but both poles are touched on the inside, or if the outside of a pole is touched and the gate is subsequently run correctly. Once the 20-point penalty has been assessed, inside touches do not bring further penalty.

50 points—If the gate is missed completely; if the outside of a pole is touched and the gate is not subsequently negotiated correctly; if the boat passes through in the wrong direction or is oriented incorrectly; if the paddler capsizes within the gate or passes through upside down; if a pole is intentionally pushed aside to permit passage.

A 10-point penalty. The racer has run this reverse gate backwards, as required, and gone through it, but he hit one pole.

For a racer to be credited with passing through a gate, the general rule is that the bow of the boat, the paddler's body, and the stern of the boat must pass through the plane of the gate, that is, an imaginary line between the two poles, in correct order. Once the body has reached the plane, no repeat attempt can be made, so if the torso of the paddler does get to the plane of the gate and passage is not completed or is in the wrong direction, no repetition will eliminate the 50-point penalty that is assessed. If passage is begun in the wrong direction or with the wrong end of the boat, but the body has not reached the plane of the gate, the boat can be pulled out and another attempt made.

Though the general rule for gate clearance is that bow, body, and stern all pass through the gate, "sneaking" with the bow, stern, or both is permitted. That is, if the competitor can speed his passage by passing the hull of the boat under one or both of the poles, he is not penalized. However, the orientation of the kayak must still be correct. The forward part of the boat must cut the plane of the gate first, the body next, and the rear part of the boat last, or the order must be the opposite one for a reverse gate.

Once a gate has been properly cleared, subsequent touching of that gate is not penalized.

Movement of a pole by the water is not penalized, even if a wave moving the pole is created by the boat or paddle of the racer, but if the moving pole touches or is touched by the competitor, the appropriate penalty is scored.

Wind movement of poles is not normally allowed for, so that if the paddler touches a pole, even if it was blown by the wind, it is counted against him. If, however, the poles are blown high out of reach and the boater passes through the space where the gate should be, he is given credit for passing through the gate.

Many penalty calls require somewhat doubtful decisions by a gate judge. If a paddler goes through a gate with his boat across it, for example, and the boat is oriented slightly in the right direction, that is, bow first or stern first, whichever is required, a 20-point penalty is assessed for hitting the poles (or the outside of the first pole), but if it is oriented slightly the wrong way, there will be a 50-point penalty for going through in the wrong direction. Where penalties are deserved, the gate judge must call them, but where there is real uncertainty in his mind, the competitor is given the benefit of the doubt.

ORDER

The gates have to be negotiated in numerical order. Reaching the next gate in the sequence before going through the correct gate automatically causes a 50-point penalty to be assessed for the missed gate, and going back to do the gate does not remove the penalty. However, only the next gate is active in this way. For example, if a competitor successfully passes through gate 4, and then reaches gate 6, he incurs a penalty of 50 points for missing gate 5. This cannot be erased, so he should complete gate 6 and go on down the course. If, however, he goes through 4 and reaches 7, he can still go back

A paddler correctly negotiating a standard forward gate without penalty.

without penalty and do 5, 6, and 7. Penalties for missing these gates are assessed only if he does not go back to do them.

BOATS

International slalom rules require boats with a minimum length of 4 meters (13 feet 2 inches) and a minimum width of 60 centimeters (23⅝ inches). These dimensions are therefore the normal ones for boats used in slalom competition, because longer craft are less maneuverable.

Boats used in slalom competitions always have pronounced rockers and relatively flat bottoms so that they can be turned quickly. Beginners can use any reasonably maneuverable boat. At the beginner stage, times and techniques are not really affected much by one's boat, unless it is so unstable or sensitive that one cannot keep it upright.

Serious slalom racers use boats that are very light and are correspondingly less durable. Such boats are an expensive hobby, particularly before you have developed the skill to treat them with the care they need in the water. Modern slalom design emphasizes small-volume boats with very low decks. Such boats allow frequent gate-sneaking. They are sensitive to nuances of balance and lean and therefore allow the expert to make the most of his technique (but may dump the inexperienced into the water very quickly indeed). Finally, the ends of a low-volume boat weigh less, so that less energy is required to turn them. Again, the difference is only really apparent to one whose skill is of a sufficiently high order that his or her turns are very efficient.

SLALOM STRATEGY

Since slalom is a race, speed is important. The competitor cannot rest between gates, drifting along with the current; he must paddle constantly, and must take the fastest way his skill will allow to get from one gate to the next. Thus, providing it will work, a direct run across the channel is preferred to a ferry.

The real key to the slalom, however, is control of the boat. Penalties are high enough so that there is always a premium on good form. Shaving 2 seconds off the time with desperate paddling is a poor bargain if it causes a touch that will cost a 10-second penalty.

The slalom racer must learn to plan his movements far in advance. Planning starts with careful inspection and memorization of the course (which will help the beginner to learn the art of memorizing complex rapids). If a trial run is allowed, it is used to learn the best way to run each gate, not for speed. Watching other racers run the course can also help you to understand the course and develop a strategy. In the actual run, planning consists of keeping your attention as far ahead down the course as circumstances permit, plotting the fastest way into the next gate and the best maneuvers to get through it that will also leave you in a good position for the gate to follow.

Actual paddling strokes through the slalom should be as vertical and as close to the boat as possible. A paddle pushed straight down into the water near the hull gives maximum forward force and minimum steering to the off-side. Strokes far out to the side, except when they are being used for course correction, simply waste energy and introduce a turning component that will have to be counteracted by the next stroke on the opposite side. A vertical paddle is also far less likely to hit a pole in the gate than one angled out to the side.

The beginner needs to learn to paddle right through the gate, both for speed and because many upstream gates will not allow coasting. Strokes should be planned so that the last stroke through the gate will initiate the turn in the direction one wants to travel next, also putting the opposite blade in position for the brace that often needs to follow. For practice, the beginner should work on a short sequence of gates, learning to connect them in various ways. With a sequence of only three gates, many combinations can be practiced over and over, since the order and direction of negotiation can be changed around.

The slalom racer needs to make his runs as efficient as possible. Besides cutting across currents efficiently, he has to cut all turns as close as he can. In approaching an upstream gate, it is important to cut into the eddy below as close to the gate as one can get, using the eddy turn to take the boat into the gate. Hitting the eddy low, so that you must paddle back against the current to the gate, wastes much precious time and energy.

The beginner and the intermediate paddler who have never done any slalom work before will both find reverse gates a real problem at first, since paddling backward is trickier than going forward. Steering is harder, and blade angle in braces must be relearned. The only solution to these problems is practice.

After passing a gate, there is always a temptation to look back at the gate to make sure that it has not been touched. Forget it and

A kayaker running a reverse gate. She has lined the boat up and is paddling through to try to maintain speed through the hole below.

concentrate on the next gate. Looking back does no good and wastes attention that is needed for what is ahead. The really proficient paddler has learned from long practice exactly where the stern of the boat is and will not have to look to see if he is clear. Flat-water practice with the English gate can help a lot with this.

More advanced paddlers should learn to drive the bow and stern of the boat under poles. A sweep stroke with a strong vertical component will drive the end of the boat underwater, particularly if it is a low-volume boat. For serious paddlers, this technique shaves off precious seconds.

It is important to get the boat lined up for passing through a gate far enough upstream so that energy and time do not have to be wasted working against the current. Lining up well in advance permits turning strokes which add to the speed of the boat toward the gate, rather than diminishing it.

Serious slalom racing is as much a battle of nerves as of boating skill, and there is no discussion of this sort of complication here. Remember, though, if you are competing in an organized race, that some participants may take it more seriously than you do. If so, they will be on edge, and small blunders or courtesies will take on exaggerated importance. Beginners should take extra care at races not to step on others' toes. Blocking put-in or take-out points while fiddling with equipment or pressing a conversation with one who is trying to concentrate, for example, may bring reactions of unfriendliness that seem disproportionate to the offense. Be particularly considerate of others at races until you have learned the ropes.

SETTING UP A SLALOM

The best way to learn how to set up a slalom is to run a few courses and assist experienced boaters in hanging the gates and taking them down. There is always a lot of work to do for those in charge of races, and you will not only learn a lot by helping—you'll earn a modest amount of gratitude that may serve you in good stead later on when you would like someone to take you down a river or lend you a boat mold.

A gate is usually hung from a light nylon line kept on a spool or winding frame. One end of the line is first carried across the river. At least two people are required for reasonable efficiency. If a bridge is available nearby, it is used; otherwise, one person has to ferry the end of the line across with his boat. (Hold the end with teeth or a hand; don't tie it onto you or the kayak.) Once the line is across the river, the gate and number are tied on and pulled over to the spot where they are wanted, and the line is secured in such a way that the gate is high enough above the water that it will not be set in motion by a periodic wave. It is usually simplest to set up a slalom at a spot where the banks are high, so that the lines can be secured easily. Large trees may also serve to hold the lines high enough over the water (small ones blow in the wind). Crossed poles are often used to hold up the gate lines, but these require much more time to rig.

Drawing the kayak over after passing through a gate. This type of kayak is specifically designed with a low deck to "sneak" under gates.

The width and positioning of gates should be designed to test the skill of the paddlers, and the level of skill of the competitors has to be considered. Gates that are set so that they will be impossible for most of the racers make for a poor course. Thus, gates for a beginners' slalom should be wider and set farther apart than gates for experts. In any case, the gates should be set to test the maneuvering skill of the competitor, rather than pure power.

Timing of a run begins when the bow of the boat crosses the starting line and ends when any part of the boat reaches the finish. Ideally, only one boat should run the course at a time, but in many races, competitors are started at fixed intervals. Scoring is communicated in various ways, but most often each gate judge either has colored signal cards with which he signals penalties to a central judging stand to be recorded, or the penalties are recorded separately at each gate and are all tallied later.

Competitors wear numbers to identify them to judges, as with most types of races. They are required to be ready in their boats at the starting line when they are scheduled to begin. It is important to be well warmed up beforehand and to get into the boat and get ready when the starting number is five or six places from you.

DOWNRIVER RACES

The downriver or wildwater race is a race from one point on the river to another. It is simply a speed race, and the only maneuvering required is that necessitated by the features of the river. The course is generally 5 or 6 miles long, and racing rules require it to be at least 3 kilometers (just under 2 miles).

Downriver racing is generally less suitable for the beginner either as a training device or for enjoyable participation. The boats used are designed for speed; they are barely stable enough and barely maneuverable enough to permit the expert to paddle them down the river without wasting energy on keeping the boat upright.

Memorization of the course and previous practice on it are as important to the downriver racer as to the slalom competitor, and since the course is not an artificially devised one, advance practice is normal. The racer must train and pace himself for much longer periods of stress, since a run will probably take a half hour or so.

Tactics in a wildwater race are to keep in fast water all the time, avoiding eddies to one side and big stoppers to the other, so as to keep the boat from slowing down. Forward strokes are used for maneuvering as much as possible, and backpaddling and ferrying are avoided like the plague. In going around turns, the competitor paddles toward the inside of the turn for maximum velocity and the shortest course, keeping just clear of the eddy around the bend. When large standing waves have to be taken head on, the racer attempts to cut right through rather than taking a rolling ride over the top, paddling hard into the waves.

Racers are normally started at intervals, though some wildwater races have mass starts. A competitor being overtaken is required to allow the boat behind to pass when the overtaking paddler calls "track."

In either type of race, slalom or downriver, it is often hard for the boater to see exactly where the finish line runs, and it is vital to keep paddling until well past. Many races have been lost when the boater stopped paddling after the last gate or bend in the river, floating sedately over the finish line some seconds later.

With local races which do not have special rescue crews, the three competitors who have arrived most recently should remain in their boats at the take-out point to rescue anyone in difficulty. Wait in your boat until three more people have come down the course.

9

Building Kayaks

This chapter is intended to serve as an introduction to the art of building kayaks. It is important for anyone considering constructing his own boat to recognize that it is only an introduction. A reasonably complete treatment of the subject would require an entire book, and that book would probably be obsolete before it was in print a year because of changes in techniques, designs, and materials.

This note is not intended to discourage the reader from building his or her own kayak—far from it. Building your own boat is well worthwhile, but the project should not be undertaken lightly. Enough information is contained in this chapter to get you started, if you are interested in making the kayak you will paddle.

An understanding of the construction techniques used to build kayaks is also valuable to any boater. To judge the capacities and limitations of a boat, the paddler needs to have some idea of its structural design and the strengths and weaknesses of the materials used to make it. Certainly, one needs to have some comprehension of these factors to make an intelligent purchase of a kayak. Finally, to protect and maintain a boat and to use it safely, there are some important facts for the kayaker to learn.

TYPES OF CONSTRUCTION

Kayaks have been made with many different combinations of materials in the past. The Eskimo used driftwood and bone to form the frame of his boat and covered it with sewed sealskins. Heavy European imitations were made for a time from wood; the wood frame

256

covered with canvas or rubberized cloth was closer to the true kayak. This membrane-covered frame was fairly standard until the postwar period, and it was used to produce some beautiful and classic boats, including designs for many purposes. The foldboats are perhaps the highest development of this method of boat building, with their ingenious collapsible frames allowing them to be stowed away and carried in a couple of packs. Some excellent slalom foldboats have been made, but because of the advantages of more modern materials in rough water, these have been largely supplanted by other types. The foldboats designed for wilderness travel or family touring on moderate water are still excellent boats for their purpose.

Plywood has also been used for making kayaks, but although it has many advantages, the quality of the boats is far inferior to that of craft made by other methods. Veneer is used for specialized flatwater racing shells, but they are useless for any other purpose and will receive little attention here. Very few kayaks have been made from aluminum, as much because of the difficulty of working with it as for inherent unsuitability.

The introduction of fiber glass as a material for kayaks was revolutionary. Here was a material that was at once extremely durable and resilient, capable of bouncing off rocks in white water with far less damage than the paddler had any right to expect, virtually maintenance free, lightweight, and relatively easy to work with, so that small numbers of boats could be made economically and experimentation with new designs was comparatively simple. Finally, the actual limitations in form imposed by the material itself were far less constricting than those of any previous material. The fiber glass formed a rigid hull and deck that needed little or no frame inside.

Fiber glass is a somewhat inaccurate term for a laminated structure, which is formed by impregnating a cloth made of glass fibers with some sort of resin that cures to create a very tough and durable form. These materials are worked into molds of the desired shape and allowed to harden. Various more precise terms are sometimes used instead of "fiber glass": "glass-reinforced plastic" or "GRP" and a good many others. "Fiber glass" will be used here except when referring to specific constructions.

Actually, many modern laminated boats do not even use fiber glass, but substitute various other synthetic cloths for some or all of the layers in the boat. Different resins are used as well, and much of the art of building boats with these materials lies in the choice of suitable combinations. More detail about some specific cloths and resins is included later in the chapter.

Several other methods of making kayaks from modern plastics have been developed, and more will undoubtedly appear in the future. One system uses a vinyl-ABS-foam sandwich which becomes plastic when heated and is vacuum-formed into a mold. Another process uses a mold that is spun with plastic material sprayed from the inside. Good boats have been produced with both of these techniques, but they have not yet supplanted the laminates and they do create some problems. They are also unsuitable for small boat builders, so the rest of this chapter will concentrate on fiber glass–type construction.

DESIGN

Some mention has already been made in Chapter 1 of basic kayak shapes, but having discussed some of the many facets of the sport, we can now go into more detail about the advantages and limitations of particular design features.

Length. The longer a boat is, the better it will track, and the more difficult it will be to maneuver. A long boat will carry more equipment and will ride higher than a shorter kayak of the same width. It will bob about less in choppy waves, but it may tend to dive after riding down a long wave. It will be faster than a shorter boat. Obviously, the shorter boat will tend to have exactly the opposite qualities and faults.

Width. Other things being equal, a narrower boat will tend to be faster, track better, and be harder to turn than a wider one.

Rocker. A kayak with more rocker (lengthwise curvature of the bottom of the boat) will be much easier to turn (whether you want to or not) than one with less rocker. A boater paddling a kayak with more rocker will find it easier to maintain a course when the water is pushing the kayak in a different direction, but in most other cases holding a course will be harder. That is to say, the boat will track poorly. Depending on the other aspects of design, leaning the boat over on its side may have the effect of increasing the rocker and making the hull easier to turn, without the negative aspects of a boat with more rocker.

Keel. A kayak with a keel—a real protrusion along the bottom center line of the boat—will track very well and be extremely hard to maneuver. Keels are rarely used in kayaks.

Bottom cross section. A V-shaped cross section will tend to be very fast, directionally stable, and hard to turn. It will also be more likely to slice into waves rather than rising over them. It will be very tippy, but will tend to become more stable as the boat is leaned over. A perfectly round lower cross section will be somewhat slower and somewhat easier to turn, and will be likely to ride up more on waves. It will be fairly unstable and will not become any more stable as the boat is leaned over. A cross section with a wide, flat bottom will track poorly, be slow, easy to turn, and will tend to ride over waves. It will be stable and hard to capsize, but if tipped beyond a certain point, it will become suddenly unstable.

Note that no kayak has a uniform cross section, and this is where the real subtlety of design begins to show. The center cross section of a boat may be flat in the middle, rounding up gently to the sides to make the boat stable and fairly maneuverable, while the cross sections toward the ends may be nearly V-shaped to make it faster and give it some tracking quality.

Form. Boats that are sharply pointed will be faster and will tend to dive through waves. Boats with width carried through toward the ends will be slower and will tend to ride up more on waves. Delta-form kayaks are those with narrow pointed bows extending in fairly straight lines to the widest point (beam) behind the center of the boat, with a more obtuse stern angle resulting. These delta-form hulls are very fast, and they can also be propelled forward more efficiently, because the stroke can be taken closer to the keel line, so that more of its power goes into the direction of travel with less torque. Delta-form boats also tend to be somewhat less maneuverable and have less volume than kayaks that are more symmetrically shaped.

Volume. The volume of a boat is equal to the amount of water it would displace if it were pushed completely beneath the surface. Since the force of buoyancy is equal to the weight of that water less the weight of the boat and paddler, it stands to reason that a high-volume boat will float better in turbulent water: in turbulent water, the strong currents often throw the kayak this way and that, and the foaming white water has less density and therefore provides less flotation for the boat. High-volume boats, with their greater buoyancy, can carry a heavy paddler or large amounts of equipment better, both because of additional flotation and because they have more room inside. In heavy water they are far less likely to be swallowed by big waves and holes. Low-volume boats are more responsive because of their lighter weight and because of the handling characteristics associated with the sharp bend between the deck and the hull of most such designs; they are tricky for the beginner to handle, and large people usually find the space cramped. Their low decks are very useful to the experienced slalom racer, because they can be slipped under gates, but this particular feature has no practical utility for dealing with any natural water phenomena.

TYPES OF BOATS

Among boats designed for competition, the extremes are the *slalom*, *downriver*, and *flat-water* kayaks. A downriver boat is designed for maximum speed in the hands of an expert. It has to be strong and usable in difficult white water, but stability and maneuverability

A typical kayak design suitable for recreational white-water touring. This is an older, large-volume slalom boat with lots of room for carrying equipment and with a seat that can be removed for ease of packing. Some paddlers would prefer a little longer boat than the standard slalom length, while others might choose a model with a little better maneuvering performance.

are sacrificed to speed as much as possible. Similar considerations apply to flat-water racing shells, except that they do not even need to be strong, nor does the cockpit have to be sealed. Slalom boats are designed for maximum maneuverability with minimum effort, but with modern slalom designs, the lowest volume practical for the paddler and the course is normally used, and the deck is kept low to allow "sneaking" gates.

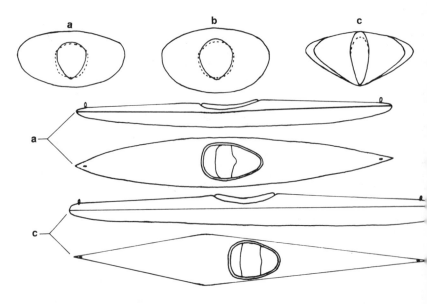

Some different kayak forms and cross sections. The cross sections at the top of the illustration show three kayaks viewed from in front of the bow.

a is a medium volume slalom design, and the outline of the widest section (which is at the center of the boat) is a flattened curve on the bottom and an even flatter curve on top. This boat will be relatively stable, though it will be a bit sensitive when leaned far over on its side, where the curve becomes sharper. The inner cross section shown by the solid line shows the shape near the bow, where a V shape has been introduced to give slightly better tracking and reduce resistance in forward paddling, while the dotted line shows a section near the stern, with a flattened curve to permit easy turning.

a in the drawings below shows the same kayak in side and top view. It has a lot of rocker for maneuverability, and tapers slowly toward the bow and stern.

b cross section shows a larger volume slalom boat than **a**. Because of its greater flotation it would ride higher in big water and would carry a larger load without becoming sluggish. Its outline would be similar to that of **a**, but with higher decks and with fullness carried a little farther forward and aft.

c shows the form of a downriver racing boat, very fast, very hard to turn, and very difficult to paddle effectively. The cross section shows both the midsection and the widest profiles. The wider section astern permits a narrower angle of entry, so that displaced water does not have to be accelerated as much, and keeps the boat from sinking so much into its own wake. Note the rockerless keel line and the V-shaped hull.

The compromises chosen by the paddler who is not primarily interested in racing will vary. Some good paddlers who paddle mainly either on day trips or on longer journeys with raft support, and whose main joy is playing the rapids, prefer modern, low-volume slalom designs. Larger paddlers, those who want more comfort, those who often carry camping gear in the boat, or those who paddle in heavy water, are likely to prefer a bigger-volume boat; but if they are nevertheless interested mainly in white-water performance, they may choose either a boat designed for heavy-water slalom courses or one of the older slalom designs, many of which are large-volume kayaks. In other words, they choose a design which is still very maneuverable and not very fast or directionally stable, but which has lots of buoyancy.

Those who are interested in general touring, both on rivers and lakes, and are willing to sacrifice some maneuverability in white water for a little more speed and easier paddling on long stretches of flat water, need a boat with less rocker and perhaps a little more pointed bottom than a slalom boat, but one which is also more stable and has more volume than a downriver racing boat. Such touring boats range from slight modifications of slalom boats to wide, stable craft that are not manageable in rapids at all. The designs most

A downriver kayak. Seen from this angle, the delta-form hull is apparent. It is narrow where the paddle stroke is taken, so that the force of paddling is exerted as close as possible to the V-shaped hull. This is a lightweight boat built for competition, not for durability. The dark bands visible are carbon-fiber reinforcement used to stiffen the lightweight deck and hull.

frequently chosen are something in between, a foot or two longer than the slalom boat, with less rocker, but still moderately maneuverable. In the hands of a good paddler with strong hanging strokes, such boats can negotiate some fairly difficult rapids, though they will not be very suitable for playing, compared with slalom boats. Some touring boats are made for two passengers.

There are all sorts of variations in design; this review should give the reader some idea of the considerations that go into making a boat. Actually putting together these factors and others into a good boat design requires a tremendous knowledge of kayak handling, imagination, technical skill, and a great deal of time and effort. Building a boat from an existing design is not too difficult, however.

HOW A BOAT IS CREATED

A designer creating a new boat that is to be made of fiber glass goes through a long series of steps before his conception can finally be made. The final *plug*, as a full-scale model is called, for a genuinely new boat is normally the result of a number of preliminary efforts that were cast much as the final boat will be, modified after trial, and used to make molds for plugs that were further refined. The first plug in the series may have been made of wood or it may have been a fiber glass boat of another design that was then changed beyond recognition. This final plug is often the result of thousands of hours of work. Once it is finished, the rest of the building process is simply a matter of mechanically reproducing boats in the shape of the plug. The real work has already been done, but it is the reproduction process with which we are mainly concerned.

Over the plug, the builder makes a mold, using techniques similar to those that will be described for building a boat, though more skill, knowledge, and care are needed to make a mold than to make a boat. The mold, like the boats that will be laid up in it, is made in two parts, so that a seam will be necessary between the top and bottom halves of the resulting kayaks. The mold is made with flanges on the edges of each of the two parts, so that the two halves of the boats made on it can be bolted together in perfect alignment. The inside of the mold, into which the outside of each copy will be laid, is finished so that it is glossy and smooth.

It is this mold that allows anyone with moderate skill and much patience to manufacture a kayak that has exactly the same shape as the plug that may have taken the designer years to create.

THE BASIC STEPS IN BUILDING A KAYAK

Before discussing boat building in more detail, it may be well to outline the necessary steps in order to give the novice an overview of what is involved.

1. Acquire the knowledge that will be needed to construct the kayak. This step may sound obvious, but it is by far the most important and the most commonly neglected.

2. Obtain all the materials that will be needed to build the kayak. This may involve some advance planning, particularly if some of the more exotic fabrics and resins are to be used.

3. Plan your building schedule, avoiding overoptimism, and line up the mold and shop to fit in with the schedule.

4. Get the mold and prepare it carefully for use.

5. Cut all the fabric pieces to be used, label them, and lay them out carefully.

6. Arrange everything that will be needed in the first session, so that you will not have to go hunting around while your hands are coated with resin and time is working against you. Good preparation is the novice boat builder's most effective weapon.

7. Mix all the ingredients you will need for your first session, premeasuring any resin components that may have to be mixed during the session.

8. Lay up the hull and the deck of the boat, working carefully. The novice should probably plan to do the hull in one session and the deck in another. Panic and impulses to do too much at a time are your greatest enemies. Above all, take care of the mold!

9. Bolt the two sides of the mold together, and seam the boat.

10. When the resin is cured, "pop" the boat from the mold.

11. Lay up the seat and coaming.

12. Clean and wax the mold, and return it.

13. Put the finishing touches on the kayak; this stage, together with seaming, will probably take as long as all the previous steps.

OBTAINING THE INFORMATION YOU NEED

Building a kayak is not exceptionally difficult, and it does not take any extraordinary amount of skill. It is messy, however, and it demands careful attention to detail, particularly if you contemplate using materials that are new to you or have tricky properties.

By far the best way to learn the techniques of boat building is to become an apprentice to an experienced person, helping with the construction of a boat he or she is making. Find out all you can in advance, and then ask as many questions as possible without making yourself obnoxious. Be helpful, without getting in the way, and respect the wishes and idiosyncrasies of your host—you may be helping with an odious job, but you are being done a favor.

If you have not been able to help someone build a boat, find out from the club, company, or individual from whom you are contemplating buying materials exactly what the directions for use are *before* you get anything. Take the directions home and read them several times, and make sure that you understand exactly every step you will go through. Unless you already know what you are doing, it is best not to try to buy from wholesale houses and manufacturers, who are not set up to deal with you. Retailers, clubs, and boat builders who sell materials on the side will be far more helpful to the novice. Be sure to tell them you are a beginner, and get the benefit of their advice and opinions. Try to learn from the mistakes of others, so that you will not have to learn from your own.

Pay attention to all the details in the directions for various systems. Temperatures are usually critical; one can do everything else correctly and ruin a boat by having the temperature too high or too low. This is one of several reasons to pay as much attention to the place where you will work as to all the other details of the project. Do not ignore safety precautions; the resins used in making fiber glass kayaks can be quite hazardous if they are treated casually. If you can't be bothered with such details, hire someone else to build your boat.

As with learning to paddle and roll, your best source of information is a local club. There will be many people in it who have had experience in building kayaks. Talk to as many of them as possible—you'll save a lot of time and trouble later on.

THE ADVANTAGES OF BUILDING YOUR OWN

It is worth mentioning at this point some of the advantages of putting your own boat together. The most obvious one, of course, is that you can save a good deal of money. The amount will depend on the type of kayak you make, your skill, sources of supply, and so on. At current prices, however, it is easy to save a couple of hundred dollars, and often you can do even better. For many kayakers, there is also a lot of satisfaction to be derived from paddling boats of their own manufacture.

Perhaps more interesting, however, is the fact that the home builder, even the beginner, can build a boat superior to those that are factory made. He can put in reinforcements and stiffeners that are too time-consuming for factories to bother with. He can use better materials if he chooses, making boats that are both lighter and stronger than those that are factory built. He can tailor the boat to his own needs perfectly. Perhaps most important, he can take the time and make the effort to do a really good job on every detail, knowing that he will be the one to paddle the finished craft.

There are many local small-production boat builders who are able to turn out really high-quality kayaks, but larger factories are at a distinct disadvantage. They must rely on machinery as much as possible, both because of high labor costs and because of the general unpleasantness of working with boat-building materials on a day-to-day basis. One day there will probably be methods of making by largely mechanical means boats that are stronger than those laid up mainly by hand, but that day has not yet arrived. Many other cost factors tend to induce large commercial boat builders to cut corners.

Finally, most of the really innovative ideas in boat building have come from amateur or small-scale builders—the long tradition of homemade kayaks in the United States has resulted in a lot of local expertise among paddlers around the country. Designing was dominated for years by European professionals, but those original boats that have been produced in America have come from amateurs and small builders.

MATERIALS

The basic "fiber glass" boat is made with a number of layers of mat or fabric composed of some synthetic material impregnated with a plastic resin. Many mats and fabrics are used, often in combination, and a large number of different resins have been tried in kayaks. New ones come along every year, so there would be no point here in attempting an exhaustive list. A few general points on materials will be mentioned, and then we will proceed to a general summary of some of the choices of construction that the builder has.

It is best to make most decisions on materials in terms of their suitability for boat manufacture, availability, ease of working, and so forth, rather than cost. Cost naturally enters into everyone's calculations, but considering the time and effort that you will put into making a boat, the cost of materials tends to be fairly low. There is no need for most beginners to obtain the latest and most expensive experimental fabrics and resins, but saving ten or twenty dollars by purchasing definitely inferior goods is usually false economy.

Cloth or *fabric* woven from long strands is superior to *mat* which is formed by compressing large numbers of short fibers. Cloth makes a boat that is both stronger and lighter. Cloths come in various widths, weaves, and weights. The most commonly used cloth in building kayaks is a standard fiber glass, or *E-glass*, of 10-ounce weight. This means that a square yard of the material will weigh approximately 10 ounces. (The weight of a *running yard* is different; this is the weight of the material per unit length as it comes off the roll, so it obviously depends on width.) A number of weights of E-glass are available, and the strength of the resulting boat depends largely on the weight of all the thicknesses of cloth used; thus, three layers of 10-ounce cloth would give a deck of the same strength as five layers of 6-ounce cloth—each would be a 30-ounce deck. One may be easier to lay up properly, but this problem will be discussed later. Since availability is often a major problem, this will enable the beginner to convert from instructions for one weight of cloth to the weight he has managed to find.

Several weaves of E-glass are available. A flat weave, which is fairly loose and in which the fibers are not twisted, is best for most purposes. Avoid satin weave and mat cloth.

Other cloths and combinations can be used. Suitable layups using more than one material are sometimes superior to those of uniform composition. Some of the popular layups use E-glass in combination with polypropylene or nylon cloth; advocates claim that the nylon or "poly" adds a good deal of strength to the laminate and does not weigh too much or absorb too much resin. Detractors feel that the synthetic cloths add only an undesirable type of strength, holding a boat together if an impact cracks the fiber glass, but not adding to its rigidity. This could allow a badly damaged kayak to fold around the paddler instead of breaking apart.

Two of the newer materials that are often used to make strong and lightweight kayaks are S-glass, a stronger and somewhat more brittle type of fiber glass, and Kevlar-49, a new synthetic material produced by Du Pont, which makes very strong, light, expensive boats. S-glass tends to absorb a lot of resin, so it should be used by builders who employ a vacuum-bag process or who are very careful to squeeze out all extra resin (see below). Kevlar is rather flexible and is best used in combination with fiber glass. For a strong and durable beginner's boat, the total layup in the hull should be 40 to 50 ounces and that in the deck, 30 to 40 ounces. With Kevlar boats less cloth needs to be used.

RESIN SYSTEMS

The other half of the laminate is the plastic resin system that the fiber glass or other fibrous material reinforces. The two main classifications for resin systems used in making fiber glass boats are polyesters and epoxies.

Polyester resin systems are the most commonly used for building kayaks. Nearly all commercially made boats, except for a few very expensive custom layups, are made with polyesters. They are cheaper than epoxies, are easier to work with for several reasons, are less toxic than most epoxies, will cure to final hardness more quickly than most epoxies at room temperature, and are generally more idiot-proof.

Epoxies, when properly chosen, are stronger and tougher than polyesters, produce better bonding between the fabric layers of the boat, and will not deform under moderate heat. (Many a polyester boat has acquired interesting but undesirable corrugations from a car roof heated by the sun or a heat lamp being used to keep the boat warm while it was being built.) Though they do not smell as bad as polyesters, many epoxies are highly toxic. Some require accurate measuring by weight, so a scale must be available. In general they are trickier to use than polyesters, but when they are used well, they make better boats.

Whatever resin system is used, it must be strong enough to make a good kayak. It must be compatible with the materials and finishes used. (Cloths may be "finished" with various treatments to make them bond with particular resins.) The resin system must be thin enough so that the cloth can be thoroughly wetted, but it must have enough cohesion when spread to stay on the cloth on the sides of the mold, rather than running down and pooling at the bottom. (A system that will do this is called *thixotropic;* an additive that gives the system this quality is a *thixotrope.*) The system must be workable at the temperatures you will use it in, and it must harden fast enough, but not too fast, at appropriate temperatures.

Thus, an epoxy system that requires heat curing to harden in a reasonable time and to develop adequate strength will not be suitable unless you have some method of effecting the cure. It would not be workable if you were using polypropylene or nylon cloth that had not been previously heat-treated, because the curing would shrink the cloth, and the boat would delaminate. Such examples could be multiplied indefinitely. This is why it is recommended that beginners either buy their materials from someone who can and will give detailed information on their use for boat building, or that they purchase them in conjunction with an experienced person. Proven combinations for which one can obtain specific instruction and information are best for the beginner.

In summary, you will need to find out several things about any resin system you are contemplating for use in building a boat. Make sure that it has been used in a number of kayaks, so that its suitability and the methods of working it are well known. Temperature characteristics are important. At what stages, if any, will it have to be heat-cured? What safety precautions and measuring devices will be required? Does it need additives for the construction method you are using, such as thixotropes? Is the curing time long enough to be suitable for a beginner, and is it compatible with the finish on the cloth you are obtaining? What are the directions for use?

BOAT-BUILDING METHODS

The best technique for the home builder of kayaks is the *vacuum-bag* method. It requires a mold that is specifically designed for vacuum bagging, since fittings must be attached for the vacuum to be applied and for excess resin to be drained. In vacuum bagging, all the cloth to be used is laid in the mold, the resin is poured in, a film of polyvinyl alcohol is laid over this, with a bleeding system for extra resin around the edge of the mold, and then sealed, suction is applied at the edges, and the resin is worked into the cloth through the film, using squeegees of Teflon or some other material. Vacuum is applied continuously while the resin cures. The vacuum aids the builder in achieving maximum strength with minimum weight. If you can find a vacuum mold, this is the best method to use, and the owner of the mold will be able to give you more details. Since vacuum molds are not generally available, however, the technique will not be described further here.

Hand layup, the most common boat-building method, uses the technique of laying each layer of cloth in the mold, one at a time, saturating it with resin, and working out the extra resin by squeegeeing.

Preparing the mold is the first step in actually building a kayak. Exact instructions should be obtained from the mold owner, so that preparation materials are not used that react badly with one another. A mold in very bad condition may have to have bad spots sanded with progressively finer wet paper down to 600 grit. Never sand without permission from the mold owner and never use power tools inside the mold. Mold restorative compound is then used on the mold, several times if it is not in perfect condition. Paraffin may be used to fill in nicks for one-time use. The mold should then be waxed several times, as is being done in this photo. Use thin coats, and buff very lightly. This is a deck mold with provision for vacuum bagging, being prepared by Bill Clark, who developed the vacuum-bagging technique for building kayaks.

Polishing a hull mold. The final surface must be perfectly smooth, with no unwaxed spots, so that the boat can be released at the end of the process. The remains of the old vacuum bag on this hull are left on the vacuum sealing material until the new material is put on.

Cutting the material from a plastic pattern to fit the mold. This is fiber glass material, and it should be kept scrupulously clean. If a pattern is available beforehand, the pieces can be cut and rolled in newspaper in advance. Label them and roll them with the bow ends out. If no pattern is provided, make one before waxing the mold. In this photo, pieces are being cut in an overlapping pattern to save cloth. The half pieces are cut to overlap 4–6″ down the centerline. It is advantageous to have such overlaps in the deck, to give it more rigidity.

For vacuum-bag molds, a strip of vacuum sealant is now stuck along the outside edge of the flange in a continuous strip. If an old strip of sealant is in place and in good condition, the old bag material can be pulled off, and the sealant can be used again.

Whatever process is being used, the mold is now coated with a thin coat of PVA (polyvinyl alcohol), to aid release of the boat. A foam brush is a good tool for applying it. Allow it to dry, and then protect the mold from any dirt or wetting.

For vacuum molds only a few strips of PVA are removed with strips of masking tape after it has dried, pieces of vacuum sealant are put on these spots, and a bleeder of polyvinyl chloride tubing is attached along the edge. The tubing is prepared in advance by cutting halfway through with a saw at 2″ intervals along the inside. A vacuum hole is visible near the builder's fingers.

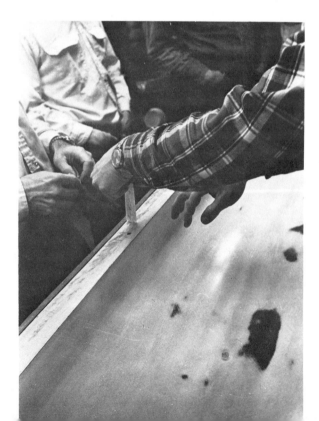

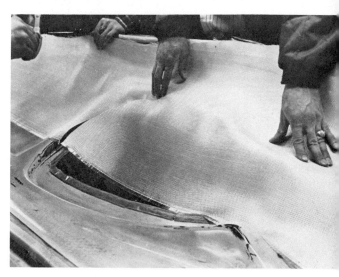

The cloth is now laid carefully in the mold. In a hand layup, it is best to paint the mold with resin before putting the first layer of cloth in. At any rate, only one layer is put in at a time, and this is saturated with resin, before the next layer is dropped in. With a vacuum mold, all layers are put in at once. This is a deck mold, and the section around the cockpit is being cut out.

Here the glass is laid completely in the mold. This is a vacuum mold, and a vacuum bleeder made with rolled burlap cloth is laid around the inside of the coaming. In a mold for hand layup, the cockpit area would be open. Vacuum sealant has also been stuck around inside the bleeder. The vacuum system should be checked for operation and leaks before mixing the resin.

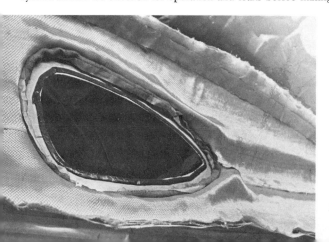

The components of the resin system should be carefully measured out according to the instructions. Here an epoxy system is being weighed. Be careful to observe safety precautions. *Resin systems are dangerous!* Wear a mask, be sure the working area is ventilated, and use gloves for handling resin. Work neatly. For hand layups, measure out a number of batches to be mixed as they are used. In a vacuum system, the exact amount of resin is weighed out in advance, according to instructions from the mold owner. Do not put extra resin in a vacuum mold, since it may fill the trap jars, boil over from heat concentration, and plug the vacuum system.

The resin system is now poured onto the cloth. For a hand layup, pour in a little at a time and work it outward with paint brushes, rollers, and squeegees. In a vacuum system, all the resin is poured in, concentrating on the end and the coaming areas, and balancing the amount of resin in each end.

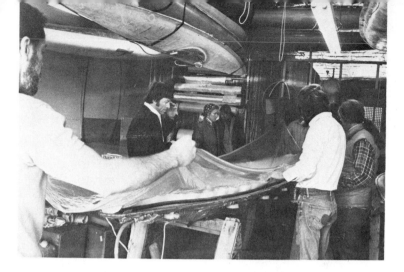

For vacuum molds, the vacuum bag, made of polyvinyl alcohol, is now dropped over the mold, pushed down to make sure no tight spots will develop, and sealed around the edge. The vacuum is turned on, and all leaks around the edge are sealed. Depending on the system and the mold, heaters on the mold but not the flange may be turned on.

Working the vacuum bag into all parts of the mold before sealing, to make sure it will not be too tight.

It is particularly important in either vacuum or hand layup to be sure that the cloth at the ends of the boat is saturated with resin and conforming to the mold. The ends are the most likely places for air bubbles to be trapped. Work the ends carefully with squeegees, and in vacuum molding, be sure to work enough resin down to the ends to saturate them properly.

OPPOSITE, TOP

Squeegeeing resin up to the edge of the hull. In both the hand layup and vacuum methods, the object is to completely saturate the cloth, beginning from the center, rolling out all air bubbles. Take care to work slowly from the middle, saturating a little cloth at a time, allowing the resin to soak up through the cloth, rather than pushing it over dry cloth and trapping air under the resin. If you squeegee resin rapidly into dry areas, the trapped air bubbles are sealed from the action of the vacuum or from escaping through the cloth in a hand layup, and they are difficult to remove. Squeegee slowly and thoroughly to assist the soaking and the vacuum and to work out excess resin and trapped air. Going too fast will simply trap more. The best squeegees are Teflon. Satisfactory ones are plasticators used for auto body work. In squeegeeing on a vacuum bag, great care must be taken not to puncture the bag. Leaks must be immediately sealed with Scotch tape. For hand layups, cheap paint brushes work well. For the main body, 2½ or 3 inches wide is about right, and for details, 1- or 1½-inch ones are best. Avoid those with nylon bristles, which will dissolve in resin.

An epoxy boat part being cured with heat under a blanket. Note the mold above with heat tapes attached. The resin has gelled when it begins to thicken and become leathery. It is not cured until it is too hard to dent with a fingernail. If some layers are allowed to cure before a part is finished, the surface must be sanded before more layers are added to avoid delamination. It is thus better to lay a whole part up in one session and to mix the resin so that it does not cure too quickly. With polyester and vinyl ester sytems, edges can be trimmed when the part has gelled. With epoxy and polyester parts, a saber saw must be used; this has to be done after the parts are removed from the mold.

With a vacuum mold the parts must be cured, removed from the mold, trimmed, and taped together with masking tape for seaming. Contact molds normally have provisions for bolting the deck and hull together to allow seaming in the mold. Provided that the parts have been trimmed before curing, the boat can be seamed before popping—removing the parts from the mold. If they have cured, trimming is best done with a saber saw, and this must be done out of the mold to avoid damaging it. Don't try to pop the parts before they are completely cured or you will ruin them. At normal temperatures (with heat for epoxy) this will take at least overnight.

For the seams you will need either 2-inch fiber glass tape made for the purpose, or you will have to cut strips from the material. The latter method is cheaper but much trickier, because rovings tend to pull out from the edges and catch everything up in a mass of resin and glass. You will need two layers of 10-ounce strips for each side, each layer 14 feet long, or the equivalent. Lay out wax paper and tape it down for saturating the layers of tape. The mold or the boat should be hung or propped on one side so that you can work through the cockpit hole on the seam at the lower side. The parts of the boat that are to be seamed must be roughened with sandpaper to get a bond.

Saturate the strips for one side and roll them up. These are then placed in the boat and carefully pushed toward the ends as they unroll, using a brush taped to the end of a stick. I like to paint the parts of the boat to be seamed with resin first. Carefully work all the bubbles out of the tape. Be sure to wear a mask at this stage, and cover your hair. Seaming is messy, and the fumes inside the boat are nasty. Allow the first seam to cure, then turn the mold over and do the other side. When both sides are cured, the boat can be popped by pulling the two halves of the mold apart. Work on a small section at a time. Use wooden wedges if any are needed. Never pry at the mold with metal tools. Patience will do the job if you have waxed and PVA-ed the mold well.

Drill holes for grab loops, insert them, tape around the outside of the ends with masking tape, and prop the boat straight up in the air on one end. The lower end is filled with enough resin to cover the grab loop. To save weight, phenolic microballoons can be added to the end pour. Otherwise, fill it with chopped glass cloth. Let the first end cure, and then do the other. A hot resin mixture (one with a lot of catalyst added) can be used because there is no harm in a fast cure.

Most seat molds are for hanging seats, including the coaming as well. They are laid up using standard contact methods with scraps from the rest of the boat. Make the seat sturdy, using perhaps a 40-ounce thickness with additional reinforcements around the coaming and edges. After the seat is popped, the mating edges on the boat and coaming are sanded rough and glassed together with resin and glass scraps. Scraps of ethafoam should be glued under the seat and on both sides with resin to brace it against movement.

Foot braces are normally glassed in, the parts sanded first to ensure a good bond. The braces can be commercially made adjustable ones or fixed fiber glass ones. My own preference is to put a styrofoam beam in the front end of the boat, slot another piece of styrofoam crossways to mate with the beam, and fit a styrofoam bulkhead in the boat braced against the beam and crosspiece. This bulkhead, fitted tightly, serves as both flotation and foot brace. The bulkhead has to be a perfect cross section of the boat, and a good deal of time is required to make cardboard patterns for the styrofoam pieces. With a similar arrangement in the stern, however, the decks are supported by the beams so that they are extremely strong, and no flotation bags are required.

10
Making Kayaking Accessories

Most of the equipment used in kayaking can be made at home without too much difficulty, either to save money or improve quality. Paddles are about the only item of equipment that cannot be made fairly easily to perform better than commercially available substitutes. Sophisticated molding techniques or good craftsmanship with wood are needed to make really good paddles.

Plans are included in this chapter for a few common items of equipment: spray skirts, wet suits, and storage-flotation bags. The directions and accompanying drawings should be studied before you get materials.

Obtaining those materials is often the main obstacle when making these or other items of equipment. Obtaining materials is often most easily done by a club, which can pool effort and buying power, particularly with material like neoprene foam, the cost of which varies incredibly with the source. A little determination should allow the individual to find all of the necessary goods in any large metropolitan area, however.

A finished accessory bag with tabs and grommets for tying to the boat. This one is sealed with the snapping PVC tubing system.

MAKING A SPRAY SKIRT

Materials needed

neoprene wet suit material, nylon backed, ⅛″ thick, about 1 yard in 36″ or 40″ widths

neoprene glue, obtainable from the same sources as wet suit material

shock cord, rubber surgical tubing, or a heavy rubber gasket 10″ or 12″ in diameter, to hold the skirt tight around the coaming

nylon webbing, 1″ wide and 12″ long

scissors, nylon or polyester string, scrap posterboard material, marker that will write visibly on the neoprene material

Directions

The spray skirt can be constructed directly on the coaming of the boat it is to fit, but ideally it should be left stretched out for a week or so during manufacture. For this reason, many makers cut a piece of wood ¾″ to 1″ thick to the shape of the cockpit rim and groove the edge for making spray

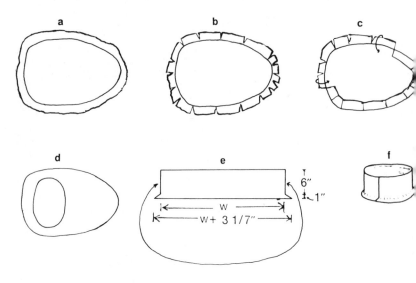

skirts. Long stretching and curing makes for a stronger skirt and better fit, but is not necessary if time is a factor.

The elastic material should first be made into a loop that stretches tightly around the coaming, but can be stretched over it without so much effort that it will be difficult to put the skirt on. Gaskets make excellent elastics, with the 10″ ones providing a tight fit on small coamings and the 12″ a looser fit on small rims and a snug one on large cockpits. If surgical tubing (available from drug stores) or shock cord is used, fit for the correct length first, overlap the ends an inch or two, and wrap the joint tightly with synthetic string or twine, securing the ends of the string well.

Now, take the wet suit material and fasten it nylon-side down over the coaming or wooden form with the elastic, arranging it so that there is a margin of 2″ extending out on all sides and so that there will be a minimum waste of material when the rest is cut off. Mark out the 2″ margin, and cut off the remaining material. The result is shown in a, a piece of neoprene rubber stretched over the coaming, secured with the elastic, with a flap of extra material extending all the way around the edge.

Cut a series of notches into the flap all the way around, so that it can be folded over without overlapping, as shown in b. Take care not to cut in all the way to the elastic; this should be completely covered after the flap has been folded over.

Coat the flap and the area it will cover with glue, including the insides of the cut notches. Allow this to dry until it is tacky. The glue is a contact-type cement; the surfaces should not be brought together until the solvent is well evaporated, and when they are pushed together they will stick immediately, so it is important to align each section carefully before allowing the coated surfaces to come into contact with one another.

Fold each section of the flap over as shown in **c.** Good fitting will ensure a leak-proof seal, but a few gaps between the flaps are of no consequence. Allow the skirt to dry in this position for 24 hours, then turn it over and leave it stretched on the coaming with the nylon side up for a week, if the time can be spared.

Measure the waist circumference of the person to wear the skirt; this is dimension w in the drawing. Cut out a strip of posterboard or other flexible material of length w and lay out an oval on the stretched skirt as shown in **d.** The oval should approximate the shape of the waist, and the rear should be directly over the back of the seat in the kayak. Cut out the oval.

From the remaining neoprene material cut out the piece shown in **e;** it will be used to form the waist tunnel. Apply glue liberally to the edges on each end of the piece. When the glue has dried, bring the two ends together so that a tube with a flange on the bottom is formed, as shown in **f.** The flange should stick out at a right angle from the bottom of the tube. This is most easily done by using a table when gluing the ends together; with the wider 1″ section on the table, bend the rest of the piece straight up, and then form a cylinder, bringing the edges of the flange together on the table first, and then joining the rest of the cylinder. Remember that once the glue has dried it will stick on contact. Mistakes at this point or any other can be corrected by cutting the material apart with scissors or a razor blade and regluing.

Orient the tunnel so that the nylon-backed side is out. Coat the top of the flange and the corner where it meets the main tube with glue. Do the same with a 1″-wide strip around the oval cut-out on the skirt on the under-side. This may require removing the skirt from the coaming or wood frame and turning it over. Allow the glue on both pieces to dry. Now glue the tunnel into the skirt to form the nearly complete piece shown in **g.** The best way to do this depends on the way one is working. If the skirt is stretched on the

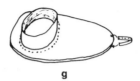

g

coaming, turn it back over if necessary, so that the nylon side is up and the glue side down. Bunch up the tube a little so that the flange can be slipped through, taking care not to let the glued section fold over and stick to itself. Press up one section at a time to glue the flange to the under-side of the skirt all the way around. After tacking all the way around, press the pieces together well to ensure complete contact. Dust any remaining exposed glue with talcum powder.

Sew the nylon webbing to the front edge of the skirt well with heavy polyester thread so that when it is yanked the pull will come on the elastic, not on the neoprene. Let the glued parts cure at least 24 hours before using the skirt. Full strength is not reached for a week or so. With nylon-backed material, the seams, particularly the one up the tube, can be sewn for reinforcement if desired, but this is not essential.

MAKING A WET SUIT

NOTE: The patterns and directions given here are my own, but they have been developed from instructions in an article by Peter Whitney and Frank Cockerline in the February, 1960, issue of *American Whitewater*, abstracted in an information sheet distributed by the National Speleological Society. Thanks to all.

These instructions are for a two-piece suit, consisting of a long-sleeved shirt and a "Farmer John" bottom, an overall-like set of pants coming up over the trunk. If both pieces are made of ⅛" material, then worn together they are ¼" thick around the vital areas of the abdomen and chest. In milder weather, either can be worn separately. Short-sleeved shirts, regular pants, or shorts can be made easily by selecting the appropriate sections of the patterns.

Materials needed

neoprene wet suit material, preferably nylon-backed, ⅛" or ³/₁₆" thick; most commonly sold in 10' x 40" sheets, one of which is more than enough for a wet suit

neoprene cement, 8 oz., and brush

zipper(s): one heavy-duty 12" nylon nonseparating zipper, one separating zipper for front of shirt, if desired, ordered to measure, four 6" heavy-duty nylon nonseparat-

ing zippers for ankles and wrists, if desired

roll of heavy brown wrapping paper for patterns

marking pens to mark on skin and on the neoprene material

heavy polyester thread and needles

measuring tape, scissors, razor blades, talcum powder, masking tape

Directions

1. With the measuring tape and a marking pen, mark the body of the person for whom the suit is being made at 2" intervals as shown in **a**, beginning with a circumference directly under the armpits. Normally, only one leg and one arm need to be marked. Measure and record the circumference of each line. Measure and record distance *a*, the distance from the line just under the armpits to the top of the shoulder.

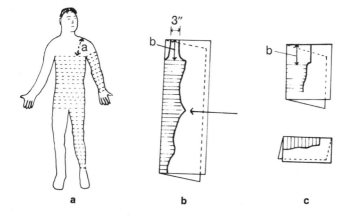

a   **b**   **c**

2. Cut a piece of the wrapping paper for the Farmer John bottom pattern. The length should be the sum of the 2″ intervals between the armpit and the ankle, plus dimension b. b is equal to dimension a, shown in drawing **a**, plus 1″. That is, b is an inch longer than the distance from the armpit line to the top of the shoulder.

Fold the paper in half lengthwise, and draw parallel lines 2″ apart on one side, starting from the bottom with the fold on the left, marking the same number of intervals as on the body. Beginning at the bottom of the pattern, measure out from the fold one-half of the leg circumference for each corresponding line, beginning with the ankle measurement at the bottom of the pattern and marking each line up to the one at the crotch. Be accurate. Above the crotch measure out one-quarter of the body circumference at each line. Draw in the curve between the measured dots as shown in **b**. At the crotch line, shown by the arrow, extend the curves to meet at a right angle. Do not round it off. At the top, mark off the 3″ top edge of the shoulder strap, as shown in drawing **b**, beginning 1½″ left of the armpit measurement. Connect the top of the strap with smooth curves, as shown in **b**.

When this curve is cut out and unfolded it will form the completed pattern, but first a minor correction has to be made in the crotch area, as shown in **d**. The actual curve of the final pattern must follow the dotted lines in the drawing, deviating from the original curve shown with a solid line. To make the correction measure 8″ along the curve from the point. Mark one arc inside the original curve, swinging ¾″ from it, and one arc outside the original curve, also swinging to a maximum of ¾″ away. With

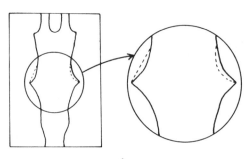

d

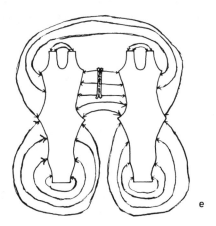

the pattern still folded, cut along the entire curve, following the outside arc above the crotch. Unfold the pattern, and cut the marked side along the inside arc. The right-hand side, with the more acute angle, will be at the front of the suit, while the left side, with the more obtuse angle, will be at the rear.

3. Lay the pattern out on the neoprene material. (It may be advantageous to cut the shirt pattern and any other items to be made before proceeding with this step, to allow fitting with minimum waste. Wet suit material is expensive.) Trace the pattern with a marking pen, turn it over, and do a second tracing with the other side of the pattern up. This will result in two mirror-image pieces which together will form the complete Farmer John bottom. Double check everything before cutting the neoprene. The two pieces should look like those shown in **e**.

4. The two pieces of the Farmer John bottom go together as shown in **e**. The suit will wear better if the nylon side is out, but most people will prefer to have the nylon facing in for ease in getting the wet suit on and off. Lay out the pieces as shown in **e** with the outside of the suit up on a floor or table covered with clean newspaper. Mark out the length of the zipper on the front edge of each piece; this will not be glued yet. If leg zippers are to be installed, do the same at the bottom of each side of each leg, where they will go. The pieces should now be glued together by coating two edges that

will mate, allowing them to dry, brushing on a second coat of cement, replacing the paper underneath with a clean sheet, and bringing the edges together. Do one section at a time.

Any order can be followed, but a good one is to glue the front torso section below where the zipper will be installed, then the back, then the inside of each leg, and finally the tops of the straps. Care should be taken to fit each of the corners that come together at the crotch correctly, since this is the trickiest spot.

To install the zipper, put a thin strip of masking tape over the teeth in the front, coat the cloth on each side with four layers of cement, allowing each layer to dry before applying the next, and apply three layers of cement to the strip on the inside of the suit along each side of the zipper opening. Press the zipper tape (the cloth on each side) onto each edge in turn. Allow the glue to cure 24 hours, and then sew the tape to the neoprene along each side, reinforcing the stitching at the bottom and top. Cut a 3″-wide strip of neoprene material 1″ longer than the zipper, and glue one edge of it along one side of the zipper on the inside of the suit, rubber side toward the zipper, to keep cold water from entering and to keep the zipper from chafing against the skin. If leg zippers are to be used, they are installed the same way.

The completed Farmer John is shown in **f.** Dust any exposed glue spots with talcum powder, so that they cannot stick to other parts of the suit, and allow all cemented seams to cure at least 24 hours before stressing them.

5. Measurements for the wet suit top are the same ones taken for the Farmer John bottom, with the addition of the arm circumferences. The measurements from the armpit to the waist are transferred to a folded pattern, as shown in **c,** beginning distance *b* (armpit line to top of shoulder, plus 1″) below the top, and measuring out from the fold one-quarter of the body circumference. The top can be made to come down as far as desired, but there is not much point in bringing it much below the top of the hip bones unless a crotch piece is added to prevent the bottom from riding up.

When the final curve is drawn to connect the points on the pattern, a curve should be drawn as shown in the detail in **g** to extend the pattern a little outside of the armpit measurement, forming the beginning of a sleeve 1½″ out, and allowing a little extra room around the armpit. Measure over 3″ from the fold at the top to allow for the neck hole and make a mark.

Make a sleeve pattern, as shown in the lower pattern in **c,** measuring

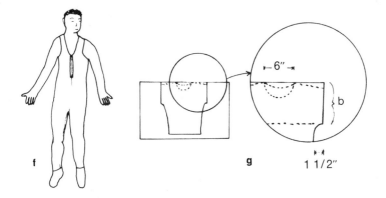

one-half of the arm circumference from the fold along each line. Cut this pattern out. The first measurement around the arm from the armpit should also be transferred to the pattern for the body of the jacket or shirt. From the armpit curve, measure up toward the top of the pattern one-half of the arm circumference. Connect this point with the point at the side of the neck hole already marked, as shown in the diagonal dotted lines in **g.** Cut the main pattern out, except for the neck hole.

6. Lay out the body and sleeve patterns on the neoprene material, trace them carefully, and cut two pieces from each pattern. Mark the arcs for the neck hole on the main pieces, as shown in **g.** The shallow one, for the back piece, should be 1″ deep, and the deeper one, for the front, should be a semicircle 3″ deep. Cut these out. For the collar, cut out a semicircle of 12″ diameter.

7. Glue the pieces together as for the Farmer John bottom, one seam at a time. Cement the lengthwise seams in the arms first, then put the sides and shoulders of the two body pieces together. Putting the arms on the main piece is tricky, and using round objects like jars inside the two pieces being fitted together helps. It is of no consequence where the lengthwise seam on the arm joins the main suit. Cement the circumference of the neck piece inside the neck hole, starting with the center of the curve at the middle of the back of the hole, leaving a 1″ space at the front. The extra material in the neck piece should be trimmed to fit tightly and comfortably around the neck after the seams have cured so that the suit can be worn.

8. If zippers are used in the top, they are best installed after the seams are glued. Short zippers can be put in the arms, and either a half-length or a full-length zipper can be put in the front, running down from the neck. Install these just as with the zippers in the Farmer John bottom, except that it is easiest to glue and sew the zipper on first and cut the material in front of it after installation, eliminating the need to align the two sides.

9. Corrections of mistakes and final fitting are quite simple when working with neoprene, since the material can be cut with scissors or a razor blade, pieces can be inserted or removed, and gluing gives a strong bond.

MAKING STORAGE-FLOTATION BAGS

Materials needed

4 yards vinyl-coated nylon or polyester material, 6–10 oz., 54" wide, or the equivalent in a different width, obtainable from tent and awning companies. Quality varies with the manufacturer, so try abrading a sample scrap; good material should be very tough

4 oz. good quality vinyl cement

3½ feet Velcro tape, 1" width. Velcro consists of two strips of backing, one covered with tiny hooks and the other with a mat, which stick together when they come into contact with each other

6 feet vinyl tubing, $^7/_{16}$" outside diameter

2 right-angle vinyl joints, $^7/_{16}$" inside diameter, flanged on one end, as shown in drawing d. These and the tubing can be obtained from some plastics supply houses. The valves listed below may be available from the same source

2 air valves, $^7/_{16}$" inside diameter, like the one shown in e. If these cannot be found, a standard hose clamp, available from chemical supply houses, can be used

scissors, talcum powder

Directions

1. Measure the kayak to obtain the dimensions for the bags. Measure along the seam of the boat between the points the bag is to reach and add 4" for the edge dimension. This would normally be from the back of the seat to

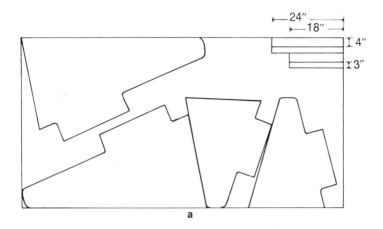

a

a little forward of the end plug for the rear bag and from the foot braces to just behind the bow end plug for the front bag. Measure over the deck from seam to seam and add 4″ for each of the cross dimensions of the bags.

2. Lay out the pieces on the material as shown in **a**, measuring carefully. Dimensions will vary somewhat from boat to boat, but the stern bag will be about five feet long and two and a half feet wide at the wide end, while the bow bag will be about three feet long and two feet wide. The flaps shown in the pattern are for the bag opening; they should project 6″. The one on the stern bag should be two feet long and the one on the bow bag one and one half feet long.

Be sure that the two pieces for each bag match each other, so that they will be easy to piece together. The rectangles laid out in the upper right-hand corner are for the sealing flaps.

3. Cut out the pieces. Mark out a 1½″ margin along the sides shaded in **b** on one surface of a bow piece and the opposite surface of the other bow piece. Do the same with the stern pieces. Cement the margins together a few feet at a time, spreading the glue on each side first, allowing it to dry until tacky, and then pressing the two pieces together. Don't apply too much glue, or the solvent will attack the vinyl coating. Dust any drips with talcum powder. At the end of this step, both bags will be glued together all around the margins, except for the flap openings with joints like the one shown on the left in drawing **c**.

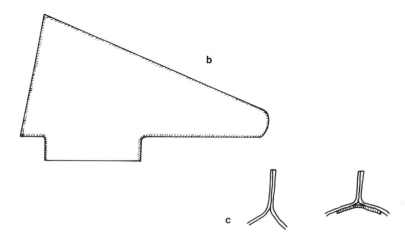

For bags that will not be subjected to pressure under hot sun, these seams should be adequate, especially since the bags are built a little over-size, so they tend to push out against the side of the boat instead of against the seams. In hot sun, however, vinyl cement will creep under stress, so if stronger seams are desired, 1"-wide strips of material can be cut from the scraps and glued around the inside of the bag as shown in the drawing on the right in **c.** This is tedious but not difficult. For a compromise, one can simply reinforce the end seams in this way, since the side seams are held by the boat.

4. Cut out four scraps approximately 3" square, and cut holes in the center of each just large enough for the tubes of the right-angle vinyl joints to fit through. Coat both sides of the flanges of the joints and one side of each of the scraps with cement, and allow them to dry until tacky. Form two sandwiches as shown in **d,** with the flanges sandwiched between the scraps, and the elbow sticking out.

Cut a hole just big enough for the tube of a right-angle joint in one side of each float bag, about a foot back from the wide end of the bag. Coat the top of each sandwich and the corresponding section inside the bag with cement, and allow it to dry until tacky. Stick the tubes through the bags from the in-side, and glue the sandwiches on, so that the tubes point toward the wide ends of the bags.

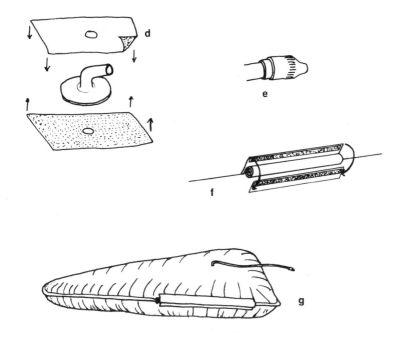

Dust any exposed cement with talcum powder.

Glue a three-foot section of tubing into the elbow of each joint and glue the valves at the ends of the tubes. These will look like the tube shown in **e** and are used to fill the bags with air after they are in the kayak.

5. Glue and sew a strip of hook Velcro along one edge of each of the wide rectangular sealing flaps and a strip of mat Velcro along each of the narrow flaps. Glue the remaining 2" of each of the narrow flaps on the appropriate bag parallel to the tunnel opening, so that the Velcro mat faces out and runs just below the tunnel. Glue the wide flaps on the other side of the tunnels so that they will hold very tight when the tunnels are rolled up, as shown in **f**.

6. The bags are completed, as shown in **g**. Fill them with air and check for leaks. Small leaks can be located with soapy water. A few folds around the seams are likely to leak, and they simply have to be glued closed. Scraps and cement should be saved for patching.

Glossary

BAR—A deposit of sand or gravel in a riverbed where the current slows down and can thus not carry as much material. Bars often block part of a river channel or form a shallow spot. Bars are common where the river widens and gradient is reduced, on the inside of bends on the downstream side, and behind obstructions where the current is relatively slow. In some rivers bars shift rapidly.

BIG WATER—Refers to a large volume of water flowing in a river and the hydraulic phenomena associated with it. Fast-moving and powerful flowing water.

BOULDER GARDEN—A section of a river where the channel is obstructed with many rocks, so that a lot of maneuvering is required to negotiate the rapid formed.

BRACE—The use of the paddle to lean against the water with the boat out of balance. A very important technique in kayaking. The term is used both as a noun and a verb. A *low brace* is one in which the paddle is held in front of the torso, and a *high brace* one in which the paddle is in front of the face or over the head.

CARRY—A **portage** (see below).

CHINE—The joint between the bottom of the boat and its side in those types of boat construction where the two are separate units. There is no true chine in a fiber glass kayak, but the term is often used to denote the part of the hull that curves up toward the vertical.

CHUTE—A steep channel, usually unobstructed, where water flows rapidly through a narrow passage.

COAMING—The concave piece fastened around the edge of the cockpit of a kayak to lend rigidity and to permit a spray skirt to be attached to the boat.

COCKPIT—The opening in the deck of a kayak in which the paddler sits.

DECK—In boats generally, any horizontal surface running between the sides, preventing the entry of water and often bearing weight. In kayaks the deck covers the top of the boat and allows it to plunge into waves or capsize without shipping water. The deck is generally curved and lends structural support to the boat, but it is not designed to support a great deal of weight. In fiber glass kayaks, the deck may refer to the whole top half of the boat above the seam.

DOWNRIVER KAYAK—A kayak designed specifically to give a competitor maximum advantage in a downriver race—a highly specialized boat. Such craft are generally very narrow throughout, reaching their maximum width (a minimum specified by racing rules) behind the cockpit. They are long and tend to have V-shaped hulls, and they are designed to allow maximum speed with only the amount of durability and maneuverability required by the course. Downriver kayaks are generally agreed to be experts' boats, of little use for any other purpose than that intended, and difficult for beginners and intermediates to paddle at all.

DROP—A place where a river makes a rapid descent between two more level sections.

EDDY—A place where the water moves in the opposite direction from the main current. Eddies form where a river suddenly widens, around bends, downstream of obstructions, and in similar situations. The term is used mainly to refer to a reversal of direction in the horizontal plane, though one may refer to vertical eddies, and real eddies often involve complicated mixtures of horizontal and vertical water movement. Eddies form resting spots where the kayaker can pull in to catch his breath and look over the river below, but the violent changes in the direction of current that they involve are major obstacles for the beginner to master and in some circumstances may challenge experienced boaters.

EDDYLINE—The boundary at the edge of an eddy between the main current and the eddy current, often turbulent and always tricky. The techniques for crossing eddylines are the most important skills that the paddler has to learn in order to boat in white water.

EDDY TURN—A method for turning into an eddy or back out into the main current by leaning into the turn and bracing on a paddle blade inserted in the current being entered.

ENDER (ENDO, END OVER END)—A maneuver (or accident) in which the kayak turns upside down lengthwise instead of sideways in a situation where the bow or stern is driven down into deep water traveling rapidly with respect to the surface of the wave on which the rest of the boat is riding. Enders occur most often on ocean surf, on the back sides of large standing waves in rivers, and in holes. May also refer to a **pop-up** (see below).

FALLS—A drop where water falls very steeply over rocks. Falls may be runnable in kayaks or not, depending on their height and characteristics.

Large falls are obviously very dangerous if they are approached unawares.

FOLDBOAT—A kayak constructed with a rigid frame that can be disassembled and which fits inside a fabric skin. Most foldboats are made in Europe, though there is also a manufacturer in the United States. In the past some excellent slalom designs were constructed, but fiber glass is so much better for this purpose that nearly all modern foldboats are made for touring on relatively easy water. Some are made for two paddlers.

GRAB LOOP—A loop of rope attached to the bow or stern (there are usually two on a boat) to provide a grip for a rescuer, a swimmer, or a kayaker landing or portaging the boat.

GUNWALE (GUNNEL)—The upper edge of the side of a boat. In fiber glass kayaks, the place where the side curves back most sharply to form the deck.

HAYSTACK—A large **standing wave** (see below), so called because its steep sides topped with spray resemble a haystack.

HEAVY WATER—A term denoting moving water exhibiting hydraulic phenomena resulting from very fast and powerful currents. Typical heavy-water formations are large whirlpools that appear and move either through a whole canyon or along eddylines, white eddies, eddylines that are very turbulent, with water sliding over the top of the eddy from the main current, and very large and dangerous holes. Heavy water is an imprecise term and may be used loosely to refer to rapids that are difficult or frightening to the user.

HOLE (SOUSE HOLE)—A depression formed in a river downstream from an underwater obstruction in which there is some backward (upstream) circulation of water. Water flows down the back surface of the standing wave below the hole and is carried away by the current below the surface. Depending on the river and the flow, holes may be small or as big as a house. They are among the most interesting river phenomena, providing kayakers both with favorite play spots and with the stuff of nightmares. See also **suck hole.**

HULL—The lower section of a boat, the part that is normally in the water. In fiber glass kayaks, the term generally refers to the lower half, below the seam.

HYDRAULIC—In general, anything associated with water. The term is also used as a noun by kayakers in two ways. "Hydraulics" may refer generally to turbulent water phenomena. A "hydraulic" often means a **hydraulic**

jump, a place in a river where the bed becomes more gentle after a steep drop, so that the water must slow down and dissipate the energy it has just picked up in its downward plunge. It does this by jumping or bouncing up again and forming a large wave, the back side of which is steep, sometimes with an upstream current. The kayaker with a buoyant boat may have difficulty getting over the top of this wave or hydraulic jump. (See **reversal** and **stopper.**)

KEEL—A projection running lengthwise along the center of the hull designed to keep a boat from slipping to the side when turning, going across waves at an angle, or following a course across the wind. A keel will also keep a paddle-driven craft like a kayak from turning easily when a paddle-stroke is made on one side, which may be desirable or not, depending on whether one is trying to turn the boat or paddle it in a straight line. Kayaks, except for foldboats, rarely have true keels, but in fiber glass boats a V-shaped projection may run down the center of the hull to serve this purpose, and it may be referred to as a keel. **Bilge keels,** used only on fabric-skinned kayaks, are additional keel strips out to either side of the main keel and parallel to it. They reinforce the effect of the keel, but their main purpose is to protect the hull fabric along the lines where it is pushed tight against frame members and is thus subject to wear. The **keel line** is the line down the center of the hull along the length of the boat where the keel does or would run.

KEEPER—A **stopper** (see below).

LINE—A nautical term for a rope; used as a verb it has the specialized meaning of floating the kayak through a rapid or shallow area while guiding it with ropes attached to the bow, stern, or (usually) both.

PAINTER—A line attached to either the bow or stern for lining, rescue, etc. For safety, painters are generally just long enough so that the end will tuck under the spray skirt. Alternatively, one painter may run the length of the boat, attached to the grab loop at one end with a snap-link or other release mechanism. A bow-stern painter is particularly favored by ocean and large lake tourers to facilitate rescue by a single boat.

PEARL—The kayak is said to pearl when the bow or stern of the boat dives into the water in front of a wave when surfing, either intentionally or by accident. If the water is shallow, there is a danger that the tip may dive into the bottom. Pearling is generally followed by an ender.

PILLOW—A cushion of water formed on the upstream side of an obstacle sticking out of the water as the current bounces off it. The pillow warns the observant kayaker of the obstacle and tends to deflect the boat around it.

PINTLE—A pivot pin attached (in one of several ways) to the stern of a kayak, on which a rudder can be placed. Like rudders, pintles are fitted only on some touring and flat-water racing kayaks.

PITCH—A section of rapids between two flat spots or resting places.

PLAY SPOT—A place in rapids where kayaks can be easily maneuvered back and forth and where there are interesting hydraulic phenomena, such as a hole or large standing waves. Characteristically, play spots are located where there are two eddies on opposite sides of a fast jet of water.

POOL-AND-DROP—A description of a river indicating that fast rapids alternate with long, calm stretches of water. The severity of the rapids of a pool-and-drop river cannot be guessed from the overall gradient of the section being considered.

POP-UP—A maneuver in which the bow or stern of the kayak is driven into a hole and the pressure of the water then ejects the boat, sometimes sending it completely out of the water. Good balance is needed to stay upright. Similar to an ender.

PORTAGE—To carry a boat and equipment around rapids, waterfalls, or otherwise unnavigable spots. Used as a noun, it indicates the act of carrying or the route followed.

POWER FACE—The side of a paddle blade that pushes against the water in a normal forward stroke. The concave side of a curved or spooned paddle.

PRY—A stroke in which the blade of the paddle is put straight down in the water parallel to the keel line of the boat and near the hull and is pushed away from the hull, often using the shaft against the hull for leverage. A common canoeing stroke that is rarely used in kayaking.

RAPID(S)—A section of a river where a fast current flows turbulently over and around obstacles and constrictions.

REVERSAL—A standing wave on which the surface current on the back side flows upstream, an extreme example of the dissipation of energy in the wave. The main current flows deeper. Reversals are found below holes, and they may provide either play spots or dangerous traps. (See **stopper.**)

RIFFLE—An insignificant rapid with very small waves.

ROCKER—The upward curvature of the bottom of the hull toward the ends of the boat.

ROLLER—A big, breaking reversal wave.

RUDDER—A steering device attached to the stern of a boat. Kayaks are rarely fitted with rudders, but flat-water racing kayaks have them, and some touring kayaks have removable ones. Strokes in which the paddle is used like a rudder are also called rudders.

S-TURN—Actually a combination of two eddy turns and the crossing of a jet of fast water between the eddies. The boater enters the jet going upstream with an eddy turn that turns the boat downstream, crosses the jet, and makes an eddy turn into the quiet water on the opposite side.

SCOUTING—Inspecting a rapid or an unknown section of water from shore after beaching the kayak upstream. To say that a rapid requires scouting means that it is dangerous to run without inspection, even with directions.

SLALOM—A kayaking competition based on the skiing slalom, designed to test the control and maneuvering skill of the competitors, generally in white water. Kayaks are maneuvered through a course of poles hung over the water and are scored on time and proper execution of the required turns.

SLALOM KAYAK—A boat designed for slalom racing, often used for recreational paddling as well. A slalom boat is designed for maximum control and maneuverability. It is as short as rules permit (4 meters), has a rockered hull and little or no keel or V-shape in the keel line, and poor speed and directional stability.

SPRAY SKIRT—A device made of fabric or neoprene material designed to form a seal between the kayak and the paddler to prevent the entrance of water regardless of leans, waves, or even capsizing. One end of the skirt fits tightly around the waist of the kayaker and the other around the coaming of the boat. Normally the elastic attaching the skirt to the kayak is easily removable for safety.

STANDING WAVE—A stationary wave in a river below a drop, constriction, or obstruction. The standing wave is dissipating the energy picked up by the water as it speeds through the drop. Normally, there is a series of standing waves of steadily decreasing size below such a spot; a solitary wave may really be covering a rock just below the surface or may be downstream from an otherwise invisible hole.

STOPPER—A reversal or roller wave, which can, at least under some circumstances, prevent a kayak from escaping the trough upstream of it. The height of the stopper requires the boat to be pushed up over it, since the kayak is buoyant, but the surface current on the back side of the wave tends to wash the boat back into the trough. Large stoppers may have strong back-currents and the water near the surface may also be very foamy, so that kayaks wallow and paddles have little purchase. A kayak which goes broadside to a stopper will tend to roll over and over; a really large stopper can even flip a boat repeatedly end over end. The term is used somewhat loosely; most reversal waves formed by natural river obstructions will eject a paddler and his boat, perhaps after a few cycles. Most dangerous stoppers are formed by man-made dams which extend across the river without break, providing no escape chute. Even very small dams can have dangerous stoppers.

SUCK HOLE—Generally refers to a souse hole, the common river formation below a large obstacle, in which the main current is diving below the surface. Though buoyant objects like kayaks and swimmers with life vests are occasionally trapped behind the stopper in a souse hole, normal holes are not usually dangerous. A true suck hole is a rare phenomenon, a place where part of the river actually dives and flows underneath some obstacles, through some sort of tunnel, for example. Although rare, such spots are very dangerous when they do occur.

SWEEP—A forward or backward stroke in which the paddler sweeps the paddle out in an arc starting near one end of the hull and going to the other, resulting in a strong turning action.

SWEEPER—A tree that has fallen over the surface of the water, often with branches extending into the water, so that a kayaker passing underneath would be swept from his boat, perhaps held by a branch or snag, perhaps pinned on the sweeper if there is a strong current. Since the sweeper is above the channel, the current will not tend to carry the boater around it, as it does around boulders and other obstacles in the riverbed. Sweepers present one of the few really dangerous river features.

SWIRLIES—Circular eddies that form like whirlpools and disappear again within a couple of minutes. The only problem they present is one of balance as currents come from unexpected directions. Common on big, large-volume rivers.

TECHNICAL—The description of a river, a rapid, or a drop as technical means that it requires considerable skill at maneuvering and precise control of the boat. The technical difficulty of particular water refers to the exactitude necessary in handling the boat. This may be distinguished from other factors requiring good balance, nerve, rolling ability in turbulent water, and the like. Some runs on large western rivers, for example, may be described as involving heavy water but not being technically difficult.

TRACK—To tend to hold a course while moving in a straight line. A boat that tracks well will be easy to paddle when touring on calm water but difficult to maneuver in a rapid. Tracking also means lining a boat up a rapid.

WHIRLPOOL—An area of water with a circular movement. Generally formed in heavy water between vertical canyon walls or along eddylines. Whirlpools are less dangerous than many think; they are normally temporary phenomena which disappear within a couple of minutes. They are likely to cause loss of balance and confusion. The paddler or swimmer trying to escape one must at first concentrate on moving away from the center, rather than toward a point on shore, until he is out of the stronger current. In general, though, simply wait and the whirlpool will disappear.

WHITE EDDY—A foaming eddy with a lot of air suspended in the water, caused by very powerful and turbulent currents. White eddies are difficult because the water is less dense than normal, giving little grip to the paddle and allowing part of the kayak to sink more than usual at the same time as it is crossing from one current to another.

WORKING RAPIDS—The action of moving back and forth and up and down a section of rapids, exploring the various currents, waves, and holes. Playing in rapids.

Checklist for Kayaking Trips

Not all of the equipment mentioned here will be necessary or wanted on every river trip. The basic rule is to take everything that may be *needed*, but to avoid carrying a lot of nonessential extras. Some items need be carried by only one member or a few in each party.

kayak
paddle
spare paddle (take-apart)
spray skirt
extra spray skirt
life preserver
float bags
waterproof storage bags
helmet
wet suit
paddling jacket
wool long johns
warm, dry clothes in storage bag
boating shoes
hiking shoes
sunglasses
extra glasses
retainer strap for glasses
sun cream
water bottle
water purification tablets or bleach
   in dropper bottle
collapsible water storage jug
food
extra food
stove
fuel
waterproof matches or cigarette
   lighter
candle or chemical fire starter
cook kit

frying pan and spatula
soap and pot scrubber
cup
bowl
spoon
pocket knife
maps (including walk-out maps)
river guide
compass
rescue line for towing lost boats
throwing line
long ropes for lining boats down
   rapids
cockpit cover for lining boats down
   rapids
first aid kit
tarp or tent and necessary items for
   pitching
ground cloth
air mattress or pad
sleeping bag
flashlight
carbide lamp and carbide
toilet paper
plastic trowel
bug repellent
mosquito netting
small towel
toilet articles
repair kit

Index